Through detailed examination of a wide variety of novels, plays, sermons, songs, popular engravings, portraiture, and propaganda, Toni Bowers examines the eighteenth-century struggle to develop new ideals for virtuous motherhood. She shows how popular representations of mothers codified and enforced a model of motherhood naturally and inevitably removed from participation in the public world, and presented other ideals as monstrous. At the same time, she points out, some of the most influential texts resisted the newly reduced vision of maternal excellence by imagining alternatives to domesticity and dependence. Addressing broad social and cultural issues, and drawing radical comparisons between past and present, Bowers argues that Western culture continues to be limited by its commitment to the contradictory maternal ideals established in eighteenth-century discourse.

THE POLITICS OF MOTHERHOOD

THE POLITICS OF
MOTHERHOOD

British writing and culture, 1680–1760

TONI BOWERS

CAMBRIDGE
UNIVERSITY PRESS

Published by the Press Syndicate of the University of Cambridge
The Pitt Building, Trumpington Street, Cambridge CB2 1RP
40 West 20th Street, New York, NY 10011–4211, USA
10 Stamford Road, Oakleigh, Melbourne 3166, Australia

First published 1996

Transferred to digital printing 1998

(A portion of part three first appeared in *Eighteenth-Century Fiction* 7:3 (April, 1995).)

Printed in the United Kingdom by Biddles Short Run Books

A catalogue record for this book is available from the British Library

Library of Congress cataloguing in publication data applied for

ISBN 0 521 55174 9 hardback

For my son,
Graham

Contents

Illustrations

Acknowledgments

For generously supporting the research that made this book possible, I should like to acknowledge the Michael J. Connell Foundation, the W. M. Keck Foundation, the Andrew W. Mellon Foundation, the Trustees Council of Penn Women, the University of Pennsylvania Research Foundation, the Stanford Humanities Center, the Stanford Institute for Research on Women and Gender, and, especially, the Huntington Library.

Other debts are more difficult to define, and impossible to repay. I must content myself, therefore, with celebrating those who have accompanied and assisted me on the long journey toward the completion of this book.

My greatest debts are to my teachers – Paul Alkon, John Bender, W. B. Carnochan, and Terry Castle – and to two extraordinary colleagues, Lois Chaber and Jayne Lewis. These friends have spent many hours reading drafts, disputing assumptions, offering advice, and giving courage. Each of them has my warmest thanks and my deepest admiration.

Felicity Nussbaum's advice more than once renewed my resolve and challenged me to think in new ways. I am grateful for her interest and faith in this project. Catherine Burroughs, Eric Cheyfitz, Elizabeth Heckendorn Cook, Carol Delaney, Frank Donoghue, Susan Frye, Barbara Gelpi, Nancy Glazener, Allen Grove, Sheila Ryan Johansson, Paul Korshin, James McGlew, Mary Clair Mulroney, Vicki Mahaffey, Stephen Orgel, John Richetti, Kevin Sharpe, Susan Smith, Daniel Traister, and Rose Zimbardo all read and commented on portions of this book at various stages in its development. Debra and Steve Wilkens provided a place to live and a multitude of happy memories during the summer of 1994; their friendship hastened and sweetened those final weeks of writing.

Jennifer Shreiner assisted in library research and manuscript preparation with intelligence and unfailing attention to detail. Thanks also to research assistants Mark Ferraro, Jennifer Won, and Ephraim Glass, and to Michael Caracappa and Jennifer Taylor for proofreading. Kate Levin cheerfully checked a long list of citations from *Clarissa* at short notice, Lisa Freeman visited the Coram Foundation on my behalf, and Frances Rouse of the Huntington Library provided expert and friendly bibliographical assistance. Thanks to Daniel Meyer of the Regenstein Library, University of Chicago; to Markman Ellis, Catherine Decker and Martha Bowden for information about Lady Sarah Pennington; and to Allen Grove for the index.

Particular thanks are due to Josie Dixon of Cambridge University Press, who sought out this project and shepherded it through publication with unwavering care, good humor, and good sense. It has been an honor and a pleasure to work with her.

PHILADELPHIA
July, 1995

Note on texts

In choosing editions from which to cite eighteenth-century texts, my first concern has been to make it possible for readers easily to examine the evidence for themselves. I make citations, therefore, to inexpensive and readily available editions wherever these exist.

There is no satisfactory and easily obtained modern edition of both parts of Richardson's *Pamela*, so citations are to the four-volume 1742 edition at the Huntington Library, unless otherwise noted.

The first edition of *Clarissa* is widely available in the 1985 Penguin edition (ed. Angus Ross), and the third edition has recently been produced in facsimile by AMS Press (ed. Florian Stuber, 1990). My citations are to the third edition, by volume and page number, with corresponding page references to the Penguin. In the few cases where quoted material appears in the first edition of *Clarissa* but not in the third, I have made note of that fact.

All scriptural quotations are from the Authorized Version. Translations from languages other than English are my own unless otherwise noted.

Abbreviations

DNB	*The Dictionary of National Biography*
JHC	*The Journals of the House of Commons.* London: 1803.
MGC	*The Marlborough-Godolphin Correspondence.* Oxford: 1975.
MP	*A Selection of Papers of the Earls of Marchmont.* London: 1831.
OED	*The Oxford English Dictionary*
PH	*The Parliamentary History of England, from the Earliest Period to the Year 1803. (Cobbett's Parliamentary History.)* London: 1806–1820. Vol. 6, 1810.
PMLA	*Publications of the Modern Language Association*

INTRODUCTION

Historicizing motherhood

" 'Surely *maternity* does not change,' said Mrs. Elliot."
                                                    Virginia Woolf[1]

In the foreground of William Hogarth's *Gin Lane* (1751; figure 1), a ragged, drunken, and diseased mother carelessly drops her infant from a dangerous height. The mother's bare, wasted breasts suggest the lost possibility of maternal nourishment and tenderness; the child's feet seem to encircle a breast as he falls, mirroring the desperate reach of his arms into the air as if in a final, futile effort to hold on. His mother remains dreamily oblivious, taking a pinch of snuff with her eyes closed, smiling. In the chaos of drunkenness and vice behind her, another mother's half-naked corpse is lowered into a coffin while her toddler weeps alone in the dirt beside her; a third mother runs after a lunatic drunk who has skewered her infant on a sword and dances around gleefully displaying his prize. On the far right, a young woman pours gin down the throat of her infant.[2] In these chilling scenes, *Gin Lane* makes central one of the most obsessive and significant plots of Augustan narrative, the plot of maternal failure.

As is well known, *Gin Lane* was produced as the companion piece to Hogarth's *Beer Street*, and the differences between the two scenes could not be more pronounced.[3] Among the bustling and prosperous inhabitants of Beer Street, according to a contemporary of Hogarth's, "Health and Chearfulness appears in every Countenance,

---

[1] Woolf, *The Voyage Out*, 133.

[2] Cf. this anonymous contemporary description of the "lower Class" gin-drinking mothers in *Gin Lane*: "their Infants [are] wretched, half naked, tho' in the coldest Weather, and half starved for want of proper Nourishment; for so indulgent are these tender Mothers, that to stop their little gaping Mouths, they will pour down a spoonful of their own delightful Cordial ... What Numbers of little Creatures, who, had they grown up to Maturity, might have proved useful Members of Society, are lost ...!" (Anon., *A Dissertation on ... Six Prints*, 16).

[3] For a detailed history and description of both works, see Paulson, *Graphic Works*, 145–48.

I

GIN LANE.

1   William Hogarth, *Gin Lane*. Second State, 1751.

[and] there can be no Want of the Necessaries of Life."[4] Significantly, there are no maternal images at all in *Beer Street*; presumably those cheerful, beer-drinking mothers stay inside, where they belong, while in *Gin Lane*, children are everywhere "lost, murder'd ... by

4   *A Dissertation on ... Six Prints*, 29.

these inhuman, unnatural Wretches, their Mothers!"[5] One might
expect, therefore, that the many shocking maternal images in
Hogarth's *Gin Lane* should have provoked comment among critics.
But the crucial importance *Gin Lane* places on criminal, absent, or
helpless mothers and their tragically misused children has gained
very little special notice.[6] This is particularly surprising when we
consider the insistent presence of similar images throughout Hogarth's corpus. Recall, for instance, the bereaved, friendless child in
The Harlot's Progress (1732); the wizened newborn who vomits as
inappropriate food is forced into its mouth by a youngster in a
frightening disguise in *Strolling Actresses* (1738); the ragged mother in
The Enraged Musician (1741), who holds a wailing infant and sings
about "The Ladies Fall"; the famous final scene of *Marriage à la Mode*
(1745), where the profligate couple's crippled and diseased child takes
a last farewell of her mother before being claimed by a cruel-looking
old woman; the impoverished street mother in the execution scene of
Industry and Idleness (1747), who hawks Tom Idle's "Last Dying
Speech"; and the insistent representation of distressing maternal
relations in Hogarth's acclaimed *The March to Finchley* (executed for
London's Foundling Hospital)[7] where, for example, two chicks cry
for their mother, who is being carried off by a soldier. All these
constitute only a sampling of Hogarth's many images of maternal
failure.[8] Nor is Hogarth's an idiosyncratic obsession. Mothers,
especially bad ones, loom large in a great many early eighteenth-
century texts, as this book will demonstrate; yet they continue to
remain invisible in most studies of Augustan culture.[9] The virtual
silence of critical discussion when it comes to early eighteenth-
century Britain's obsessive representation of maternal figures is too

[5] Anon., *Dissertation on ... Six Prints*, 16.
[6] Kunzle examines Hogarth's depiction of children, but pays little attention to their mothers.
George provides anecdotal data to indicate that gin drinking and monstrous maternity
were understood by Hogarth's contemporaries to go hand-in-hand (e.g. 54. Cf. Anon.,
Mother Gin). McCormick, who denies that "negative portrayals of women in art are
politically motivated and culturally enforced" (xx), notices eighteenth-century literary
representations of motherhood briefly, as "backgrounds" to nineteenth- and twentieth-
century representations.
[7] Hogarth painted *Finchley* for the Hospital in 1746; it was engraved for popular consumption
in 1750.
[8] Cf. the perversion of motherhood in *Credulity, Superstition and Fanaticism* (1762), where a
woman gives birth to rabbits. *The Times*, Plate 1 (1762), like *Finchley*, pictures mothers and
children as victims of war.
[9] Cf. Armstrong's *Desire and Domestic Fiction*, one of the most important recent discussions of the
early novel (see 21–22 below).

pervasive to be the result of simple oversight or coincidence. On the contrary, it signals the continued investment of contemporary critical discourse in a maternal mythology that Augustan texts were producing, a mythology that at once exploits and denies explicitly maternal agencies and subjectivities, especially as these operate in the public world.[10]

The distressing maternal images in *Gin Lane* make explicit reference not only to failed mothers in Augustan society, but also to their unfortunate offspring. In the early decades of the eighteenth century, abandoned or exposed children – in Augustan slang, children who had been "dropped" – constituted a social presence that could not be ignored; their bodies, dead or (barely) alive, littered London and the countryside. Hogarth's contemporaries grimly noted the ubiquity of abandoned children and the nation's alarming rate of infanticide.[11]

By the 1720s, the situation had become very serious. Queen Anne's administration (r. 1702–14) had supported relief for orphans, charity schools, and other progressive measures, but under her Hanoverian successors, largesse toward impoverished children measurably decreased. Poor laws were continually modified, making it ever more difficult to qualify for the dwindling amount of available relief. In 1722, the legislation that established workhouses as places of refuge for the poor in effect created a system of deathtraps for small children, who died in workhouses in large numbers.[12] Meanwhile, laws requiring parishes to care for any child born within their jurisdictions were leading to increased desperation among indigent pregnant women who were refused lodging, even physically chased out, by townspeople unwilling to assume responsibility for infants born within their borders. On April 8, 1727, Nathaniel Mist's *Weekly Journal*, an early news miscellany, recounts the story of a woman in Wolverhampton who was acquitted of the murder of her newborn in just such horrific circumstances.

It appeared that she was a poor Woman, and that her Husband was gone from her, that she wander'd about the Parish, and no Body would take her

---

[10]   For one examination of present-day critical investments in eighteenth-century assumptions about motherhood, cf. Bowers, "Critical complicities."

[11]   Old Bailey *Proceedings*; Hoffer and Hull *Murdering Mothers*, 66ff. George provides an excellent summary of gin's role in eighteenth-century London's social crises (44–54).

[12]   Nichols and Wray, *History of the Foundling Hospital*, 1–2.

in, so that she was suffer'd to be brought to Bed in a House of Office, to shelter her from the Weather, where the Infant dy'd of Cold and Want, and the Mother forc'd to live many Days on Bread and Water only, the Parish refusing her any Assistance for Fear of bringing a Charge upon them.

For this, Mist declares, "the Parishioners themselves ought decently to be hang'd for the said most shameful Murder." Both Mist's sentiment and the Wolverhampton mother's reprieve were, unfortunately, highly exceptional. Mist's pages are full of grisly accounts of child abuse and abandonment, and of the suicides of unmarried mothers (mostly young servants); in the nineteen months between May, 1725 and December, 1726, the *Weekly Journal* reports the death sentences of no less than fifteen infanticidal mothers.

As early as 1713, Joseph Addison argued for "a Provision for Foundlings, or for those Children who, through want of such a Provision, are exposed to the Barbarity of cruel and unnatural Parents ... Monsters of Inhumanity" (*Guardian* no. 105, 366).[13] Addison's contemporary Thomas Coram, a prosperous shipbuilder, also observed the miseries of abandoned children. Traveling in London and its environs, Coram, it is said, "frequently saw infants exposed and deserted in the public streets" and was grieved at such "a departure from humanity and natural affection."[14] Perhaps inspired by Addison's essay,[15] Coram began in 1720 to solicit patrons and governmental approval for an institution dedicated to the relief of foundlings; in 1739, he finally received from George II a royal charter for the establishment of the "Hospital for the Maintenance and Education of Exposed and Deserted Young Children," commonly known as the London Foundling Hospital.[16]

According to its royal charter, the hospital was established "in

[13] Addison is not entirely without sympathy for the "profligate women" he decries. What "overcomes the tenderness which is natural to them" he says, is "fear of shame, or their inability to support those whom they give life to" (*Guardian* no. 105, 367).

[14] Nichols and Wray, *History of the Foundling Hospital*, 1. Cf. Paulson, *Life, Art, Times*, 37; George, *London Life*, 324, n. 61.

[15] Nichols and Wray, *History of the Foundling Hospital*, 13.

[16] For brief, readable histories of the Foundling Hospital from its inception to the present, cf. McClure, *Coram's Children*, 249–51; George, *London Life*, 55–60. For a description of Coram's stated intentions in setting up the hospital, see Brownlow, *Foundling Hospital*, 2–3. According to Brownlow, Coram saw himself as setting up a refuge not primarily for *children* but for their *mothers*, who were often "the unsuspecting victim[s] of treachery" (3). The hospital was originally conceived as a "sanctuary" where these "wretched mothers" might "deposit" their illegitimate offspring "and be thus enabled to return to that path from which they had unguardedly strayed" (Brownlow, *History and Objects of the Foundling Hospital*, 3).

behalf of great numbers of helpless Infants daily exposed to Destruction" or even murdered by their "inhuman" parents.[17] From the first, however, the infants admitted to the Foundling Hospital were much less likely actually to have been exposed than to be brought to the door by desperate, indigent mothers who parted from their children with great reluctance and hoped to reclaim them under better circumstances. The hospital's minute book describes the terrible grief of those impoverished mothers who were lucky enough to find a place in the hospital for their children, sorrow only matched, according to one observer on the night the doors first opened, by "the Expressions of Grief of the Women whose Children could not be admitted ... so that a more moving Scene can't well be imagined."[18] Thirty children were admitted that first night. According to the Hospital's minute book, all but three were "dressed very clean," though some were "almost Starved" and one was in the last stages of malnutrition, "too weak to Suck, or to receive Nourishment."[19] The cleanliness of these children, their desperate physical condition and their mothers' grief, all suggest that poverty, not "Barbarity," was behind their abandonment at the Hospital.[20] Coram himself seems to have reached this conclusion. From early in his campaign, he defended the mothers the Hospital was to serve from the charge of "inhumanity," arguing instead that the main reason for the high rate of infanticide and child abandonment was the "inability of parents to maintain" their children.[21] Ironically, then, the Foundling Hospital was less engaged in reclaiming the "dropped" offspring of negligent monster-mothers like the one in the foreground of *Gin Lane* than in adopting the children of loving, but hopelessly impoverished, mothers. The hospital officially set out to

---

[17] Anon., *Royal Charter*, 1–2. Soon after the Charter was granted, the governors drafted a bill revising it. The amended preamble said that the hospital was "for infants who are *liable* to be exposed in the streets, or to be murdered by their parents." This avoided the problem of "giving license to that which was contrary to law" (Brownlow, *History and Objects of the Foundling Hospital*, 5).
       It was also the stated goal of the Foundling Hospital to return the children to their parents eventually, when the parents were economically stable enough to maintain them. The ideal narrative is imagined in Hogarth's "The Foundlings" (1739; Paulson, *Graphic Works*, 424) where a mother who tearfully abandons her child eventually reclaims him. Cf. Brownlow, facing 6. In fact, only a small minority of the children who entered the Foundling Hospital ever returned to their birthparents.

[18] Nichols and Wray, *History of the Foundling Hospital*, 39; Jarrett, *The Age of Hogarth*, 74–5; Paulson, *Life, Art, Times*, 39–40; Cf. McClure, *Coram's Children*, 247.

[19] Nichols and Wray, *History of the Foundling Hospital*, 39.

[20] Cf. McClure, *Coram's Children*, 247.

[21] Brownlow, *History and Objects of the Foundling Hospital*, 5.

2   William Hogarth, *Moses Brought to Pharaoh's Daughter*. Second State, 1752.

fill vacancies created by maternal *abdication*; but in fact, it engaged in a more problematic *usurpation* of destitute mothers forced unwillingly to fail their children.

Hogarth was an original governor and a lifelong supporter of the Foundling Hospital. He was present when Coram's charter was received, and was one of four governors who presided over the opening of the hospital on March 25 and witnessed the heartrending scene described above. He was among the inspectors who selected and supervised the wetnurses to whom the children were sent. Hogarth consistently donated time, money, and art to the Hospital.[22] But in 1747, he presented the Foundling Hospital with his most important gift, the celebrated painting entitled *Moses Brought to Pharaoh's Daughter* (figure 2). The painting was executed especially for the Foundling Hospital, as part of an agreement between Hogarth and fellow artists Hayman, Highmore, and Wills that they

---

[22]   For Hogarth's involvement in the charitable work of the Foundling Hospital, see especially Paulson, *Life, Art, Times*, 37–42, 56.

3   The original Seal of the Foundling Hospital.

would each present the hospital with a large painting on a biblical theme.[23]

In choosing as his subject the biblical story of young Moses' adoption by the daughter of Egypt's Pharaoh, Hogarth followed Coram, who had recently based the design for the hospital's official seal (figure 3) on the same narrative.[24] "The affair Mentioned in the 2nd of Exodus of Pharaoh's daughter and her Maids finding Moses in the ark of Bulrushes," Coram said, "... I thought would be very appropo [sic] for an hospital for foundlings, Moses being the first

---

[23]   Hayman's painting appears here as figure 4. Highmore produced a scene from the biblical story of Hagar and Ishmael, and Wills represented the little children coming to Christ. Hogarth's *Moses* was unveiled at the Foundling Hospital in April, 1747, and Hogarth produced an engraving of it in 1752. The engraving is reproduced here. See Paulson, *Graphic Works*, 156 for descriptions of all versions.

[24]   Paulson, *Life, Art, Times*, 44.

4 Francis Hayman, *The Finding of Moses in the Bulrushes*. 1746.

Foundling we read of."[25] Francis Hayman, as we have seen, followed suit, illustrating the same story in the painting he donated to the Hospital, which was displayed with Hogarth's (figure 4). But Hogarth's rendering of the Moses story is vastly different from Coram's and Hayman's; indeed, it diverges from nearly all previous depictions of the Moses narrative in European art which, like Coram's seal and Hayman's painting, picture the moment when the infant Moses is discovered in the bulrushes by Pharaoh's daughter and the baby's mother joyfully accepts a position as his wetnurse.[26] Hogarth, by contrast, represents a later scene, when Moses' mother delivers her

[25] Nichols and Wray, *History of the Foundling Hospital*, 20–21.
[26] Cf. Van Dyck's two versions of *The Finding of Moses*, which Hogarth knew (Paulson, *Life, Art*, 156). I was convinced of the ubiquity of the "finding" scene by browsing through Gibbs's *Kitto Bible* at the Huntington Library, where scores of images represent the discovery in the bulrushes, but not one before or after Hogarth pictures the later, sadder moment of exchange.

weaned child to Pharaoh's daughter, who names him and takes him for her own son.[27]

Moses Brought to Pharaoh's Daughter makes disturbingly visible the money that Moses' mother, obviously poor, is paid for her services, and – especially in the 1752 engraving – emphasizes the grief of both mother and son during this exchange. Thus Hogarth recasts Coram's analogy: Moses stands for the London foundlings not by virtue of having been "exposed and deserted," but because his mother, though attentive and affectionate, is forced to resign him to a surrogate for economic and social reasons. In *Moses Brought to Pharaoh's Daughter*, Hogarth suggests that social and material injustices made problematic the well-intentioned activities of the Foundling Hospital. He revises the reductive assumptions behind Addison's characterization of scandalous or impoverished mothers as "cruel, unnatural" and "profligate women,"[28] presenting a more complicated view of maternal "dropping" of children and the agencies behind it.

According to one of Hogarth's most esteemed modern interpreters, *Moses Brought to Pharaoh's Daughter* is in the tradition of "choice" pictures, modeled ultimately on the choice of Hercules. "Moses," Ronald Paulson says,

is choosing between Virtue, a hard but honest life with his true mother, and the languid reclining Pleasure, the easy life of the court. Lurking within a simple, very classically-conceived history is a blunt statement about the social function of the Foundling Hospital and an admonition to its charges. (*Life, Art,* 45)

One might wonder, however, exactly what "admonition" the

---

[27] The Egyptian princess's naming of the "first foundling" seems to have set a precedent for Foundling Hospital procedures. According to Brownlow, "it has been the practice of the Governors, from the earliest period of the Hospital to the present time, to name the children at their own will and pleasure, whether their parents should have been known or not" (73). The first boy and girl taken in were named Thomas and Eunice Coram (Nichols and Wray, *History of the Foundling Hospital,* 21). Children were routinely given the names of noble sponsors, historical luminaries, and even fictional characters: Marlborough, Pembroke, Laud, Chaucer, Milton, Bacon, Cromwell, Michael Angelo, William Hogarth, even Tom Jones and Clarissa Harlowe were all residents of the Foundling Hospital (Brownlow, *History and Objects of the Foundling Hospital,* 73–74). Eventually, the governors found it inconvenient to name the children after themselves since "when they grew to man or womanhood, they were apt to lay claim" to the privileges associated with their names (75).

[28] Cf. Cadogan's influential treatise on infant feeding, written for the use of the governors of the Foundling Hospital, where parents bring to the Foundling Hospital children whom they "did not care to be encumber'd with" (*Essay,* 10). Interestingly, Cadogan closes his treatise by referring to his text as a foundling left at the hospital (34).

painting might have been making to the Hospital's young inmates. For the life offered the children of the Foundling Hospital was hardly one of "languid reclining Pleasure," as Hogarth surely knew. The children took cold baths and were put to work early doing handicrafts, outdoor chores, and silk winding for the benefit of the hospital. When old enough, they were apprenticed out – girls to domestic service and boys to the army or navy, or to master "mechanics" (i.e., laborers).[29] Moreover, the Foundling's children had no choice about entering the Hospital in the first place: when Hogarth produced *Moses*, it was still the rule that only children less than two months old were admitted (Brownlow 38). And even in the relatively few cases where parents did return to reclaim their children, this was hardly the result of the children's own choice.[30] In fact, the children admitted to the Foundling Hospital were like Hogarth's Moses precisely in their *lack* of choice.

As Hogarth presents the scene, there is no reason to assume that the child Moses even knows that the woman who has served as his nurse is in fact his mother. Nor does Hogarth's Egyptian princess show signs of that knowledge (as she does, for instance, in Hayman's painting); all eighteenth-century commentators agree that the princess seems not to imagine who the nurse really is. (Whether such knowledge would make any difference is, of course, another question.) The servants whispering behind the princess may suspect the truth,[31] but Moses' mother is the only person who we can be sure knows the secret. If the painting is indeed, as Paulson says, "a story

[29] Nichols and Wray, *History of the Foundling Hospital*, 130–31; Brownlow, *History and Objects of the Foundling Hospital*, 79. Nichols and Wray reproduce the children's spartan diet in the mid-1740s (128–29); cf. 149 for the rigorous daily routine of Foundling children in 1799.

[30] Until 1764, parents wishing to reclaim a child were required to repay the costs of its care and "post security for its future maintenance" (McClure, *Coram's Children*, 124). That the policy prevented many poor parents from reclaiming their children is demonstrated by the fact that when these financial requirements were eliminated in 1764, there was an immediate and dramatic rise in the number of parents who returned to claim their children: there were forty-nine reclamations in 1764, whereas the largest annual total before that time had been four.

The Coram Foundation's art collection includes a fascinating 1858 painting by Emma Brownlow King, which pictures the return of a young foundling to her birthmother. The scene might be interpreted as an answer to Hogarth's *Moses*. The painting is reproduced by Nicolson (n.p.).

[31] There are tantalizing differences between these figures in the 1746 painting and in the 1752 engraving. In the painting, the maidservant throws up her hands in amazement, her eyes fixed on the Hebrew "nurse"; apparently the slave is whispering the secret of the nurse's identity. In the engraving, it is the slave who shows concern and amazement; the maidservant listens with serious attention, but does not seem to be aware of the secret.

of choice," then the person most reasonably construed as making a choice is not the frightened toddler but his mother, who consciously sells her relation to her child. The question then becomes not a matter of simple choice ("hard but honest Virtue," "languid reclining Pleasure") but of what it might mean for this woman – a slave whose son would have been murdered except for the surrogacy of the Egyptian princess – to "choose" maternal abandonment. How free is such a "choice"?

Before returning to the crucial question of the mother's "choice," and as a way of framing it more precisely, we should pause to note that the figure most emphasized in *Moses* is neither the child nor his mother, just as Hogarth's painting is not finally a celebration of foundlings or their impoverished parents. To the extent that any figure is central, that figure (as Paulson notes with some discomfort[32]) is the princess – an implausibly white Egyptian, representative of the hospital, who beckons from a position of exotic otherness that is also comfortingly the same. By embodying European standards for beauty, including the white skin that was both a racial and a class marker in Augustan England, the princess upholds (even as she draws our attention from) the hierarchies of race and class represented by the waiting woman and whispering slave on the left and by the desperate poverty of the Hebrew mother on the right. It is crucial to see that these hierarchies are essential to the benevolence of Pharaoh's daughter – a benevolence at once sincerely charitable and culpably complicit. For Moses, we recall, was the lucky exception; most male Hebrew babies of his generation were murdered by the genocidal edict of this princess's father. Not only is the "choice" of Moses' mother problematic and overdetermined, then; so is the Egyptian princess's "choice" to save this child, insofar as it represents the caprice and co-optation of benevolence that functions uncritically within, and is enabled by, scenes of oppression.

In a similar vein, despite the humanitarian language of the Foundling Hospital's official documents and alongside the sincere philanthropy of many of its supporters, we must recognize another motivation behind the establishment of an institution devoted to

---

[32] Paulson observes that "the visual pattern does not correspond with complete faithfulness to the psychological: Pharaoh's daughter ... dominates the picture instead of Moses ... The curious dominance of Pharaoh's daughter ... requires some explanation." On the same page, Paulson finds it "offensive" that the "tattling negress" draws attention from the Hogarthian "line of beauty" created by the figure of Pharaoh's daughter (*Life, Art*, 48).

reclaiming the lives of destitute children – the staffing of the burgeoning British empire, an empire devoted to remaking social and racial others like the daughter of Pharaoh into useful, attractive versions of the British.[33] The charitable work of the Foundling Hospital, while by no means rendered fraudulent, is nevertheless complicated by similar motives. Coram himself, after all, had built his fortune trading in the American colonies. According to a eulogy delivered by a friend shortly after his death, Coram had hoped to draw "the Indians in North America more closely to the British interest, by an establishment for the education of Indian girls"; this, the friend enthuses, "would be a refined stroke of policy; for he is the wisest ... of all politicians who, by promoting the glory of God, interests the Divine Providence in extending the power of any nation."[34] By proffering its charity without addressing the social injustices that made such charity both necessary and inadequate, the Foundling Hospital was helpful to a few at the expense of many, and ironically contributed to the very situation it was designed to relieve.[35]

But to return to the painting. Despite her "dominance," even the Egyptian princess is not quite at the formal center of Hogarth's vision; nor is the diminutive Hercules who approaches, but does not occupy, center stage, and whose agency, as we have seen, is decidedly minimal. The real center of Hogarth's painting is not a figure at all, but an empty space filled only at a distance by stereotypical features of Egyptian landscape and architecture: we detect, for instance, a sphinx and a pyramid. This gap separates Pharaoh's daughter – with her exotic iconography (incense, angel, crocodile), her white companion, and her black slave – from the scene of exchange, loss, and grief on the other side of the painting where Moses, his mother, and the steward enact the tragic drama of overdetermined maternal "choice." The painting, in fact, constitutes not one scene, but two, separated by the central gap between the privileged hand of mercy that chooses one child while allowing hundreds to die, and the laboring hands that exchange coins over a commodified toddler.

Finally, then, Paulson is right when he observes that the narrative

[33] Cf. Cadogan, *Essay upon Nursing*, 6; Nichols and Wray, *History of the Foundling Hospital*, 1, 13.
[34] Brownlow, *History and Objects of the Foundling Hospital*, 33. Cf. Paulson, *Life, Art, Times*, 36–37.
[35] During the 1750s, Parliament tried opening the doors to all eligible children. The experiment was brief and catastrophic. Cf. George, *London Life*, 44–45; McClure, *Coram's Children*, chs. 7 and 8.

depicted in *Moses Brought to Pharaoh's Daughter* is "a story of choice" –
or, more precisely, a story about the possibility of choice in a scene of
such profound overdetermination. The key questions suggested by
Hogarth's fable of maternal renunciation are questions about the
relative agencies of the reluctant mother and complacent princess.
Where does agency lie in this painting? Who has choice, and what is
being chosen? In light of the complicated network of complicities we
have observed, can Moses' mother be said to "choose" to relinquish
her son? Is she the active *agent* of her own maternal erasure, or is she
the *victim* of social structures that make her motherhood impossible?
Does she abdicate, or is her position usurped? In the moment of
tragic good fortune depicted in Hogarth's *Moses*, we see distilled a
generation's struggle to understand the multiple agencies and
complex accountabilities behind maternal failure – both individual
women's failures as mothers and the social conditions that made
maternal failure inevitable.

This book will make two central arguments. First, that the struggle to
define maternal virtue, authority, and responsibility was critical to
the construction of models for legitimate power and allegiance in
Augustan England, a society where relations of authority on all levels
were undergoing revision. And second, that the increasingly narrow
definition of maternal virtue that emerged during the first half of the
eighteenth century was vital to the containment of matriarchal
authority at a time when patriarchal authority was undergoing
radical reconception and was therefore particularly vulnerable.
Augustan discourse was preoccupied with motherhood. In novels,
visual art, conduct literature, and printed ephemera of all kinds,
questions about maternal agency and the scope of maternal authority
emerge as central. Again and again, as we shall see, the maternal
becomes a crucial (though frequently denied) site on which battles
over agency and authority were fought.
    Our focus on the first half of the eighteenth century sets this work
apart from virtually all related accounts of the eighteenth-century
revolution in maternal behaviors, most of which assume that the
most significant changes in assumptions about motherhood and in
maternal behaviors were late-century developments.[36] Our purpose,
by contrast, is to discover where the much-noticed mid-century

[36]   There is an increasing body of important work on the cultural status and functions of
       motherhood in the late eighteenth century, just after the period of interest here. See for

boom in manuals and treatises devoted to extolling and controlling a particular version of motherhood came from. As we shall see, though the ideal of the tender, noble, self-sacrificial, and ever-nurturant mother may have been put to new political uses in the second half of the century, it was codified at least a generation earlier, in texts whose maternal agendas are often overlooked. Attention to early eighteenth-century constructions of maternity allows us to accommodate phenomena that literary historians have found puzzling, such as the late seventeenth-century practice of feeding infants "by hand" (i.e., replacing breastmilk with a kind of gruel that almost invariably killed them). Perry dismisses this trend as an "extraordinary" and "peculiar" "fad" (218–19), and finds no connection between it and the intense rhetoric advocating maternal breastfeeding which she sees as a later phenomenon. I see feeding "by hand" as part of the seventeenth- and early eighteenth-centuries' growing attention to the maternal role in infant feeding, attention which mid- and late-century texts continued to revise and expand, but did not inaugurate.

Some historians of motherhood seem to consider Rousseau's *Emile* (1762) as something like a sufficient cause of the profound changes that took place in the eighteenth century in infant feeding, maternal presence with children, the relative authorities of fathers and mothers, and men's increased interest and control over childbed and nursery (especially among the economically privileged).[37] But I am convinced that England constitutes a separate case from France, and that the most frequently noted developments in eighteenth-century maternal behaviors were in place in England well before mid-century. The texts examined here demonstrate that Rousseau's formulations of the 1760s, and even those of Cadogan in the 1740s, functioned to codify and accelerate trends already underway in England more than to initiate new ways of thinking and behaving.[38]

Augustan representations of maternity are most often representa- ·>

[37] example Greenfield, "The maternal bosom," Nussbaum, " 'Savage' mothers" and "Polygamy"; Perry, "Colonizing the breast."
Fildes, *Breasts, Bottles and Babies*, 115–16; Kaplan (following Badinter), *Motherhood and Representation*, 18–22, 210. Shorter earlier had criticized this reduction: "It is unlikely that *Emile* itself played much part in initiating the movement [to maternal breastfeeding], partly because such ideas had long been circulating, and partly because in the 1760s we find the switch to maternal nursing already well underway among the middle classes" (182). Shorter refers to social developments in France, which lagged considerably behind England.

[38] Gelpi, "The nursery cave," 44; G. Sussman, *Selling Mother's Milk*, 6–7.

tions of failed authority and abdicated responsibility. Conduct books and sermons are constantly scolding mothers, who are presumed to be only too prone to error. Novels consistently represent inadequate maternal characters: passive and ineffectual, devious and selfish, silent or absent when most needed. Furthermore, Augustan texts display great uncertainty about the causes of – and responsibilities for – maternal failure. Most often, such failure is seen as an individual moral problem: mothers fail because they are not properly virtuous. Augustan establishment writers were much occupied with defining and enforcing virtuous motherhood (a procedure that often took the form of distinguishing "natural" from "unnatural" maternal behaviors), prescribing particular maternal behaviors and pro-scribing alternatives. But sometimes in early eighteenth-century representations, even those mothers who follow all the rules for maternal excellence find their authority compromised, their "virtue" productive of injustice and suffering. Augustan discourse relentlessly holds these mothers accountable for their failure to prevent evil, while also, sometimes, admitting that failure to be inevitable. In situations of great stress, mothers' adherence to normative standards for maternal virtue can make them ironically guilty, as we shall see: though unquestioning submission to husbandly authority is always required (even when particular husbands are in error), yet mothers who allow their husbands to harm their children are guilty of abdication. Yet at the same time, acts of maternal *abdication* in Augustan texts also look disturbingly like experiences of *usurpation*, involving coercion and force, not simple choice.

That abdication and usurpation might be difficult to distinguish had been brought home to English minds during the debates surrounding the "Glorious Revolution" of 1688–89, when King James II fled to France leaving room for his son-in-law and daughter, William and Mary, to assume the throne. The nation was profoundly divided over these developments. Parliament struggled to find language that would account for what had happened and fought bitterly about who was responsible. A resolution passed by the House of Commons early in 1689 placed blame squarely on the king: after having "endeavoured to subvert the Constitution" by his tyrannical Catholicism, it said, James had "withdrawn himself" from England; in a paradoxical exercise of royal authority, he had "abdicated the Government; and...the Throne is thereby vacant" (*JHC*: 10 [28 January, 1688]: 14). Or as Gilbert Burnet would put it later, James "did choose ... to abandon all."[39] But the House of Lords had great difficulty agreeing to this language, and particularly resisted the words "abdicated" and "vacant." After much debate, Commons's language prevailed: it was decided that William and Mary's right rested on James's "abdication." But many remained uncomfortable with the ambiguity of the act that had unseated the king and unsure about their own subsequent allegiances.[40]

For a brief period early in 1689, controversies over agency took the form of open debates – in Parliamentary sessions, coffee houses, pamphlets, and homes – concerning the location of agents responsible for the king's fall and the legitimacy of the proposed settlement. But soon it became dangerous to side with James publicly or even to express reservations about the process that had transferred his authority.[41] By the end of 1689, the question of who would sit on the throne was (uneasily) settled. But more fundamental and disturbing questions were brought forward by the Revolution, and persisted even when it was no longer prudent or practical to frame them in terms of the event itself. The so-called Glorious Revolution, in other words, provided the occasion for the formulation of questions whose significance extended far beyond it – questions about the loss or failure of authority structures on many levels, about the location of political legitimacy and responsibility, and about the possibility of integrity for those who swore allegiance to the new administration. As an official site of debate, the revolution was largely (though by no means entirely) defused after the negotiations of 1689. But the wounds it exposed continued to fester, its divisions and hostilities continued to be waged on other sites.[42]

---

39 Burnet, *History of His Own Time*, 1: 796.
40 For very different contemporary estimates of these debates cf. Burnet, *History of His Own Time*, 1: 795–96, 815–17; Clarendon, *Correspondence of Henry Hyde*, 2: 260–62.
41 Clarendon, *Correspondence of Henry Hyde*, 2: 252–70. I do not suggest, of course, that the Glorious Revolution was never a subject of debate again after the installation of William and Mary. The Advertisement to Millar's 1758 edition of Swift's *History of the Four Last Years of the Queen*, where the writer objects to Swift's deliciously ambiguous deployment of "abdicated" as a passive verb in reference to King James (176), demonstrates the marked longevity of the debate over agency at the Glorious Revolution. Cf. Hume, *History of England*, 6:514; Kenyon, "The birth of the old pretender," 11.
42 The events of 1688–89 have by now been largely divested of both their glory and their revolutionary status. During the 1980s, historians led by J. C. D. Clark argued that the exit of James and the installation of William and Mary did not much change English society: traditionally authoritative institutions survived intact, and were only transfigured in the early nineteenth century. In the past few years a more moderate view has emerged. J. R. Jones grants aspects of the Clark thesis (e.g., the revolution was not "in itself... an epoch-making event"), but argues that the events of 1688–89 should not be pronounced

One of those sites was motherhood, a vexed and threatening *topos* throughout the early eighteenth century. The transgressions of failed mothers in Augustan writing epitomize early eighteenth-century anxieties by being neither active nor passive, but, strangely, both at once.[43] Even when apparently most powerless, these maternal figures exercise a paradoxical kind of control, constraining and limiting those who look to them for direction, leaving obedient children (like James's loyal subjects) without satisfactory options. In the texts we shall consider here, the struggle to define and limit maternal authority participates in, complicates, and specifies the Augustan need to make sense of any relationship of authority and subordination, and to assign degrees of responsibility to all those involved when such relationships change.

A few caveats are in order. First, even though Augustan texts relentlessly metaphorize parenthood, including maternity, as a figure for political authority, we shall resist the temptation to proceed in entirely the same way. In this book, motherhood is not primarily a facilitating metaphor, though it will function that way to some extent. Our primary subject is motherhood as an object of knowledge and a category of political experience in its own right, not "motherhood and," "motherhood for," or "motherhood as" something else.

Indeed, even speaking of "motherhood" as a finite subject is unsatisfactory, for part of our purpose is to resist the construction of motherhood as a single, changeless function or a limited set of

---

negligible, either. Instead, Jones argues that we might see so-called Glorious Revolution as an "important stage" in ongoing "processes of change" (2; cf. T. Harris, "Property, power and personal relations," 140–42). I find such formulations more reasonable than the tendency of what has, ironically enough, been called "The Jonathan Clark revolution" (Elton, *Tudor and Stuart Politics and Government*, 303) to reduce 1688 to the point of insignificance. Of course the powerful institutions of the seventeenth century (church, aristocracy, monarchy) remained powerful through the eighteenth century; but new explanations and alternative models of authority were also gaining ground.

What we need now is not another assessment of whether the events of 1688–89 brought about enough change to qualify as "revolutionary," but a recognition of the positivist thinking behind the debate itself. The most interesting question is not *when* or even *whether* a triumphal "rise" in new ideas and power brokers occurred, but *how* new explanatory paradigms and social structures interact with, respond to, and are conditioned by those already in existence, and how societies over time become transformed versions of themselves. Such an approach to the processes of cultural change may be found in the strategies adopted by J. G. A. Pocock, John Bender, and Michael McKeon, who variously complicate the reductive idea of discrete, competing epochs.

43   Cf. *New Atalantis*, 202–03, where Manley portrays the abdicating King James as a tragically victimized-yet-responsible mother. Cf. Part 3, 213, below.

positions, the same throughout history. The myth of eternally changeless motherhood is a central pillar upholding patriarchal privilege; it is part of the assumption everywhere implicit in contemporary Western societies that motherhood is somehow more "natural" and "instinctual" than fatherhood (which has long been recognized as a fluid, socially constructed category, available for legal and philosophical theorizing and practical revision[44]). This book starts from the premise that motherhood, far from a static, "natural" experience, is a moving plurality of potential behaviors always undergoing supervision, revision, and contest, constructed in particularity. It is precisely this excessive, organic, historically contingent motherhood that Augustan writing tried to reduce to manageable proportions, not least through metaphorization. We shall trace the processes of that reduction, asking how it was achieved, what purposes it served, and where it failed.

Secondly, this book does not engage in a search for the origins of the ideas about motherhood that it examines. The eighteenth century did not invent the confinement of maternal power within systems of masculinist domination; there was no previous golden age. On the contrary, in historical periods when the figure of the mother has carried greatest social authority and enunciative power in Western tradition, its delimitations have been most striking. The supreme example of this paradox is the Virgin Mary, whose iconology successfully represented ideal motherhood and informed fantasies of female power for many generations of Christians. But as feminist theorists have noted, the Virgin's power depended on her difference from all other women and on her subordination to her son.[45] And in similar fashion, Freudian psychoanalytic theory and its transformations – sacred articles of the post-Christian West – privilege the formative influence of the pre-oedipal mother to the exclusion of nearly all other early influences, but tend to deny her subject status equivalent to that of the child for whose development she exists. So even when Western discourse has accepted and promoted the idea of maternal authority, it has remained difficult to imagine that authority outside patriarchal definition and exploitation.

Nevertheless, there are degrees of historical difference. Until the

---

[44] Hume, "Of Chastity"; Delaney, "The meaning of paternity."
[45] Suleiman, "Writing and motherhood," 368; Irigaray, *This Sex Which is Not One*, 95; M. Warner, *Reading Clarissa*, 57–8, 104–5.

eighteenth-century emergence of the full-time housewife/mother as
the crucial – though invisible and supposedly non-productive –
facilitator of a newly reduced notion of productive labor (i.e., capital-
based, wage-earning, male), the separation of motherhood and
public life was never as complete as it would be subsequently, and
the dilemmas faced by many middle-class mothers today would not
have been imaginable.[46] The specific assumptions about motherhood
most characteristic of eighteenth-century discourse – that motherhood naturally and necessarily stands apart from productive labor
and public authority, that it is neither participant in politics nor
affected by historical change – could emerge in England only after
the religious and social upheavals of the sixteenth and seventeenth
centuries, and developed recognizably modern form during the first
half of the eighteenth century. We shall look at this important
revisionary moment in motherhood's complex, continuing history.

It is perhaps also necessary to note that an effort to recapture
imaginable Augustan motherhoods is not the same as the documenta-
tion of *actual* maternal behaviors. We are looking at how the
discursive construction of particular ideals for maternal identity and
behavior, and the effort to eliminate other options, worked to uphold
the developing apparatus of male bourgeois power and liberal
ideology in eighteenth-century England. To understand how Augustan maternal mythology served particular cultural interests, we need
to see what that mythology left out; but we shall not delve far into
maternal demographics or trace long-term historical developments
in maternal ideology. Neither recovering data nor setting up comparative before-and-after narratives is the point. Our goal is to hear
in eighteenth-century voices echoes of past and future possibilities
that, though perhaps never quite present, are never entirely absent,
either. To make visible many alternatives present at various levels in
eighteenth-century texts about motherhood – some consciously
valorized or denigrated, others barely recognized or hardly imaginable – is of greater interest here than constructing progressive
teleologies or deciding what "really" happened.

Accordingly, we shall look at eighteenth-century texts not only to
see what maternal behaviors and attitudes they recommended, but
also to see what they can tell us about varieties of maternal possibility

---

[46]   See Armstrong, *Desire and Domestic Fiction* for the invention of the "domestic woman," a
       newly idle, privatized function in the early eighteenth century. Cf. Irigaray, "And the one
       doesn't stir without the other," 83; B. Hill, *Women, Work, and Sexual Politics*, 47.

denied credibility in the effort to create a monolithic version of maternal excellence. What silencings, abandonments, and abortions became necessary to bringing forth Augustan Britain's ideal mother? Any answer must be legion. But in the largest terms, as we shall see, what Augustan discourse excluded from its vision of virtuous maternity was *maternal difference* – differences within mothers, differences between and among them. With rare exceptions, Augustan writing assumes a limited (middle-) class-bound set of norms for virtuous motherhood, and refuses to admit that differences of economic privilege and historical position might make possible other, equally valid models. But maternal difference is everywhere apparent, even in texts that deny it most insistently.

The increasing dominance of a single correct version of maternal virtue in early eighteenth-century Britain was facilitated by what Foucault might have called various "technologies of motherhood." The popular press functioned as one such technology. So did the carefully staged representation of symbolic royal maternity during Queen Anne's reign. The ever-increasing proliferation of conduct literature aimed at women of (or aspiring to) middle-class sensibility and circumstances was yet another technological agent that helped to create a particular ideal of motherhood for Augustan culture. And so was emergent novelistic discourse, an especially powerful technology. The novels we shall consider, like the conduct books to which they respond and with which they overlap, seem to concern themselves with feminized, domestic matters by definition not part of the public world. Indeed, what Nancy Armstrong says of conduct books may also be said of the many Augustan novels produced primarily for female consumption:

By developing a language strictly for relations within the home, conduct books for women inadvertently provided the terms for rethinking relationships in the political world, for this language enabled authors to articulate both worlds while they appeared to represent only one. (*Desire*, 75)

Armstrong traces the eighteenth century's creation of a feminine ideal defined by domesticity, subjectivity, and the dubious power to order reality conceptually without seeming to participate in it materially. But *Desire and Domestic Fiction* virtually omits consideration of the eighteenth-century domestic woman as a mother, obscuring motherhood's central status in Augustan women's lives. The virtual absence of motherhood from so fine a work as Armstrong's ironically indicates the success of the eighteenth century's denial of political relevance to maternity. For Augustan women did not merely supervise servants, order households and regulate the consumption of goods; their main task, and the activity that most clearly established their gendered identities and social value, was reproduction.

Once the central element of maternity is restored to the picture, allowing us to see that the eighteenth-century "domestic woman" Armstrong describes might better be thought of as a "domestic mother," new problems emerge. One might presume, for instance, that by virtue of their supposedly apolitical affective role, domestic mothers would escape accountability for public events. We might imagine that mothers would have been considered innocent victims or hapless beneficiaries of social forces and institutions over which they had no control, not responsible agents. But as we shall see, the mothers who figure prominently in Augustan narratives, though supposedly without political agency and authority, never escape accountability. Insistence on the momentous responsibility of maternal ciphers appears in each of the texts we shall examine, signaling a profound duplicity at work in the creation of the middle-class mother, a figure always both innocent and guilty, victimized and victimizing.

Indeed, in the representations of maternal failure that fill Augustan narratives, reductive distinctions between power and powerlessness are radically complicated, and we begin to glimpse the complex dependency that so often links the resistance of the oppressed to collusion – even identification – with their oppressors. Maternal guilt is always overdetermined, maternal innocence always interested and compromised. The possibility disappears of inhabiting a definitive, stable position as *either* agent or object, aggressor or resister. Instead, everyone is complicit in the processes of maternal failure, including mothers themselves, even though they often find themselves in positions so disabling and contradictory that satisfactory action is impossible. To borrow the language one critic has used to describe women "choosing" abortions, the bad mothers represented in Augustan texts are "subject and object of violence at the same time."[47]

It is in this complicated sense that I treat the mothers in question here as agents, and see their represented experiences as part of the

---

[47]   B. Johnson, "Apostrophe," 33.

Augustan struggle to define and locate political agency. The point is not that they act autonomously, choosing freely amongst a rich field of options, or that they fully control the effects they produce. But neither are they helpless. They exercise *some degree* of choice, and are *to some extent* complicit in its results, though seldom to the extent that they are held accountable.[48] The mothers whose stories we will consider are not merely forced or fooled into conformity with standards for maternal virtue that deny reality to their subjective experience; instead, as we shall see, those who conform – and not all do – do so in varying degrees and contexts, believing they have something to gain from certain aspects of the dominant model of virtuous and effectual motherhood.[49] Neither their conformity nor their resistance is an all-or-nothing matter. Our effort will be to recognize the many shapes resistance takes in these texts, while remaining alert to the compromises and complicities always inherent in its manifestations.

A final explanation is in order. In a book about motherhood, the virtual absence of psychoanalytic methods and assumptions may constitute a silence that some readers find resounding. There is no doubt that over the past twenty years most influential critics and theoreticians of Western bourgeois motherhood have shared a psychoanalytic orientation: Chodorow, Gallop, Hirsch, Homans, Ian, Irigaray, Kristeva, Sprengnether, and Suleiman, to name only a few. Their work has changed feminist theory and practice, and makes studies like this one possible. Yet I am convinced that the psychoanalytic rubrics within which these critics (variously) work necessarily undercut efforts to understand motherhood in history. While there are great variations of scope, purpose, and method within the heterogeneous body of material I am grouping together as psychoanalytic feminist writing on motherhood, yet there are a few assumptions which even the most sophisticated feminist re-workings of Freudian paradigms share with "classical" psycho-analytic theory. Psychoanalytic feminist theories of motherhood still tend to work from the assumption that relations between mothers and their children are necessarily and exclusively private, deployed outside (even in opposition to) public life and discourse.[50]

---

[48] Cf. Giddens, *A Contemporary Critique*, 56–63.
[49] Cf. Hollway's notion of "investment," 237–38.
[50] Suleiman, "Writing and motherhood," 359; Daly and Reddy, "Introduction," *Narrating Mothers*, 7, 18.

The oedipal narrative, on which depend the empowering potentials
of the pre-oedipal mother, assumes as natural and inevitable a
domestic setting of egregiously bourgeois dimensions: remote
father, ever-present mother, isolated nuclear family, normative
heterosexuality. It is the naturalization of this scenario that I am
trying to dethrone here; to the extent that psychoanalytic feminist
considerations of maternity are driven by it, I find them unhelpful.

Further, psychoanalytic rubrics make it too easy to proceed as if
motherhood were a finite category, constant in history. According to
one pyschoanalytically oriented critic of maternal relations, "the
question that needs to be confronted is a question of definition:
'What is a mother? What is maternal?' " (Hirsch, *Mother-Daughter Plot*,
163). I suggest that there are more pertinent questions. Rather than
ask what "a mother" (any mother, every mother) *is*, we shall be
interested here in seeing what a particular past culture could (or
could not) imagine mothers *doing*, what spaces and positions it could
imagine them inhabiting. And we shall ask how we might use such
knowledge to recognize maternal difference(s) in the present and to
construct future motherhoods that do not necessarily entail abjection, withdrawal, or passivity.[51]

This is not to say that psychoanalytic methods, *tout ensemble*, are
necessarily (i.e., ahistorically) inappropriate for feminist examina-
tions of maternal politics. Quite the contrary. In 1978, Nancy
Chodorow's monumental *Reproduction of Mothering* demonstrated the
possibility of reimagining motherhood from within psychoanalytic
paradigms at that time. But all discourse exists in history; and the
history of maternal theory has brought us to a place where psychoanalytic assumptions, once very helpful, are now proving more a
liability than an asset to feminists thinking about motherhood.
Ironically enough, writing like Chodorow's has contributed to a
situation where feminists working to develop genuinely alternative
critical/maternal practices could now better employ more historically sensitive theoretical models.[52]

The problems inherent in psychoanalytic feminist thinking about
motherhood have been most clearly recognized by its best practi-
tioners who, to their credit, are often seriously troubled by disso-

---

[51]   Cf. Ruddick, "Maternal thinking," 214–15. For work in this direction, cf. Daly and Reddy,
       especially the fine introduction to that volume.
[52]   Daly and Reddy "Introduction," *Narrating Mothers*, 2–7; Garner "Constructing the
       mother," 87–93; Roof, "This is not for you," 158–66.

nance between their purposes and their method.[53] Yet despite the dissatisfaction and even despair that these critics express over psychoanalytic discourse, it seems to them inescapable. This I believe to be an error. Psychoanalysis is a very powerful discourse, but it is not *discourse itself*. It is true that women and other "others" are forced to speak in phallocentric languages. But we can choose among (and within) those languages, and we are responsible to choose bravely. If indeed we hope for change, then we must ensure that the limits we struggle against really are, at our own historical time and place, frontiers.

To be sure, Western motherhood traditionally has been, and still is, defined and contained by patriarchal privilege, and there is much to be learned from careful consideration of exactly how this has occurred in specific historical contexts. This book will be largely occupied with that kind of consideration, asking how influential Augustan writers imposed specific limits on motherhood by representing it in particular ways. But this book may also be seen as an experiment in doubting that maternity must necessarily exist in relation to primary patriarchal power, and in celebrating the incompleteness that always bedevils processes of cultural containment. Though silenced, mothers remain authoritative; though complicit, resistant; though co-opted, outside. Recognizing this incompleteness, we can move beyond a concentration on first one and then the other of the dyadic positions offered by totalizing myths of difference (silence-authority, complicity-resistance, inside-outside). Instead, we can gather the alternatives together, imagining abdication that produces a byproduct of authority, forms of complicity that constitute forms of resistance, places supposedly outside that redefine what inside might mean.

Difference, in other words, need not be imagined as a matter of hierarchical, fixed positions authorized by virtue of their exclusion of other fixed positions – the model of formal debate, warfare, traditional heterosexual en-gendering and its relation to homosexuality monolithically conceived. Instead of thinking this way, we might learn to see difference as a fluid relation between shifting positions that incorporates, interchanges, and continually revises all imaginable possibilities while never finally obliterating any – the model of dance or of what we call bisexuality, both of which admit the

[53] Sprengnether, *The Spectral Mother*, 8; Hirsch, "Incorporation and repetition," 11–12, 67, 167, 131–32; Gallop, "Mother tongue," 319–27.

possibility of continuous, profound revisions of always-changing subject positions.[54] Motherhood provides an especially fruitful site for this kind of experiment. Ambidextrous and multiple, irreducibly public *because* it is so intensely intimate, motherhood undermines the cultural systems that would delimit it, threatening (that is, promising) to expose the ludicrous distinction between what is relational and what is political, a distinction eighteenth-century discourse labored to construct, enforce, and naturalize. In this light, the effort to reimagine maternal difference offers us an opportunity to practice reimagining difference itself. The reason for paying close attention to long-silenced maternal voices and forgotten maternal stories is that they might help us to inhabit (maternal) difference differently, and so to transform familiar patterns of dominance and subordination into something new.

Motherhood was a precarious and anxious undertaking in Augustan England.[55] Midwifery manuals described in grisly detail the problems to be expected during pregnancy and childbirth,[56] and influential conduct books carried chilling warnings. To be "in readiness for her departure," John Dunton's *Ladies Dictionary* intones, is "the duty of a *big-bellied woman*" (142). Augustan women took such advice seriously: they were acutely anxious about pregnancy and

[54]   I distinguish between the *model* bisexuality and the *term* "bisexual." The model seems to me to promise more than the currently dominant dyadic model, in which "homosexuality" is posited as the debased opposite of "heterosexuality." This division relies on narrowly phallocentric notions of what is "sexual" in the first place, and serves the interests of ideological homogenization, exclusion, and hierarchy. But the *term* "bisexuality" remains problematic because it still makes reference to the dyadic framework where homosexuality is pitted against heterosexuality (and indeed, where male is opposed to female) as if these were exclusive options. It might be instructive as well as amusing to substitute "sexual" for "bisexual" in the familiar list of alternatives, thus: "homosexual," "heterosexual," or "sexual."
       For the historical constructedness of our notion of bisexuality, cf. Rackin "Foreign country;" Zimbardo, *At Zero Point*, esp. chapter 4; Laqueur, *Making Sex*, 133; Wittig, "The straight mind," esp. 107–8. For a fine example of how we might begin to complicate "the contrastive (and heterosexual) model of gender" see Gwillam, *Fictions of Gender*, 14. For the political costs of binary notions of difference, cf. Mohanty, "Under western eyes," 64. On the importance of resisting absolutized notions of power and static positions of dominance and subjugation, cf. Porter, "History and literature," 262–65.

[55]   The most useful place from which to begin a general study of experiences of pregnancy, birthing, lactation, and childrearing in eighteenth-century England is Fildes's collection, *Women as Mothers in Pre-Industrial England*: see especially essays by Crawford and Pollock in that volume. Cf. Fildes, *Wet-Nursing*; Fildes, *Breasts, Bottles and Babies*; G. Sussman, *Selling Mothers' Milk*; Illick, "Child-rearing in seventeenth-century England and America."

[56]   E.g., Sharp's *Midwives Book*. Cf. Hobby, *Virtue of Necessity*; Peters, "The pregnant Pamela," 432–42.

delivery, and many expected to die in childbirth or shortly afterwards. Their fears seem to have been justified. Puerperal fever, milk
fever, and long, agonizing deliveries were not only "ever-present," as
Fildes reminds us, but were "unrelieved by analgesics or anesthetics"
(*Wet-Nursing*, 90). In the unpaged "Approbation" (a kind of editorial
preface) to Elizabeth Joceline's famous letter to her unborn child, we
read that the author bought herself a winding sheet as soon as she
learned that she was pregnant, called for it "instantly" upon giving
birth, and died of a fever nine days later.[57]

The dangers of pregnancy and childbirth extended not only to
mothers, of course, but to their children as well. Once again,
historians disagree on exactly how dangerous those dangers were.
Where one decries the "appallingly high levels of infant and child
mortality" in Augustan London, another argues that "the infant
mortality rate has been greatly exaggerated," and asserts, with rather
cold comfort, that "80 to 85 per cent of all babies" survived, "at least
for a few years" (Earle, 230; Pollock, 51). The physician William
Cadogan grimly noted in 1748 that anyone looking over the "Bills of
Mortality" would surely "observe, that almost half the Number of
those, that fill up that black List, die under five Years of Age" (6).

As debates continue over the precise hazards of the undoubtedly
hazardous business of childbearing in the early eighteenth century,
we might turn attention to the less-frequently noted menace maternity posed in the more cerebral realm of (male) intellectual discourse.
For it is not too much to say that in late seventeenth- and early
eighteenth-century England the maternal functioned as a pivotal
category in virtually all forms of discourse, a place where ideas about
legitimacy and authority were routinely contested.[58] As an overtly
political category, maternity proved immensely threatening to patrilineal inheritance structures and, as we shall see in Part One, was
gradually divested of potency. The major means of this divestment

[57] Cf. Mendelson, "Stuart women's diaries," 196; Stone, *Family, Sex, and Marriage*, 64. Roger
Schofield expresses skepticism: although "many women died needlessly," he argues, the
rate of death was only about 1 per cent and chances were better of dying from infectious
diseases. Likewise, Dorothy McLaren finds it unimpressive that of the fourteen wealthy
women she studies, "only two" died in childbirth "after producing ten and eight infants
respectively at almost annual intervals" (McLaren, "Marital fertility and lactation," 46).
Against such use of statistics, Fildes observes that childbirth was especially fearsome
because it was a particularly painful and conspicuous cause of death, even if not an
inordinately frequent one in statistical terms. Chaber provides an eloquent rebuttal to
skepticism like Schofield's and McLaren's (" 'This Affecting Subject,' " esp. 211–20).

[58] Cf. Bruce, "The flying island," 66; Part One, below.

was an increased delimitation of maternal influence to the private sphere. During the Augustan period, motherhood came to epitomize the radical withdrawal of the domestic woman.

Augustan writing on motherhood – including conduct literature, sermons, fiction, visual images, and all sorts of popular writing – participated in recasting the multiple, contingent *experience* of mother-hood as a more easily controlled social *institution*,[59] an institution defined according to a limited set of supposedly timeless behaviors and sentiments: all-engrossing tenderness, long-term maternal breastfeeding, personal supervision and education of young children, complete physical restriction to domestic space, absence of sexual desire, withdrawal from productive labor. These were the criteria for virtuous motherhood outlined in texts directed at women of the developing middle sectors of Augustan society. Moreover, despite their class-specific nature, these criteria became, by the middle of the eighteenth century, the exclusive markers of motherhood itself, universally imposed on women of all social positions.

This imposition was facilitated by the powerful implicit thesis of virtually all of the most influential work on motherhood in the early eighteenth century: that maternity exists apart from historical con-tingency, that it is not "classed." In engendering this assumption, eighteenth-century bourgeois discourse almost succeeded in invali-dating notions of legitimate motherhood that did not presuppose the exclusion, passivity and silence that were coming to characterize middle-class female existences. The combined efforts of texts like many of those we shall consider came close to neutralizing resistance not only to a domestic ideal of maternal virtue, but also to the increasing social dominance of "the middle sort" of men, whose economic and cultural interests that ideal served.[60]

The portion of maternal history we shall consider begins with the public career of Anne Stuart, Princess of Denmark between 1683 and 1702, and Queen of England between 1702 and 1714. Focusing on Anne's efforts to construct political authority from symbolic mater-nity, Part One argues that changes in the political valences of royal motherhood as Anne experienced it contributed to an increased

---

59   I borrow Rich's famous language.
60   The term is from Defoe's *Review* for 1709 (see Part Two, note 16). Cf. the anonymous *Dissertation on Mr. Hogarth's Six Prints*, 9. In 1753, James Nelson divided English society into five parts, which he called "classes": the nobility, the gentry, wealthy traders and merchants, peasants, and urban dwellers (156–57).

distance between maternity and public authority during her lifetime. Anne's tragic maternal history, the birth and early death of her son William, Duke of Gloucester, and the desperate hopes for children that her subjects continued to cherish even when such hopes had become unrealistic – all created an apt context for Queen Anne's use of symbolic motherhood when physical (and hence, directly political) childbearing was finally admitted to be out of the question. Unfortunately, Anne's timing was bad. By the time she chose motherhood as the symbol of her political power, it was already too late to construe public authority from figural maternity. Yet despite its failure to define and create political viability, Queen Anne's maternity remained a continual locus of anxiety in patriarchal writing long after her death: Pope, for example, used Anne's signature phrase "nursing mother" in his *Dunciad* to describe the detestable and threatening Queen Dullness. Part One examines the failure of maternal imagery to create political authority for Queen Anne, and considers ways in which that failure remained incomplete.

Part Two considers representations of maternal monstrosity among thieves, whores, and workers in early eighteenth-century England, arguing that the Augustan fascination with "unnatural" motherhood may be read as part of a two-pronged effort: an effort to construct by default a particular version of "natural" motherhood, and an effort to alleviate an increasingly visible ideological contradiction – the contradiction between the perceived necessity of competitive self-construction and the perceived necessity of maternal abnegation. Augustan narratives of monstrous motherhood implicitly valorize the maternal behaviors advocated in conduct writing for "middling" women as instinctual and universal, even in material circumstances that make such behaviors impossible, inadequate, or inappropriate. Defoe's Moll Flanders and Roxana, for instance, invoke abstract, culturally correct standards for "natural" motherhood that render their own maternal behaviors – constrained as they are by desperate economic circumstances and disreputable social positions – negligent at best and sometimes criminal. The result is not narratives that bring those standards into question, but myths of maternal monstrosity in which the narrating heroines deny their own gendered humanity and maternal viability. By putting into the mouths of impoverished and criminal mother-narrators an insistence that behaviors possible only for comfortable domestic mothers are exclusively "natural," Defoe (like many another Augustan writer)

admits only one definition of maternal virtue and transforms
material differences into moral hierarchies – or nearly so. For in the
effort to reduce motherhood to a monolith, narratives about monstrous mothers instead reveal maternity to be a multitude of
changing behaviors and attitudes, taking shape within specific
material conditions.

At the same time that Defoe published *Moll Flanders* and *Roxana*,
Eliza Haywood produced very different maternal stories. In the three
tales by Haywood that we shall consider, motherhood signifies apart
from patriarchal influence and confers unique authority on women,
even providing them access to the public world. Haywood's vision of
maternal strength and possibility goes far beyond Defoe's representation of mothers hopelessly encumbered by their children, and
suggests more than Defoe's infanticidal novels imagine: that it is
patriarchal authority and economic dependence, not children's
competing needs, that make motherhood and personal autonomy
seem mutually exclusive. Haywood, however, remains uneasy about
the costs of maternal autonomy and ambivalent about the public
legitimacy and viability of powerful maternal figures, who thrive only
so long as they remain sequestered. Like Defoe's, Haywood's tales
partake of the central assumption at work in the majority of
Augustan representations of motherhood: the assumption that virtuous motherhood and public authority are incompatible.

Again and again in early eighteenth-century representations of
motherhood, there is an attempt to place blame for perceived
maternal failure wholly on the exceptional deviance of individual
mothers, to deny the necessarily corporate nature of such failure –
and of its definition *as* failure. This reductive strategy re-enacts and,
implicitly, criticizes Augustan attempts to make individual agents
wholly responsible for the many failures of public authority that
characterized seventeenth- and early eighteenth-century English (or,
after 1707, British) politics. In some of the tales of maternal failure we
shall examine in Part Two, the inadequacy and interestedness of this
procedure are so egregious that the effort obviously undermines
itself, creating space for new ways of interpreting both failures of
political authority and changes in maternal practice, a species of
political practice.

The texts considered in Parts One and Two, then, represent
mothers of the very highest and very lowest social stations. In Part
Three, we turn to Richardson's depictions of "middling" mothers in

Pamela, Part 2 (1741) and *Clarissa* (1748–49), where conduct writing's norms for virtuous motherhood might be expected to be most appropriate.[61] In the second part of *Pamela*, Richardson is concerned to control the subversive potential of conduct literature, especially the possibility that mothers might adhere to the prescriptions of conduct writing in defiance of their husbands' authority. This is precisely the possibility that tempts Pamela as a new mother. Her eventual submission to Mr. B. in their dispute over maternal breastfeeding – a submission which entails repudiation of conduct literature's authority and denial of her own autonomous subjectivity – defines Pamela as a virtuous mother. But this dubious triumph is achieved at considerable cost, and is vulnerable to the same criticisms as Richardson's depiction of female virtue in *Pamela*, Part 1: Pamela's maternal virtue, like her sexual virtue before, often looks disturbingly crafty, hypocritical, and morally reductive. But as in the first *Pamela*, these problems are mystified, and all ends in apparent, if superficial, harmony.

Clarissa, on the other hand, faces squarely the issues that *Pamela*, Part 2 sidesteps, ruthlessly exposing vast gaps between operative Augustan mythologies of motherhood and the particular sociodomestic and material situations within which mothering actually takes place. First published in the same year the Foundling Hospital opened its doors, *Clarissa* presents its own vision of maternal failure, and again abdication and usurpation are hard to tell apart. In the person of Mrs. Charlotte Harlowe, failed maternity slowly emerges

---

[61] As many critics have by now pointed out, the atmosphere of both *Pamela* and *Clarissa*, like the attitudes of their protagonists and the readers imagined in conduct books, are distinctly "middle class," even if it is impossible to say exactly what this means. In Part Three, I follow this tradition, considering Pamela's home and Harlowe Place as households to which the standards set forth in conduct literature should be applicable.

I recognize that this procedure is vulnerable to criticism. The two families are not especially similar: Mr. B. is from an old, landed family, while Mr. Harlowe is a self-made tradesman. And neither family seems especially concerned with business and frugality, traits prominent in paradigmatically middle-class figures (Franklin) and in definitive treatments of middle-class mentalities (Weber). Yet I see both the B.'s and the Harlowes as "middle-class" families insofar as they formulate and critique recognizable outlines of that still-unfixed social category. I use "middle-class" inexactly, but the idea of "middling men" was broad and vaguely applied in the early eighteenth century, too. I align my practice with that of Earle (who defines "the middling people" as those "who worked but ideally did not get their hands dirty" [3]), Neale ("the absence of a contemporary language ... should not prevent historians from categorizing the past in ways unknown or only vaguely understood by men in the past" [99]), and Nussbaum, who argues persuasively that "the categories of class may exceed an individual's own understanding of that position" (*Autobiographical Subject*, 50–51).

as the embedded causal plot behind the machinations that lead to Clarissa's disturbing rape/seduction, the hidden matrix of a catastrophe for which agency appears to be clearly defined, but is in fact diffuse and multiple. *Clarissa* interrogates the maternal norms inculcated in *Pamela*, and demonstrates that even a comfortable domestic woman can be denied the authority to construct her own motherhood, since motherhood cannot be separated from the historical, political, and economic positions of particular mothers. And it asks, in the barely audible voice of a failed and grieving mother, Augustan England's most troubling questions about agency, responsibility, and lost authority.

We conclude with a short consideration of a famous text from 1762, Lady Sarah Pennington's *An Unfortunate Mother's Advice to Her Absent Daughters*. Pennington was separated from her daughters by their father, and forbidden even to correspond; yet she longs to communicate with her children and especially to fulfill the indispensable duty of maternal instruction. So she "goes public," publishing the letter that she says she would have preferred to send privately. The expedient worked: the girls (along with hundreds of other readers) got the letter, and – surprisingly enough – Lady Sarah became famous not as a transgressive woman, but as a devoted mother and wronged wife. Indeed, she emerges from the *Advice* as a new kind of virtuous mother: a mother whose virtue is demonstrated not by her private feelings or domestic behaviors, but by her public resistance to tyranny. In *An Unfortunate Mother's Advice to Her Absent Daughters*, Pennington speaks in a new kind of maternal voice, a voice at once public and private. Rejecting the code of passive obedience enjoined repeatedly on Augustan mothers, she develops physical means of demonstrating the legitimacy of both her text and her maternal authority.

Like the images from Hogarth with which we began, Lady Sarah Pennington's *Advice* is concerned with forced maternal abdication and the problems of authority and responsibility it makes visible. Can an absent mother be a good mother? Can mothering be done properly by any agent besides the mother herself? To what extent, in short, is motherhood re-presentable, and who is responsible for its representations? Pennington mothers her children through the proxy of print, and so defies not only her tyrannical husband, but also the tyranny of maternal politics in her day, with its insistence that mothers be invisible, inaudible, and without political agency, but nevertheless always accountable. Her success – not only at communicating with her daughters, but at convincing her contemporaries of her maternal virtue – definitively indicates what we shall see repeatedly in the texts this book considers: that though many influential Augustan writers labored to produce and enforce a particular, limited set of norms for virtuous motherhood, the ideals engendered in their discourse never entirely eliminated maternal difference. *An Unfortunate Mother's Advice* straightforwardly enacts a politics based on the revolutionary notion that maternal virtue and authority take a multitude of forms, and can even inhabit absence, abdication, and transgression.

PART ONE

Royal motherhood: Queen Anne and the politics of maternal representation

She felt a mother's fondness for her people, by whom she was universally beloved with a warmth of affection which even the prejudice of party could not abate.[1]

[1] Smollett, *History of England*, 2: 111.

On June 10, 1688, Queen Mary of Modena, consort of James II, gave birth to a son. The king and queen had already lost four children in their fifteen years of marriage, and since a recent miscarriage the queen had been continually ill; no one expected that she would produce any more children. So the pregnancy came as a great surprise to the nation. James's supporters eagerly welcomed the little prince as the guarantor of the king's faltering authority: "Hail, Royal BOY!" enthused Aphra Behn before the baby was even born, "whose Coming is design'd / To calm the Murmurs of all Humane Kind" (Behn, "A Congratulatory Poem," 3). But such rejoicing was by no means pervasive. What celebrations did take place upon the child's birth, according to Gilbert Burnet, "were very cold and forced ... only to make a shew" (1: 754). Burnet, of course, was no friend to James's government and can hardly be called an objective observer. His biases, however, are representative; for the baby's arrival terrified and galvanized the Protestant majority, who feared the establishment of a Roman Catholic dynasty and the perpetuation of James's unpopular policies.

In need of strong rhetoric to discredit the unwelcome infant's claim to the throne, Whiggish Protestants called into question the possibility that the queen might actually have brought forth a healthy child. The likelihood of Queen Mary's motherhood was attacked from every possible angle: the queen's poor health and reproductive history, difficulty in determining possible dates of conception, ambiguities at the moment of delivery, and so on.[2] Burnet again exemplifies his contemporaries' preoccupations in the detailed attention his history gives to Queen Mary's bodily capacities. "The Queen," he notes,

had been for six or seven years in such an ill state of health, that every winter brought her very near death. Those about her seemed well assured that she, who had buried all her children soon after they were born, and had now for several years ceased bearing, would have no more children ... She had great and frequent distempers ... which put all people out of their hopes or fears of her having children. Her spirits were ... much on the fret ... In the end of *September*, an accident took her to which the sex is subject ... She was in the progress of her big belly let blood several times (1: 748–49)

[2] Burnet, *History of His Own Time*, 1: 748–90. Cf. Weil, "Politics of legitimacy," 68. Comparisons were maliciously drawn between Mary of Modena and the Virgin Mary, both of whom were described as having conceived "without the aid of a husband" (Weil, 76). Cf. Kenyon, "Birth of the old pretender"; Speck, "Orangist conspiracy."

– and so on. Such intimate and yet also entirely public speculations on the maternal potential of the queen's body prompted a powerful and widely disseminated rumor: that the royal pregnancy had been a hoax, and that the infant baptized as James's heir was actually a substitute smuggled into the palace in a warming pan. The near-impossibility of such a fraud – more than forty people were in the room when Mary delivered – did not stop many Protestants, including the baby's half-sister Princess Anne, from relying on it for decades.[3]

What is interesting about the effort to cast the infant as supposititious is that it did not take the form of a debate over whether he was really James's son, the usual strategy for defining illegitimacy. Instead, the debate focused on whether the child was really *Mary's*: much evidence was marshaled by Protestants to prove the queen's maternal incapacity. Of course, the point of attacking the baby's maternity was to invalidate his right to the throne, an essentially patrilineal right; there is no question that James's government was the real object of the attack. Nevertheless it remains significant that the maternal potential of Mary of Modena's particular female body was the site of political contest in the texts that constituted what historians have come to call "the warming-pan scandal."

A generation later, another queen of England – also famous for failed motherhood and poor health – would find that her child-bearing was a political issue. But Queen Anne's experience was unlike Mary of Modena's in important respects, and the differences can teach us much about developing Augustan maternal ideology. For in the decades following the birth of Mary of Modena's unfortunate son, changes in the political position and function of queenly motherhood were taking place. The queen's maternity remained a crucial site for competition between various patriarchal interests; but Anne's own physical capacity for childbearing – the particularities of her maternal body – played a much less significant role in that competition than had her stepmother's. Instead, during Anne's reign the queen's maternity became increasingly abstract, a bargaining chip in a newly reformulated game of patrilineal inheritance.

---

[3] Boyer, *English Theophrastus* (1722), 3. Cf. Burnet, *History of His Own Time*, 1: 749–54; Clarendon, *Correspondence of Henry Hyde*, 2: 198. In 1730, Oldmixon finds it regrettable that King James did not follow the example of German Emperor Henry VI, who put his wife Constantia in a "publick" place during her labor, "that no suppositious Child might possibly be convey'd to her and there in sight of the Citizens … none being excluded, she brought forth a Prince, who was afterwards the Emperor *Frederick* II" (*History of England*, 729).

Queen Anne unintentionally precipitated attention to her maternity exactly twenty years after the warming-pan scandal. In the wake of her husband's death in 1708, Anne decided to remove from the collect for the Anglican service for March 8th these words: "And that these blessings may continue to after ages, make the queen, we pray thee, a happy mother of children, who ... may happily succeed her in the government of these kingdoms" (*PH*, 777). But Parliament objected to the queen's emendation, suggesting that instead of removing the prayer for heirs, she marry again and produce "issue" at last. "No greater happiness," they said, "can be desired for your kingdoms" (*JHC*, 16: 72; *PH*, 778; cf. Gregg, *Queen Anne*, 285). Anne's famous reply silenced Parliament forever on the issue of remarriage. "The provision I have made for the Protestant Succession," she wrote, "will always be a proof, how much I have at my heart the future happiness of the kingdom. The subject of this Address is of such a nature, that I am persuaded you do not expect a particular Answer" (*JHC*, 16: 75; *PH*, 778).

In commenting on this response, Anne's biographers traditionally refer to her overwhelming grief for Prince George and the tactlessness of Parliament's timing and request. Both are undeniable. Anne was devastated after George's death, and Parliament's brutal hurry was widely remarked in the popular press, in broadsides bearing such titles as "The Hasty Widow, or the Sooner the Better." Yet the "subject of the address" was not only Anne's remarriage, but also – indeed, more fundamentally – its hoped-for "issue." If we take the subject of the exchange between queen and Parliament to be maternity, not just remarriage, Anne's response resonates in new ways. For as everyone in Augustan England was aware, Queen Anne's decision to remove the prayer for heirs had a long and painful history. Despite seventeen pregnancies (once with twins), Anne had assumed the throne without living children. For a few years after her accession in 1702, supporters and petitioners had continued to insist on Anne's potential motherhood. "I pray God, that your Majesty may soon embrace a son of your own," the Earl of Marchmont wrote to the new queen that year, "that would be a healing and composing blessing to this wavering nation" (*MP*, 3: 242 [July 1, 1702]). In the same year, the House of Commons expressed the hope that God would "bless these kingdoms with royal issue of your majesty" (*PH*, 12); and Mary Chudleigh prayed that heaven would "let You in a num'rous Offspring live."[4] Against these bright hopes, Anne's poignant words in a 1703 letter to the Duchess of Marlborough seem measured and realistic: the queen still hopes for "the inexpressible blessing of another Child," but "I do not flatter myself with the thought of it."[5] In any case, hopeful rhetoric was becoming increasingly impractical in the face of Jacobite threats to Protestant succession. By the Fall of 1705, Parliament had renewed old debates about the establishment of a Hanoverian presence to ensure a smooth transition and pre-empt Jacobite action at the queen's eventual death.[6] And then in 1708, Prince George died.

By removing the prayer for heirs, Anne signaled her unwillingness to participate in the pretense that she – at forty-three years old and a virtual invalid – would ever produce another child, whether she remarried or not. Anne saw that Parliament's request was not really about her physical maternity at all: it was a ploy designed by certain partisan factions to delay the arrival of a representative of Hanover.[7] The Duke of Marlborough understood this at once when his wife wrote to him of the remarriage request. In a letter to the Duchess dated February 13, 1709 Marlborough wrote,

As to the adress made to the Queen to lay aside grief and to think of marrying, [it] is a very good antidote against the invitation for this sessions, but may be a strong argument for it at another time. (*MGC*, 3: 1217)

By refusing Parliament a more "particular answer," Anne showed that she too understood "the nature" of royal maternity as it figured in Parliament's request: her maternity had become abstract, a convenient category outside political decision-making and action.

In the rhetorical wars of 1688, Mary of Modena's actual motherhood, the "Sacred VESSEL" (Behn, "A Congratulatory Poem," 4) of her particular body and its ability to bear children, had been crucially important. It had mattered that the queen was believed by many to be physically unable to give birth. But by 1708, it did not really matter; in the exchanges over the prayer book, Anne's maternity had been severed from Anne herself. But the *idea* of the queen's maternity as a rhetorical place subject to political manipula-

---

[4] Chudleigh, "To the Queen's Most Excellent Majesty," 44.

[5] *MGC*, 1: 186, n. 7.

[6] This idea Anne successfully opposed throughout her reign. Her resistance parallels Elizabeth I's to a similar proposal. Cf. Gregg, *Queen Anne*, 404.

[7] For the politics of the Hanoverian invitation cf. Gregg, *Queen Anne*, 183; *MGC*, 3: 1217. One result of the debate was the Regency Act (1706), which designated officers to serve at the queen's death until the arrival of a Hanoverian successor.

tion was still very useful. This is why the widely recognized fact that Anne would never produce an heir – made virtually indisputable by George's death and Anne's determined removal of the prayer for heirs from the prayerbook – did not put an end to discursive connections between queenly maternity and public politics. On the contrary, the finality of Anne's bodily maternal failure after 1708 actually *renewed* such connections: now the queen's maternity could be represented as entirely symbolic, divested of its earlier potential as a political activity at once physical and female. Little wonder that Anne told Parliament she was "persuaded that you do not expect a particular Answer."

The twin anecdotes of Queen Mary and Queen Anne illustrate complex changes in the way royal maternity functioned in the political discourse of Augustan England. Traditionally, queens had been public figures whose maternal bodies were, literally, political agents: a queen bodily engendered the political state, and representations of her maternity helped to define the political status of motherhood. Accordingly, in the crisis of 1688 the queen's motherhood figured (at least rhetorically) as political *while* particular, public while personal, physical, and female. But twenty years later, queenly maternity had been defined as a symbolic category indicative of the distance *between* political agency and female experience. At the time of the Glorious Revolution it was still possible to imagine that public legitimacy and authority might be derived, to a considerable extent, from maternity; but in the early eighteenth century, the connection between maternity and political legitimacy came to function much less as a challenge to patrilineal systems of power and inheritance than as a facilitator for those systems.

This shift was a gradual, almost imperceptible, process. Its lineaments may well have been invisible to eighteenth-century eyes, and will remain partly in shadows for us even after careful analysis. Nevertheless, we can trace its large outlines, borrowing light from smaller, more manageable explanatory narratives. One such narrative concerns the difficulties Queen Anne encountered in her attempt to use maternal imagery to build political authority. Understanding why the queen's efforts could not but fail can help us begin to understand how, why, and to what extent maternity was separated from public authority during the Augustan age.

From the earliest days of her political career (Princess of Denmark

1683–1702; Queen of England 1702–07; Queen of Great Britain 1707–14), Anne Stuart encouraged her subjects to imagine her as the perfect embodiment of two ideals: virtuous mother and powerful ruler. Indeed, as we shall see, Anne deliberately conflated the two ideals at her coronation, explicitly using maternity as a figure for royal authority. But the cultural position and political efficacy of both halves of Anne's double image – mother and monarch – were changing radically, and Anne found it increasingly difficult to forge political authority from maternal self-representation.

Many factors contributed to the growing distance between royal maternity and public authority during Anne's lifetime. For one thing, rules for effective authority on all levels – including monarchical authority – were being rewritten in the wake of the seventeenth century's many political upheavals and in the gradual shift – begun before Anne became queen and continued well after her death – from aristocratic to middle-class cultural dominance. As English men came to believe themselves authorized to choose their rulers should blood lines fail or legal heirs prove unacceptable, the continuance of a particular dynasty, though still a matter of concern, was less important than ever before. What mattered more was that a ruler could be depended upon to protect the economic, political, and cultural interests of elite Protestants. By the time of Anne's accession, it had become more necessary that the new monarch could be defined (and her definition manipulated) representationally than that she could engender history physically.

The problems inherent in Anne's maternal self-representation were exacerbated by the growing insistence in Augustan conduct books and sermons that maternal authority could only be legitimate – indeed, could only be imagined – in the context of isolated, private households, not as a constitutive presence in public affairs.[8] Though this rhetoric was designed for middle-class consumption, Queen Anne's maternal self-representation was peculiarly vulnerable to its implications. For Anne took pains to present herself in terms attractive and accessible to the majority of her people; she linked herself representationally to the increasingly powerful ideals of Augustan society's "middling" sectors and invested herself with the trappings of equality with commoners, effacing her royal difference to a significant extent. In 1691 she assumed the name "Mrs. Morley"

---

[8] Cf. Part Three, below.

when communicating with her friend Sarah Jennings Churchill ("Mrs. Freeman") because, in the words of Anne's biographer, she wished "to establish in private a relationship of equality between herself and the countess" (Gregg, *Queen Anne*, 81). Sarah herself would later recall that Anne had a "different taste" from most monarchs: "a friend was what she most coveted; and for the sake of friendship ... she was fond even of that *equality* which she thought belonged to it" (*Conduct*, 14).

Publicly, too, Anne carefully cultivated her image as an ordinary domestic woman: she loved to eat, to gamble, and to have babies. She was a submissive wife, a soft-spoken mistress, temperamentally amenable to suggestion, and exemplary in her devotion to the English church. "The *colder Airs* of MAJESTY alone," Elkanah Settle wrote,

> Attended Her not farther then [sic] the *Throne*.
> In her *Recesses*, all serenely Mild,
> That tend'rest condescending SWEETNESS *smiled*.
> ("Threnodia Britannica" [1714], 13)

Likewise, Anne's marriage to Prince George was routinely represented as companionate, a private refuge from the royal spotlight. Eulogies on the Prince's death typically refer to him as Anne's "*Friend*."[9] "Heavens!" Theobald cried in an elegy published in the year of the queen's death, "How she shines, divested of her State; / And only, in *Connubial Virtues*, Great" (14). Anne's very popular relinquishment of the "first fruits" in 1704[10] was another act understood to level the difference inherent in her position: by resigning part of her own income to impoverished clergymen, Settle enthused, "*ANNE* disroab'd her own *Prerogative*" ("Threnodia Britannica" 14). As late as the nineteenth century, the incorrect notion that Queen Anne's grandmother was a washerwoman remained popular[11] precisely because it perpetuated the image of Anne as simultaneously royal and of the people. Even today, Anne is said to have been oddly

---

[9] E.g., Marshall, 10.

[10] The tradition thus established of royal donation to needy members of the clergy came to be called "Queen Anne's Bounty." Gregg gives the annual sum thus relinquished as £16,000–£17,000 in early eighteenth-century money (*Queen Anne*, 179). Anne was still much loved for this act after her death (see figure 7, below). She also won lasting popularity early in her reign when she donated £100,000.00 of her personal revenue to the war effort. These acts of largesse take on new significance in light of a contemporary truism: a woman who is "full of good Works ... may thus be a Mother when she ceases to bear" ([Steele,] *Ladies Library*, 2: 357).

[11] Cf. Strickland, *Lives of the Queens of England*, 12: 106.

ordinary: one modern writer calls her "by nature and inclination, a mirror and a mouthpiece for the middle-of-the-road English attitudes" (Curtis, *Life and Times of Queen Anne*, 92).

Now of course, Anne was not an ordinary woman, and her social position necessarily created critical distances between the queen and the majority of her subjects. Moreover Anne (a Stuart, after all) zealously defended her royal privilege. Despite her desire for "equality" with Sarah Churchill, for example, the queen was quite capable of asserting her monarchical privilege when the ambitious Sarah pushed too far (as she often did).[12] Nevertheless, Queen Anne's considerable popularity was largely due to the fact that unlike any monarch before her, she was defined in terms of what she *shared* with her subjects: she was a model for women insofar as she was ordinary. So Anne enjoyed and exploited a special relation to the emerging ideal of domestic womanhood, defining, representing, and deploying the interests and values of her increasingly-powerful "middling" subjects. Her representation shaped contemporary expectations for attainable female virtue and acceptable female authority. And because she adopted a maternal self-representation, Anne helped to construct Augustan ideals for virtuous motherhood.

"THE TEEMING PRINCESS OF DENMARK":
ANNE AS MOTHER, 1684–1700

During the 1680s and nineties, the maternal body of the Princess of Denmark was the hope of Protestant England and a political force to be reckoned with. Anne's political authority was routinely represented in maternal terms, as in a portrait from 1688 (figure 5). The political nature of Anne's maternity and the public authority it provided are evident in the captions to this portrait, where Anne proclaims herself (in faulty French) one who would be either queen or the mother of a king – significantly, it does not seem to matter which.[13] The declamatory Dutch at the bottom of the portrait ("O Virtue and Courage Reward My Hope and Crown it with Glory"[14])

---

[12] Cf. B. Brown, *Letters and Diplomatic Instructions*, 286.
[13] Cf. Manley: at the time of her father's accession to the throne, the Princess Albania [Anne] "was certain in her self or Posterity to succeed her Father" (*Queen Zarah*, 54).
[14] My thanks to the staff of the Dutch Consulate's office in San Francisco for assistance with this translation.

5 J. Gole, *Anne of Denmark*. c. 1688.

reinforces the message that Anne's motherhood was a public phenomenon of international importance. Indeed, to Princess Anne it must have seemed that maternity *was* political authority. As one contemporary chronicler put it, Anne was famous at the end of the seventeenth century as "the teeming Princess of *Denmark*" whose maternal potential presented an even greater political threat to her deposed father than her own potential to be queen.[15]

Princess Anne and her supporters became adept at using the promise of her female body for political ends. During 1687, when Anne wished to avoid potentially damaging association with her unpopular father without openly offending him, she excused herself from attending James's court by pleading problems related to

[15] Boyer, *The English Theophrastus*, 2.

pregnancy.[16] In 1688, she again used pregnancy for political ends, this time to avoid hearing the report of the council James appointed to verify the legitimacy of the newborn prince.[17] James himself recounted this incident in his memoirs:

On the fifteenth [of Oct., 1688] the prince of Wales was named. His birth was proved, in a council extraordinary, on the twenty-second. The princess Anne waved [sic] being at it; pretending danger in coming abroad, being with child.[18]

"None believed that [pregnancy] to be the true reason," Burnet says, "so it was looked on as a colour that shewed she did not believe" in the child's legitimacy (1: 786). Throughout that Autumn, Anne continued to plead pregnancy to avoid appearing in public or seeing her father; but in December, when Anne and George had safely defected to William, the Prince revealed to Clarendon that Anne had not been pregnant at all. "Good God bless us!" Clarendon wrote in his diary, "nothing but lying and dissimulation in the world" (2: 216).

Anne's maternal stratagems continued during William and Mary's reign. When William maneuvered to cashier Sarah Churchill as Anne's principal attendant, the princess used her current pregnancy to create public sympathy and to put reciprocal pressure on the childless king and queen.[19] Even as late as 1701, when the Act of Settlement had been passed and William tried to bring the Electoral Prince of Hanover to England, Anne prevented this threat to her own authority "by falsely informing the king that she was again pregnant."[20] So it was no secret to Princess Anne that political leverage lay in her bodily ability to reproduce and in the secrets and mysteries surrounding pregnancy. Throughout the treacherous years surrounding the Glorious Revolution, and all through the reign of her estranged and hostile brother-in-law, Anne managed to retain her position as heir-apparent by means of carefully timed exploitations of the political possibilities of physical motherhood.

The birth of her son William Henry (later Duke of Gloucester) in the year of the Revolution settlement gave increased lustre to Anne's image as the hopeful Protestant princess (figure 6). Little William's relative health, the fact that he was male, the assurance that he

16 Cf. Clarendon, *Henry Hyde*, 2: 196; Gregg, *Queen Anne*, 51.
17 Cf. Burnet, *History of His Own Time*, 1: 785–86.
18 MacPherson, *Original Papers*, 1: 155.
19 Gregg, *Queen Anne*, 86–7. Cf. Brown, *Letters and Diplomatic Instructions*, 53; Green, *Duchess of Marlborough*, 74–5.
20 Gregg, *Queen Anne*, 123; Gregg, "Jacobite," 368.

6   Studio of Godfrey Kneller, *Anne of Denmark with the Duke of Gloucester.* c. 1694.

would be raised Protestant – all seemed to promise a smooth Protestant succession in the Stuart line, to vindicate the Revolution itself, and, not least, to enhance Princess Anne's political importance *as a mother*. Decades later, Thomas Salmon would recall not only that the nation reached consensus on the revolution settlement after Gloucester's birth but also that "upon the Birth of a Son, the Interest of the Princess of *Denmark* seemed to be much advanced, and all the

World began to make their Court that Way, how much soever they had slighted her before."[21]

Besides Gloucester, Queen Anne had four children: her daughters Mary (b. June 1, 1685) and Anne Sophia (b. May 12, 1686) died (probably of smallpox) in February, 1687 – the "fatal February" when Anne also had a miscarriage; another Mary (b. October 14, 1690) lived for only a few hours; and a son George (b. April 17, 1692), died shortly after birth. Anne also seems to have suffered at least thirteen miscarriages or stillbirths and two episodes of pseudo-cyesis – an indication of how desperate was her need to give birth.[22] Indeed, we will never be sure exactly how many times Anne was pregnant, since Augustan uncertainty about whether to count miscarriages and stillbirths as children has resulted in discrepancies in the records.[23] We do know, however, that her formidable maternal history was not especially unusual: many wealthy women of the time gave birth to twenty children and at least one bore thirty.[24]

But every one of Anne's children was dead before their mother was thirty-five. In the language of one contemporary, "tho' there was a child born every year for many years, yet they have all died: So that the fruitfullest marriage of the age was fatally blasted as to the effect of it."[25] Gloucester lived the longest, and his death in 1700 – just five days after his eleventh birthday – was the hardest of all his mother's heartbreaking bereavements. Two years later, Anne assumed the throne as a paradoxical and unprecedented figure: a "childless parent"[26] whose health had been broken by almost continuous childbearing, and a monarch of disputed right whose claims to authority rested on a failed maternal body. Despite the

---

21 Salmon, *Life of Her Late Majesty*, 1: 30. Cf. Harrison, *An Impartial History*, 26; Gregg, *Queen Anne*, 72.

22 Gregg, *Queen Anne*, 54–6; 100–06.

23 My estimates are derived from Boyer, *The English Theophrastus*, Chester, Conyers, Harrison, Gregg's biography, and the *DNB* (1: 443ff).

24 McLaren, "Marital fertility," 22. Disease and cultural practices (e.g., sending out to nurse, feeding "by hand"), of course, often made it uncertain whether even a single child would survive to adulthood. Cf. Fildes, *Breasts, Bottles and Babies*, 83. It is chilling to observe the very low value placed on women's labor and health under such conditions. The situation was hardly better in the middle sectors where, according to one estimate, mothers averaged one delivery every twenty-three months and just three out of five children born could be expected to survive to age fifteen (Earle, *The English Middle Class*, 230).

25 Burnet, *History*, 1: 563. Cf. Rapin-Thoyras, *Histoire d'Angleterre*, 4: 534.

26 Anon., "Generous Muse," 9.

careful deployment of her politicized maternal body, Anne's physical motherhood proved insufficient at last.

Queen Anne's authority as maternal monarch, then, was acutely compromised. As monarch under Parliament, she was by definition a kind of cipher; and as *maternal* queen, her public authority was further reduced, not only by the developing ideology of domestic motherhood which it is this book's task to trace, but also by her physical failure to produce and sustain heirs. Increasingly, representations of Anne as national mother "backfired," as Carol Barash puts it, "inadvertently calling attention to her lack of offspring" and diminishing her political authority.[27] By 1714, Delarivier Manley felt compelled to defend the queen from political attacks made explicitly on the basis of her childlessness.

> The Loss of the D. of *Glocester* [sic] and the want of Hopes of Posterity from Her present Majesty, are Misfortunes never enough to be lamented: But is it not a very ungenerous way of proceeding instead of Comforting and Supporting their Prince under this Calamity, to Insult and Despise Her for it? To multiply their Affronts and Indignities, because She wants Posterity, who might possibly revenge them? ... God be thanked, Her Majesty wants not those faithful Subjects who ... would serve Her in the last Moments of Her Life with as much Fidelity and Zeal, as if She had Twenty Sons and Daughters to inherit after Her. ("Modest Enquiry," 18, 24)

Such spirited defenses, unfortunately, were rare. By the end of her reign, the nation's "Nursing Mother" was little more than a person to be gotten around, a patroness, a metaphor put to use in the interests of others' power.

In helping to define the attributes of a proto-middle-class mother – despite both her aristocratic descent and her lack of living children – Queen Anne found herself an outsider and an anomaly, like neither the ideal aristocratic mother described by the Marquess of Halifax, whose dignified and undemonstrative behavior is directed at every moment by considerations of class difference,[28] nor the paradigmatic "middling" mother Richardson would provide for emulation in the second part of *Pamela*, whose apparently more individual and spontaneous mothering style provided a powerful alternative model, as we shall see. Caught in a moment when popular notions of royal authority, female subjectivity and maternal

---

27 Barash, *Augustan Women's Mythmaking*, 366–67.
28 Cf. Part Three, note 26, below.

identity were all undergoing fundamental redefinition, Anne ended her reign in frustration, isolation, and loss, a disenfranchised monarch and a bereaved mother.

This situation affected not only Queen Anne's political authority or the authority that women could conceive for themselves in reference to her, important as these repurcussions were.[29] It also affected directly the possibilities for authority inherent in motherhood, the queen's chosen self-representation. Both victim and perpetrator of her own failure to create a politically influential maternal self-representation, Queen Anne was caught up in and helped to engender the fiction that maternity and public political authority are mutually exclusive experiences.

"THY NURSING MOTHER": SYMBOLIC MATERNITY AND ROYAL AUTHORITY AT THE CORONATION OF QUEEN ANNE

As Princess of Denmark, Anne used literal, bodily motherhood as a political agent, as we have seen. But after Gloucester's death, when it was becoming difficult to pretend that "the teeming Princess" would ever leave an heir, Anne needed to find a new strategy. So she attempted to shift the values behind the maternal image that had so far abetted her power, and to use *symbolic* rather than *literal* motherhood to engender royal authority.

As early as her coronation on April 23, 1702 (ironically, the seventeenth anniversary of her father's coronation), the new queen began to revise her maternal image, deliberately adopting a new persona as symbolic national mother in an attempt to occlude the failure of her physical maternity. The coronation was Anne's first opportunity to represent herself definitively to the nation; she used it to present herself not only as ruler, nor even as woman-ruler, but as mother-ruler, choosing as the text of the coronation sermon Isaiah 49: 23, "Kings shall be thy nursing-fathers, and their queens thy nursing-mothers." The relation between this text and the sermon preached on it at Anne's coronation is worth considering in detail, because it demonstrates how the queenly-maternal power Anne sought to project was undercut even at this, its earliest manifestation. The figure of motherhood did not provide autonomous power for

---

[29]   Cf. Gallagher, "Embracing the absolute," esp. 37; Barash, *Augustan Women's Mythmaking.*

Queen Anne. Instead, Anne's maternal image became, even at her coronation, largely an image of displacement *from* authority, of co-optation and redefinition by patriarchal forces and figures. And the use of motherhood as the privileged figure for Anne's royal impotence contributed in its turn to a reduction and displacement of maternity itself during Anne's reign.

To understand how this might be so, it is necessary to remember that uncertainty about Anne's right to the throne remained alive throughout her reign; indeed, the queen herself seems to have felt it keenly. Anne's famous remark in a letter to her sister Mary on the birth of James Edward Stuart ("it may be our brother, but God only knows" [B. Brown, *Letters and Diplomatic Instructions*, 37]), and her concern that the deaths of her children may have been God's punishment for her role in her father's demise, suggest Anne's discomfort with her position. According to the Duchess of Marlborough, "it was a great trouble" to Anne "to be forced to act such a part" against her father (*Opinions*, 3). At the end of Anne's life, Tories even detected willingness on her part to instate her half-brother.[30]

Be that as it may, Anne's right to rule was indisputably a subject of debate, even a potential cause for invasion and civil war, during the whole of her reign. As a poem published during the Sacheverell controversy put it,

> Since Monarchs were Monarchs, it never was known,
> That so little Power belong'd to a Crown,
> Or that, made by a Mob, they may so be pull'd down.[31]

Under such circumstances, much necessarily depended on Anne's self-representational strategy. She needed to find a style of queenship that would confer legitimacy after the fact, silence dissent, and allow her to transmit the crown to the right kind of successor (that is to say, a Protestant). Her claim to legitimate inheritance arguable, her authority in need of definition and reinforcement, her ability to ensure succession in doubt, Anne appeared at her coronation as the embodiment of the most characteristic crises of her age.

It seems odd that in such desperate political straits, and after the loss of eighteen children, Anne should have chosen *maternal* imagery to delineate her authority and defend her legitimacy. True, the

---

30 E.g., MacPherson, *Original Papers*, 2: 288–89, 528. Cf. Boyer, *Memoirs*, 36; Gregg, *Queen Anne*, 83–4, 149–50, 364–6, 402; Gregg, "Jacobite."
31 Anon., "A New Ballad," 22

metaphor of the monarch as parent already had a long and powerful history in English politics. Elizabeth I was famous in the eighteenth century for having built her authority on the filial affections of her people,[32] and James I, Charles I, and both of Charles's sons had made something of a trademark of being "parents" to the realm[33] – indeed, Charles I's use of this rhetoric made his execution a matter of patricide as well as regicide. Robert Filmer's enormously influential *Patriarcha*, and the identity between father and king that it insisted on, were common coin in 1702.[34] Female writers exploited the familial metaphor to protest women's subordination,[35] and Locke's *Second Treatise*, a text that gained authority throughout the century, assumed a metaphorical relationship between political and domestic relations.[36] So Anne's use of parental political imagery was by no means unprecedented. On the contrary, the metaphor had entirely *too* rich a history, and carried too many dangerous valences: simply evoking the monarch-as-parent trope was a way of conjuring up the troubled seventeenth century and the radical challenges to both domestic and royal authority that the metaphor had partly enabled.

"Kings shall be thy nursing-fathers, and their queens thy nursing-mothers." The text seems a peculiar choice for Anne's coronation not only because it features motherhood in the context of a maternal history that must have given listeners pause, but also because it subordinates the queen's authority to that of a king strangely absent from the occasion at hand. Though Anne was married, she was not the consort of a king regnant. Her Danish husband Prince George appeared to his contemporaries as a nonentity of unprecedented proportions, and seems to have had virtually no interest in governance.[37] Swift's view of George is representative: "the Prince being

---

[32] Cf. Rapin-Thoyras, *Histoire d'Angleterre*, 2: 59.
[33] Orgel, "Prospero's wife," 59; Goldberg, "Fatherly authority," 3. Anne's decision to figure herself as national mother constitutes one of many instances in which she reverts to earlier, especially Elizabethan, representational structures.
[34] Cf. Kay, *Political Constructions*, 111.
[35] E.g., Astell, *Reflections upon Marriage*, 85–87.
[36] Locke cast the authority of mothers as a potential rival to that of fathers, but only within a domestic sphere which it is Locke's explicit project in the second treatise to de-politicize (38). Cf. Kay, *Political Constructions*, 166. For a closer examination of the complex phenomenon of patriarchalism, cf. Schochet.
[37] Of course it is possible that George was excluded from politics by Anne's notoriously self-aggrandizing and devious ministers, or even, as one writer suggests darkly, that he had more political influence than appeared (Strickland, *Lives of the Queens of England*, 12: 21). In any case, Queen Anne's marriage seems to have provoked none of the anxiety England felt at the mere prospect of marriage for Elizabeth (cf. Tennenhouse, *Power on Display*, 23–24).

somewhat infirm and inactive, neither affected the Grandeur of a Crown, nor the Toils of Business" (*Memoirs*, 75). So for Anne as for no English queen before her except Elizabeth, a public recognition of queenly subordination to kingly authority was, it would seem, unnecessary.

To make matters worse, the mention of king-fathers in the absence of a reigning consort must have suggested Anne's own king-father (who had died in exile just seven months before Anne's coronation), thus resurrecting the very questions about her legitimacy that the ceremony at hand was supposed to bury. It is painfully ironic that the troubling specter of James, known to contemporaries for his special "tenderness" to this favorite daughter,[38] should have been summoned by the very words Anne chose to represent her royal authority, an authority which depended on her father's exclusion. In the peculiarly compromised circumstances of Anne's accession, the choice of a text emphasizing vaguely proprietorial king-fathers served more to mystify and even to undermine the queen's authority than to define and bolster it.

Why then would Anne have chosen such a text to represent her authority at her coronation? Perhaps she was relying on the familiar. As we have seen, motherhood had always been Anne's trump card, essential to her political survival. And her survival had always appeared essential for reasons that transcended (even while they seemed to justify) personal ambition: Anne was seen, and saw herself, as the last preserver of an English Protestant tradition seriously at risk from French imperialism and the continued threats of Jacobite invasion. The child she longed for could have provided English Protestantism with a native leader of defensible legitimacy, neutralized the threat of her Roman Catholic half-brother, and, not least, restored to Anne herself political authority born of maternity, the only authority she had ever really possessed but which by 1702 had been seriously damaged.

Furthermore, the coronation text is merely a fragment. Like many

---

[38] Boyer (1722): "King *James* was ever an indulgent Father to all his Children, and had even a particular Fondness for the Lady *Anne*" (2). James himself claimed in his *Memoirs* to have "always cherished her beyond expression" (MacPherson, *Original Papers*, 1: 246). James's special tenderness for Anne and the despair he felt at her betrayal became legendary after 1688. "God help me," he is said to have cried, "my own Children have forsaken me!" (Salmon, *Life of her Late Majesty*, 1: 15; Hume, *History*, 6: 513). Cf. "Generous Muse," 10; Macpherson, *Original Papers*, 1: 591; Clarendon, *Correspondence of Henry Hyde*, 2: 208. On his deathbed, James extended forgiveness to his three greatest enemies: the Hapsburg emperor Leopold, the Pope, and his daughter Anne (Gregg, *Queen Anne*, 127; *DNB*, 1: 443).

of her subjects, Queen Anne read the Bible every day as part of a
regimen of private worship and prayer. Combined with her vigorous
loyalty to the English church, this practice made her renowned for
"exemplary Piety and Devotion" (Sherlock, *A Sermon Preach'd*, 21),
virtues closely associated with feminized domestic experience. According to Elkanah Settle, Anne gave "her dearest Hours" to "her
Closet, [her] *Altars,* and her GOD" ("Threnodia Britannica" [1714], 7).
Edward Young argues that though Argyle and Churchill enjoyed
"the Glory" of military campaigns, England's enemies were in fact
"subdu'd by *ANNA*'s Pray'r" ("On the Late Queen's Death," 3).

> How Great her Zeal! how fervent her Desire! . . .
> Constant Devotion did her Time divide . . .
> Though *Europe*'s Wealth and Glory claimed a Part,
> Religion's Cause reign'd Mistress of her Heart   (4)

And in *Tatler* 130 (February 7, 1710), Steele calls the "Publick
Triumphs" of Anne's reign "the natural Consequences" of the
queen's "Private Virtues" and "Religious Retirements" (*Tatler* 2:
258). For Queen Anne and her subjects, who were deeply steeped in
scripture, any biblical phrase would have resonated beyond itself.
So we might consider Anne's choice of the coronation fragment as
a gesture toward a larger context, and specifically toward Isaiah 49
which, as we shall see, makes a powerful case for maternally-imaged
public authority. Unfortunately, the use to which the fragment was
put in the sermon preached at Anne's coronation largely subverts
the maternal power depicted in Isaiah, and has surprisingly destruc-
tive implications for the new queen's claims to authority and
legitimacy.

Isaiah 49: 23
Defining maternal authority

Isaiah 49 describes the restoration of children to a bereaved parent
of ambiguous or androgynous sex (the parent appears as "him
whom man despiseth," but also as one whose children are "begotten" by another and as "Israel" and "Zion," entities personified
as female throughout the Old Testament). After a period of loss and
debasement, this speaker is restored by God's faithfulness to a place
of power and fulfillment through the birth of children. In church
tradition, the bereaved-then-comforted parent had been identified

as Christ. And in the sermon he preached at Anne's coronation, John Sharp, Archbishop of York briefly defends this traditional identification, then goes on to expand the text's reference to include the new queen. "This Chapter out of which I have taken my Text," Sharp declares, "hath always been understood to be, and it certainly is, a Prophecy of our Lord *Jesus Christ"*; at the same time, however, *"Kings* and *Queens"* may also be considered *"Nursing-Fathers* and *Nursing-Mothers* to his *Church* and *People"* (3). In light of Anne's own repeated bereavements and the fact that she herself chose the text, we may follow Sharp's lead and assume that Anne may well have identified with the speaker, understanding the parental voice of Isaiah 49 to be an echo of her own supremely disappointed maternal voice.

Furthermore, the language of the chapter emphasizes explicitly maternal experience to a much greater extent than the excerpt might suggest. From the first words, the speaker forges a direct link between maternity, inherited legitimacy, and a public authority based in and exercised by means of a female voice:

Listen, O coasts, unto me; and hearken, ye people, from far: The Lord hath called me from the womb; from the body of my mother hath he made mention of my name. (v.1)

The "mother" harks back to her own fetal existence, the period of complete symbiosis with *her* mother, as the originating moment of her empowering naming by God. The relationships are between a mother, her child, and God; there is no human paternal figure present. Obviously, this triangle suggests the immaculate conception of Christ. But in the expanded context of Anne's coronation, a uniquely female form of authority is suggested as well, an authority inaugurated in maternal experience: "from the body of my mother hath he made mention of my name." Indeed, it would be hard to imagine a text more fraught with images that link maternity to traditionally male forms of power. The unborn speaker is still *in utero* when the Lord empowers her voice in starkly phallic terms: "He hath made my mouth like a sharp sword," she tells us, "he hath ... made me a polished shaft; in his quiver hath he hidden me" (v. 2).

The speaker complains, as Anne might well have done in a maternal context, that "I have labored in vain, I have spent my strength for nothing, and in vain" (v. 4). She is comforted by God, who promises her renewed maternity originating from divine faithfulness greater even than that of a mother to her child, the supreme (though fallible) manifestation of human faithfulness:

Can a woman forget her nursing child, that she should not have compassion on the son of her womb? Yea, they may forget, yet will I not forget thee ... Thy children shall make haste ... and come to thee. As I live, saith the Lord, thou shalt surely clothe thee with them all, as with an ornament, and bind them on thee, as a bride doeth ... The children whom thou shalt have, after thou hast lost the other, shall say again in thine ears, The place is too narrow for me; give a place to me that I may dwell. Then shalt thou say in thine heart, Who hath begotten me these, seeing I have lost my children ...? Behold, I was left alone, these, where had they been? (vv. 15–21)

Furthermore, God promises that the world's acknowledgment of the queen's political power will be the direct result of the promised extra-patriarchal maternity. It is in this charged context that the fragment used at the coronation appears:

Thus saith the Lord God: Behold, I will lift up mine hand to the nations, and set up my standard to the peoples; and they shall bring thy sons in their arms, and thy daughters shall be carried upon their shoulders. *And kings shall be thy nursing fathers, and their queens, thy nursing mothers*; they shall bow down to thee with their face toward the earth, and lick up the dust of thy feet, and thou shalt know that I am the Lord: for they shall not be ashamed who wait for me ... for I will contend with him that contendeth with thee, and I will save thy children. (vv. 22–25)

What is perhaps most striking about this passage is the very small concern it shows for the nurturing capacities of kings, capacities only too much in evidence in the coronation fragment. Taken whole, Isaiah 49 is much more concerned with the ability of the female speaker to produce progeny and by this means to exercise authority over the world. Indeed, the words singled out for the coronation text are the only place where the chapter even mentions kings or fathers. And even then, the only action in which kings engage in Isaiah 49 is the act of bowing down before the queen-mother; they most decidedly do not take precedence over her as nursing-parent. The initial problem presented by the coronation text, in other words, the fact that it seems to be primarily about kings and fatherhood, is not present in Isaiah 49 as a whole.

In Isaiah, the mother-monarch is addressed by God, who promises that she will find nursing fathers and nursing mothers in other kings and queens. She herself will be nurtured as a result of her motherhood. But at Queen Anne's coronation, the addressee has been changed to the nation: Sharp claims that the text describes "the Relation between Christian *Princes* and their *People*." The difference is significant. In Isaiah the queen exercises an authority that is at once expressly political and embodied in her female voice – she speaks publicly and with authority ("Listen, O coasts, unto me") and is addressed directly ("Thus saith the Lord God"). But in the coronation text – "Kings shall be thy nursing fathers and their queens thy nursing mothers" – the nation is addressed *about* the maternal queen, who stands silent, not part of the exchange.

There are other important differences between the verse as it appears in Isaiah 49 and as it worked at Queen Anne's coronation. In Isaiah's dream, political peers (the rulers of "the nations") take on oddly subordinate parental roles which include acknowledging the maternal speaker's pre-eminent legitimacy and authority: "they shall bow down ... and lick up the dust of thy feet." But at the coronation, the queen exists as a mother only, unconnected to parents or parental legitimation, inhabiting an isolated space in relationship to her subjects/children. Isaiah's queen is connected in many ways to a matrilineal inheritance. Called in her mother's body, she is both mother and daughter, and inhabits these as plural positions; she breeds not only children, but parents. Progressive time, linearity, even parental priority – all are subverted; the monarch's legitimacy resides outside patrilineal forms of inheritance. And her divinely ordained maternity creates a new kind of political authority, a matriarchy associated from conception with the female voice. In Isaiah, motherhood is productive of – even tantamount to – political power.

All this is lost in the truncated version of verse twenty-three and in the sermon Sharp preached on it, to which we now turn. As we shall see, the powerful and potentially subversive image of the queen as "nursing mother" to the nation is the central figure on which Sharp's sermon focuses. But Sharp's strategies do not quite succeed in enabling Anne fully to inhabit the public authority she tried to claim at her coronation. Instead, the queen's position as self-sufficient maternal cause becomes a glaring reminder of expunged ancestry, an image of isolation and weakness. And ironically enough, it is in Sharp's use of maternity as the central metaphor for queenly authority – the metaphor that worked so powerfully and subversively in Isaiah –that this compromise occurs.

The Coronation sermon:
Defending maternal authority

Sharp begins his defense of the queen's authority by asserting that as nursing-parent, the monarch's first duty is to the church. Christian princes must, he says,

think themselves obliged above all things to take care of the *Church* of God; remembring that it is chiefly with respect to *That* that they have the Charge of being *Nursing-Fathers* and *Nursing-Mothers*. (6)

The queen's duty to the church is paired with her responsibility "to secure and promote [the] *temporal* Peace and Happiness" of her people (9). The spiritual side Sharp considers the "chief" duty, but secular obligations are, paradoxically, "no less" important. Thus Sharp divides and hierarchizes Anne's queenly responsibility, then denies having done so. The mother/queen's responsibility to the Church is subtly privileged (as "chief"), but a direct mitigation of the importance of her "temporal" (material, economic, overtly political) influence is avoided.

The duplicity of Sharp's logic reveals how delicate a move he was performing when he attempted to distinguish between the new monarch's authority over the church and her authority in political affairs. This was not a routine distinction in 1702: temporal and spiritual matters had long been virtually indistinguishable in England. So the fact that Sharp would construct even a rhetorical hierarchy for the two is revealing. It suggests that while politics and religion were still very closely entangled when Anne ascended, this was *less* true than in the past.[39] Further, Sharp subtly suggests that the queen will be more involved in spiritual than in temporal affairs. Christian rulers, he says, may be expected to "make it their business to maintain and defend true *Religion*; To encourage *Piety* and *Virtue*" and "in their own *Persons* to set good Examples to their Subjects of *Piety* and *Devotion*" (6,7). Despite the rather vague terms in which these monarchical tasks are described ("piety," "virtue," "good Examples"), the passage invokes the image of rulers who actively promote religion "in their own *Persons*." The queen's secular duties, by contrast, may in Sharp's scheme of things be carried out by deputies. Nurturant rulers should "look into the Affairs of the

[39]   Cf. Speck, "The Orangist conspiracy," 91–93; McKeon, *Origins of the English Novel*, chs. 2 and 3; Sharpe and Zwicker, *Politics of Discourse*, 8–10.

Kingdom with their own Eyes; and ... see that all the *Magistrates* under them did their duty ... they [should] provide that *impartial Justice* should be administred" (9–10). So far as securing "temporal Peace and Happiness" (9) is concerned, the queen's job is to *supervise ministers*, not to act directly. She is to be a comparatively distant manager, overseeing subordinates "with her own eyes" but not participating directly in the administration of justice.[40]

The point is a small one in the context of the coronation ceremony. It is unlikely that those present, even if they had noted the slight distinction made between the spiritual and temporal aspects of the queen's authority, would have objected. In all likelihood, Sharp's words would have been interpreted by his audience as placing proper emphasis on spiritual matters; to be "defender of the faith," after all, had long been a central aspect of royal privilege and responsibility. Nevertheless, Sharp's emphasis subtly shifts the mother-queen's authority away from temporal, public affairs and into a relatively symbolic and sequestered sphere, much as conduct writers of Anne's generation took pains to separate the "temporal" and "Eternal" duties of mothers.[41]

Sharp's division of monarchical labors, then, works against its supposed aims. It excludes the monarch, at least in relative terms, from the practical, secular, public activities that were, in the early eighteenth century, assuming the central place that religion had previously occupied in English society. It sets the stage for what would become a pattern in Anne's reign: the monarch's authority, defined in maternal language, is first said to operate in two separate-but-equal spheres, the spiritual and the temporal; then that authority is subtly redirected away from the latter sphere. Throughout her reign, the queen's efforts to exercise explicitly maternal authority would enjoy much more success in the spiritual realm than in the world of practical politics.

Between Anne's coronation and her death, both flatterers and detractors tended to avoid the phrase "nursing mother," with its suggestion of bodily and peculiarly female power. Anne was imagined instead as the nation's abstracted and de-gendered "parent" (Shute, "A Pindarick Ode," 3), and the maternal metaphor was

---

[40] Gregg, *Queen Anne*, 135.
[41] In a chapter entitled "The Mother," for instance, Steele's *Ladies Library* (1714) makes it clear that though some of its reflections "have been purely *civil*, and related only to *Temporal* Life, yet our main View has been to the *Eternal* one" (134).

euphemized with code-words like "tenderness,"[42] and an emphasis on reciprocal affection betwen monarch and people. At the opening of Anne's first parliament (October, 1702) the House of Commons employed typically abstract language, praising "your majesty's tender concern for your people" and "intire confidence in their affections" which "must engage them to make your majesty the utmost returns of duty and gratitude" (*PH*, 48). Like Elizabeth before her, Anne was said to exercise an "affective rule" by which she could compel obedience more effectively than any tyrant. Matthew Prior was one of many who spelled out the strategy for the queen:

> Entire and Sure the Monarch's Rule must prove,
> Who Founds Her Greatness on Her Subjects Love ...
> Our Vanquish'd Wills That pleasing Force Obey;
> Her Goodness takes our Liberty away.[43]

When local officials from Peterborough were granted audience with the queen in May, 1710, they praised her as "a constant and indulgent Mother to our Holy Religion"[44] – but not as its "nursing" mother. The phrase virtually disappears during Anne's lifetime.

It re-emerged with a vengeance, however, at her death. The caption at the bottom of a celebratory engraving (figure 7) calls the dead queen "the greatest Lover of her Subjects, the most tender Nursing Mother to the CHURCH, the best Mistress, the best Wife, the best Mother, and the best Christian, the Age in which She liv'd produc'd." And in the preface to his dirge on the queen's death, Francis Peck also reverts to the coronation language: "Consider Her either as a Woman, or a Christian; As a Nursing Mother of the Church, or a Parent of Her People, and She was the Delight of all good Men, and the Glory of the Age She liv'd in!" (vii–viii). Such

---

42 For the supreme importance of "tenderness" to the developing code of virtuous domestic motherhood, see Part Three. Like a domestic mother, the queen was vulnerable to critics who felt she was *too* tender. Joseph Smith, for instance, called Anne's tendency to be controlled by ministers the result of "Tenderness to a Fault" (Smith, *Duty of the Living*, 13–14).

43 Prior, "Prologue, Spoken at Court," 2. Cf. Defoe's "Hymn to Peace" (1706):

> *You* have found *the Passage* to our Hearts.
> Despotick Rule can there no Grievance prove,
> *For Arbitrary Power's no Crime in Love.*
> MADAM, this Title makes you absolute,
> Where *Love's the Bondage,* Subjects ne'er Dispute;
> Prerogatives and Laws are Foreign things,
> *The Hearts of Subjects are the Strength of Kings* (51–52)

For the parallel "affective rule" recommended to domestic mothers in Augustan England, cf. Part Three, below.

44 Anon., *Collection of All the Addresses*, 38.

Her Auspicious
BIRTH
Feb.6th 1664

And Happy
ACCESSION
March 8th 1701

Her most
Glorious
CORONATION
April 23d 1702

And much
Lamented
Death
August 1st 1714

This Plate is humbly Dedicated,
To all true Lovers of the Pious & immortal Memory of our late
GRACIOUS SOVEREIGN QUEEN ANNE.

The *Royal Psalmists* wondrous Son,
And all that was in *Salem* done,
Ne'er had so good a Right to Fame,
As ANNA, Matchless ANNA'S Name
In Her a SOLOMON we See,
Abstracted from Idolatry.
She many *Temples* caus'd to rise,
Whose Airy Turrets dare the Skies.

Chast was her Life, and pure her Pray'r,
Her Peoples Good her only Care.——
But 'tis for ARON'S Sons to Praise
The *Monarch* in immortal Lays.
Her ROYAL-BOUNTY do's demand.
This gratefull Tribute at their Hand;
And ANNA and the STUART-LINE
Require a Pen that is *Divine*.

She was the greatest Lover of her Subjects, the most tender Nursing
Mother to the CHURCH, the best Mistress, the best Wife, the best Mother,
& the best Christian, the Age in which She liv'd produced. Sold by J. Clark, Engraver
in Castle Yard Holborn. pr. 6

7 J. Clark. An engraving memorializing Queen Anne, "the most tender Nursing
Mother to the Church." c. 1714.

tributes exemplify the marked resurgence of the "nursing mother" trope at Anne's death (and the vigilance with which Augustan writers maintained the distinction between the queen's secular "parent-hood" and her role as "nursing mother" to the Church.)[45] Even Anne's enemies could safely deploy the "nursing mother" trope once she was gone. In 1742 the Duchess of Marlborough sniffed, "the church of England, one would naturally think, could not be in any *immediate* danger of perishing under the care of such a *nursing mother* as the QUEEN" (*Conduct*, 39). The coronation's "nursing mother" language, in short, failed to augment Queen Anne's personal authority, even over the Church, during her lifetime; contemporaries simply avoided the image of the monarch as the nation's "nursing mother" until it could no longer resonate powerful physical presence for the maternal queen.

Like its defense of the new queen's maternal authority, the sermon's defense of Anne's right of inheritance also proved inade-quate. Sharp attempts to provide Anne with a legitimizing gen-ealogy, broken into two distinct parts: from apostolic times to Queen Elizabeth I, and from the Civil War to Anne *via* William and Mary, but omitting James II. The effort to avoid the delicate problem posed by James is palpable, and the strategy is unique: Sharp reconstructs Anne's genealogy so as to make her the *distant* heir of *kings*, and the *direct* heir of *queens*. Anne's hereditary claim becomes sororal (*via* Mary) rather than filial. But the fact that this female inheritance is presented as the culmination of an otherwise uniformly patrilineal dynasty, and the duplicitous language used to expound its legitimacy, largely undercut the ostensible argument that the queen's right may be derived in terms that might be described as gynolineal.

After listing a series of "nursing-fathers" whose place in English history is dubious (King Lucius, Constantine) or whose claims to the tenderness that "nursing-father" evokes are arguable at best (Henry VIII), Sharp's genealogy pauses triumphantly at Elizabeth, whose excellence demonstrates that queens are "equal Sharers with *Kings*, in making up the *Blessing* ... promis'd to GOD's People" (16). The return of Charles II in 1660 is celebrated for having restored English

---

45   Cf. Collier, *Queen Anne's Death*, 21–22; Smith, *Duty of the Living*, 15; Peck, "Lamented Death of Queen Anne," 35; Blower, *A Sermon Preached*, 13 (Blower wrote six months before Anne's death, when the queen was already seriously ill). Manley, again the exception, uses the nursing mother metaphor without limiting its reference to the Church ("Modest Enquiry," 9–10).

religion, laws, and liberty, but Sharp treats the rest of the seventeenth century more gingerly. Only the vaguest allusions appear to the Civil War (euphemized as *"Factions* at *Home"*) and to the most problematic figure of all, James II (hurriedly depersonalized as "a *Faction* from another Quarter"). With obvious relief, Sharp's narrative reaches the happy moment when William and Mary are "raised up" by God to "rescue" the nation from the still-unnamed James, and concludes with a bright vision of contemporary England, which possesses "the same *Religion,* the same *Church,* the same *Government* . . . the same *Rights* and *Liberties,* and *Properties,* that ever we did" (17).

Anne figures in this largely fictional (and decidedly Whiggish) account of English history as "A Sister of our never to be forgotten QUEEN [Mary II]" (18). But the legitimacy derived from sororial relation is compromised even as it is asserted, as an expanded quotation will make immediately apparent: God, Sharp says,

hath preserved to us another *Branch* of the same *Royal Stock* to repair our Losses. *Ramo uno avulso non deficit alter Aureus.* A Sister of our never to be forgotten QUEEN is yet left us. (18)

Ostensibly, of course, the "Royal Stock" is the whole line of kings and queens leading to Anne. But the violence of the "breaking off" language in the Latin tag ("One branch having been broken off, there does not fail another similarly golden"), combined with the suggestion that Anne and Mary are similar branches springing from a common trunk, destabilizes the fragile genealogy Sharp has constructed. The revolution of 1688–89 and especially the death of James II just seven months before Anne's coronation were still too recent for Sharp's audience not to have been uncomfortably aware that both Anne and Mary were of the same stock in a more troubling sense: both were daughters of the deposed king and sisters of the exiled prince born in 1688, who – if laws of inheritance were to be the criteria – should have preceded them to the throne. Sharp's language, ironically enough, brings to mind the very question he is trying to avoid: from where does Anne's legitimacy derive, if not from James?

Despite Sharp's insistence on Anne's sororal inheritance, then, the never-quite-absent patriarch looms threateningly in the image of two branches extending from one common trunk, overshadowing Anne's coronation despite all attempts to exorcise him, and reminding those assembled that as of 1688, royal succession had become more problematic and tenuous than ever before. Once, right of succession had been (at least in theory) reliably indicated by physical descent; but now that both King James and his eldest son had been bypassed in favor of James's two Protestant daughters, that comparative certainty had been undermined. Moreover, the fact that hereditary succession had become newly debatable further separated political authority from maternity. Legitimate inheritance had once resided quite literally in the bodies of queens; but during Anne's lifetime, royal legitimacy became less a fact than an interpretive issue, and interpretive authority rested with powerful male subjects. The combination of all these factors rendered Sharp's genealogical gymnastics not only unconvincing, but even somewhat beside the point.

In a kind of final irony, Sharp's attempt to write out Anne's paternal lineage undermines the power of the biblical text's matriarchal imagery. In Isaiah, motherhood alone provides lineage, right of inheritance, and political authority; fatherhood does not count. But the coronation sermon attempts to have it both ways: to place Anne in a fundamentally patriarchal line of succession while avoiding the dangerous – but still necessary – admission that in the final analysis, whatever legitimacy she enjoyed was derived patrilineally. In its effort to transform Anne from daughter to sister-and-mother, Sharp's sermon denies her a coherent descent. She stands in a genealogy based on patrilineal inheritance as the lone figure legitimated by sororal ties – ties necessarily compromised by their inescapable link to a disinherited patriarch.

To note the many fatal contradictions in the coronation sermon is not to accuse Sharp of deliberately undercutting the new queen's already precarious authority. The fact is that the archbishop was assigned an impossible task. In order to distance Anne from her father, Sharp emphasized her maternal role and sororal status rather than her troubling filial position; indeed, the sermon avoids direct mention of the queen's patriarchal inheritance altogether. But James is eerily present nevertheless in every evasion, every euphemism, every exclusion. At some moments, indeed, the irony of the dead king's presence may have reached near-comic proportions. For centuries, new English monarchs put on the ring of Edward the Confessor at their coronations; but it is said that Anne had to use a replica of Edward's ring because her father had taken the original with him into France.[46]

---

[46]   Strickland, *Lives of the Queens*, 12: 61.

SYMBOLIC MATERNITY AND PRACTICAL POLITICS
IN QUEEN ANNE'S ENGLAND

Anne was not the first queen of England to assume the throne amid doubts about her legitimacy or to use symbolic maternity as a defense against political enemies. When Elizabeth I was crowned in 1558, her circumstances were in many respects remarkably like those surrounding Anne in 1702. Elizabeth was unquestionably the daughter of Henry VIII, but her legitimacy had been undermined by her maternal inheritance: Henry had divorced and then executed her mother Anne Boleyn – whose position had been controversial in any case during her brief tenure as Henry's queen – and had expressed a preference for his heirs in the Suffolk line over Boleyn's daughters. When Elizabeth came to the throne, therefore, she was haunted by a contradictory legacy much like Anne's: her right to rule was disputed by her own father, from whom it supposedly derived. And crucially, Elizabeth was also childless. An eighteenth-century chronicler's description of Elizabeth's precarious position might well have been written with Anne also in mind: "her Right to the Crown was always contested openly or tacitly; ... the Papists in general considering her but as a Queen *de facto*, believed they might with a safe Conscience assist in dethroning her."[47]

In presenting herself as the symbolic mother of her people, Anne closely followed the early rhetoric of Elizabeth, who insisted early in her reign that her subjects were her children.[48] But "the Second Elizabeth" (as Anne was frequently called[49]) failed to construct political power from maternal symbolism. Why, we might wonder, did Anne fail where Elizabeth had succeeded? The question is important, because the processes that contributed to the failure of Anne's maternal representation not only reduced the public authority of the maternally imaged queen, but also reveal changes in the political functions of maternity itself between Elizabeth's time and Anne's.

---

[47] Rapin-Thoyras, *Histoire d'Angleterre*, 2: 57.

[48] Cf. 67, below.

[49] Virtually all forms of contemporary writing used this designation for Queen Anne, from sermons preached at court to partisan diatribes like Manley's "Modest Enquiry" (1714), to the catchy drinking song "England's Triumph," where ordinary sailors are called to acts of heroism now that "the Second *Elizabeth* sits on the Throne" (n.p.). Cf. Blackmore, "Eliza," 219–21. Chudleigh offers an extended comparison of the two queens ("To the Queen's Most Excellent Majesty," 122–24), as does Blackmore's "Eliza."

The many similarities between her own situation and Elizabeth's were not lost on Queen Anne, who throughout her reign deliberately modeled both her iconography and her policy on that of the Virgin Queen. The costume Anne wore for her first address to Parliament, for instance, precisely reproduced a famous ensemble worn by Elizabeth;[50] and before the end of the first year of her reign, Anne had adopted Elizabeth's motto (adopted from *her* mother), *semper eadem*: "always the same."[51] As late as 1713, Anne wrote to England's Dutch allies that "she had ever in her Eye the Example and wise Conduct of that great Queen her Predecessor," and said she considered her emulation of Elizabeth to be "one of the greatest Glories of her Reign."[52] In the year of her death, Anne resisted a proposed bill that would have limited religious toleration, arguing that it had always been "the Glory of her Reign" to follow "the Steps of Queen *Elizabeth*."[53] And if Montrose is correct in observing that "the image of the queen as a wetnurse seems to have had some currency" in Elizabeth's day ("*A Midsummer Night's Dream*," 67), then even Anne's adoption of "nursing mother" language may have been part of her effort to exploit Elizabethan metaphors.

When confronted with threats similar to those Elizabeth had faced – her contestable right to rule and her childlessness – Anne attempted, characteristically, to meet the case as her predecessor had done. She declared herself the mother of the nation, rather than of birthchildren, and effaced as much as possible her own complicated and tenuous place in patriarchal inheritance. Following Elizabeth, Anne attempted to use symbolic maternity as an escape from legitimation crisis, a way of stepping out (or appearing to step out) of the issue of patriarchal inheritance altogether to create a kind of alternate matriarchal order instead. The move had worked for Elizabeth, at least in the short term and so far as her own retention of power was concerned;[54] but it did not work for Anne. A combination of problems rendered Queen Anne unable to bolster her authority by means of maternal symbolism.

---

50 Gregg, *Queen Anne*, 152.
51 Ibid., 152; Curtis, *Life and Times of Queen Anne*, 93.
52 Swift, *Memoirs*, 199.
53 Ibid., 295.
54 In the long view, Elizabeth's failure bodily to secure the Protestant succession helped make inevitable the violence of the seventeenth century. The long-term results of Anne's similar failure were arguably better: Britain got Hanoverians, not Stuarts, and enjoyed comparative stability and prosperity.

For one thing, there were not only striking similarities but also great differences between Anne's situation and Elizabeth's, differences that Anne underestimated to her cost. Take the crucial matter of childlessness, for instance. Elizabeth made it clear from the first that she did not wish to marry and have children (though she also specialized in sending conflicting signals on this question[55]). She deliberately sublimated maternal experience into her public relationship with her people, as she explained to her first Parliament on February 4, 1559.

The House of Commons addressed the Queen in a very dutiful manner, and represented to her, how necessary it was for the happiness of the Nation, that she should think of marrying. The Queen graciously thanked the Commons, and ... added, that by the Ceremony of her Inauguration, she was married to her People, and her Subjects were to her instead of Children: They would not want a Successor when she died, and for her part, she would be well contented, that the Marble should tell Posterity, HERE LIES A QUEEN THAT REIGNED SO LONG, AND LIVED AND DIED A VIRGIN. (Rapin-Thoyras, *Histoire d'Angleterre*, 2: 53).[56]

When nagged by her second Parliament to marry, Elizabeth instead intensified her symbolic maternal image: "I assure yow all that though after my death yow may have many stepdames, yet shall you never have any, a more naturall mother, than I meane to be unto yow all" (*State Papers, Domestic Elizabeth*, 12.27.36; cf. Heisch, "Persistence," 50).

So when Elizabeth said her subjects would be to her "instead of" children, "instead of" carried a message of choice, the willed exclusion of one option (physical motherhood) in favor of another (symbolic motherhood). Elizabeth's maternity was always *designedly* symbolic – as, indeed, was Elizabeth's entire persona: she was to a great extent an icon, a sign of the nation.[57] She made what might

---

[55] For more than twenty years Elizabeth teased her realm with a large cast of possible husbands, effectively playing her potential maternity as a political trump card. See Chamberlain, *Sayings of Queen Elizabeth*, 70–96 for a collation of numerous "sayings" attributed to Elizabeth in which she trifles with suitors and subjects alike. I am indebted to Susan Frye and Mary Claire Mulroney for helpful conversations concerning Elizabeth's manipulations of her own potential marriage and maternity. Cf. Frye, *Elizabeth I*, 38–40; 154, n. 40.

[56] I quote Rapin's seventeenth-century paraphrase. Allison Heisch's forthcoming *Queen Elizabeth: Political Speeches* promises to provided a fine edition of the original speech, "The answere of the Quenes highnes to ye peticion proposed vnto hir by ye lower howse concerning hir mariage."

[57] Cf. the famous portrait by Gheeraerts the Younger where Queen Elizabeth is less an individual woman than a symbol, like the map on which she stands (reprod. Tyacke, *English Map-Making*, fig. 8).

have been her most vulnerable spot – motherhood – work in her own interests by transforming it from physical absence to symbolic presence. It was a strategy calculated to outwit patriarchy on its own ground, so to speak, by magnifying rather than denying or ignoring the importance of maternity for queenly authority, while redefining maternity as a symbolic matter separate from Elizabeth's particular female body.

Anne, on the other hand, was always a *woman* in her subjects' minds; much was made of her homely, domestic attributes (submissive wife, tender mother), her health, her squabbles with favorites. For her, symbolic maternity was not a first choice but a last resort. Unlike Elizabeth's, Anne's public persona had always been constituted in maternal terms. From her birth, Anne's life had held significance – not only for others, but for Anne herself – largely because she might produce an heir. But by the time of her accession, as we have seen, Anne's physical motherhood was a public failure. The figure of symbolic motherhood, a personal innovation and an act of resistance for the twenty-five-year-old Elizabeth, became the epitomy of co-optation and defeat for the ailing, middle-aged Queen Anne, ironically foregrounding her unwilling childlessness and so undermining, rather than bolstering, her authority as monarch.

It may also be that Elizabeth was able successfully to exploit figural motherhood because the symbolic order was, simply put, *available* to her in ways that it was not available to Anne. Margaret Homans has argued that women have traditionally been identified with the debased literal – the body and its needs, the daily routines of housekeeping, and also with literal meaning – while men are traditionally associated with more-highly valued figural constructions, especially metaphorical language. These "differential valuations of literal and figurative," Homans says, have implications for "the way our culture constructs masculinity and femininity" (*Bearing the Word*, 5). For

to take something literally is to get it wrong, while to have a figurative understanding of something is the correct intellectual stance. [The masculine] symbolic order, both the legal system and language, depends on the identification of the woman with the literal, and then on the denial that the literal has any connection with masculine figurations. (5, 10)

Homans's arguments cannot be applied equivalently to all historical periods. They are far less relevant to Elizabethan England, when the female images of the Virgin and the Queen *were* strongly associated with the figural, than to Augustan England, when the kinds of gendered associations Homans describes were beginning to take hold in British imaginations, delimiting representational and interpretive possibilities for women and men. This historical distinction, indeed, is precisely the point: keeping it in mind, we can follow Homans's insights to a better understanding of Anne's representational predicament.

As we have seen, Anne initially tried to deploy literal motherhood as a means toward political power, and when that strategy failed she tried to exploit the power of figuration instead. But in fact *both* procedures were doomed. To insist so strenuously on actually, physically bearing a child was, for Anne, "to get it wrong" – not only because she proved unable to bear healthy children, but because literal motherhood, even if it had lasted, would always have been already co-opted by patriarchy. Indeed, the greatest fiction surrounding Anne's maternal experience may well be the idea that physical motherhood could really have freed the queen from the reductions and exploitations of androcentric culture, or brought her political authority. Ironically, it was perhaps only because she *never was* literally a maternal queen that Anne was able to cherish the cold comfort that things might have been essentially different for her. The failure to sustain heirs, in other words, did not in any simple sense *cause* Anne's failure to construct and maintain royal authority in her female person; the more fundamental problem was the imbeddedness of all maternal authority – literal or figurative, queenly or not – in gendered (that is, politicized) systems of meaning.[58]

Unlike Anne, Elizabeth shrewdly recognized maternity to be not an end in itself, but one of many signs pointing toward the real signified: her own power. As a result, she was able to keep everyone guessing. Against all expectations, for instance, Elizabeth chose not to attempt a vindication of her mother, and so avoided resuscitating the issue of her own much-contested maternal inheritance. And Elizabeth was shrewd enough to shift the grounds of her self-representation, manipulating signals, playing off popular hopes. She dispensed with figural maternity when it no longer served her purposes, and manipulated other images instead. Anne more naively chose maternal self-representation and stuck to it. And perhaps because of her many maternal losses, Anne – unlike Elizabeth – saw

[58]   Cf. Gallagher, "Embracing the absolute," 38.

literal and symbolic maternity as distinct, mutually exclusive options. (This belief may have partly fueled her refusal in 1708 to cooperate with the pretense of maternal potential.) Anne seems to have realized too late what Elizabeth knew all along: that maternity's relation to political authority was neither inevitable nor consistent, and that neither symbolic nor physical motherhood would ever be enough.

Further, Anne seems not to have recognized that Elizabeth's rhetorical formula would function quite differently in a different historical situation. In Elizabeth's day, symbolic and empirical structures were still practically interchangeable. Renaissance processes of comparison and substitution made metaphors, allegories, analogies and symbols especially potent as explicators of the physical world, and representation itself was still often understood as a semiotic, not a mimetic, undertaking.[59] Metaphysical representation worked to guarantee ontological significance to empirical experience and political importance to ideational forms. But canons for politically operative representation had changed between Elizabeth's day and Anne's: by the eighteenth century, reliable representation was increasingly understood to be a matter of faithfulness to empirical detail, not the deployment of a set of decipherable symbols.

The popular vitality of symbols in the sixteenth century is indicated by the need for Elizabethan Protestantism to construct a symbolism of its own in response to Roman Catholic imagery.[60] Elizabeth benefited from this necessity. She successfully appropriated Marian symbolism – including symbolic maternity – because those symbols were still powerful and positive enough during her reign to be worth exploiting. But they would never again be so after the 1640s. As John Phillips has argued, the Puritan revolution destroyed forever "the correspondences of the natural world to the supernatural," metaphorical correspondences "possible only in a material world graced by the medieval view of the incarnation of Christ and guided by the traditions of the [Roman Catholic] Church."[61] By Anne's day, the continual possibility of violent conflict between English Catholics and Protestants, the impending threat of French imperialism, and popular fears of Jacobite retaliation all converged to make maternal

---

[59] Van Dyke, *Fiction of Truth*, esp. 165; Gordon, *The Renaissance Imagination*, 18–23; Siemon, *Shakespearean Iconoclasm*, 57–62. Thanks to Rose Zimbardo, Mary Claire Mulroney, and Kevin Sharpe for enlightening conversations about the changing status of representation between Elizabeth's day and Anne's.

[60] Montrose, *A Midsummer Night's Dream*, 66; Yates, *Astrea*, 78.

[61] Phillips, *The Reformation of Images*, 208. Cf. Aston, *England's Iconoclasts*, vii.

imagery, with its lingering traces of Marian myth, far less appealing than it had been to Elizabeth's contemporaries.[62] What C. L. Barber calls the "ritual resource" of Marian mythology (196) was less a part of cultural consciousness under Anne, and to the extent that Marian imagery was still a resource, it was not a positive one.

Even if maternal symbolism *had* carried the positive charge in Anne's day that it did in the early sixteenth century, the attributes of the Virgin Mary, the maternal icon *par excellence*, simply could not have worked for Anne as for Elizabeth. Anne could figure herself, with some difficulty, as queen-mother; but by no means could a woman who had been pregnant seventeen times represent herself as a *virgin*-queen-mother. Anne's iconography is like Elizabeth's in many of its features, often deliberately so; but it necessarily lacks the element of divine mystery, the unique, magical immanence of the "virgin scepter-swaying mother" that Elizabeth's all-encompassing imagery had been able to recoup for Protestantism and for queenly authority.[63]

Before the 1630s, royal authority was powerfully represented as parental power, as we have seen. For Elizabeth to call herself a symbolic mother was to create real political authority. But by Anne's day, the practical power of domestic imagery had considerably diminished. The attack on Filmer's patriarchalism mounted by Locke in his treatises on civil government is representative of a new set of attitudes toward the traditional equivalence between rulers and parents after the Glorious Revolution. Kings could no longer be unproblematically represented as fathers; the idea that homes were merely smaller versions of public political spaces no longer went unexamined.

If symbolism itself, and domestic symbolism in particular, failed by 1700 to carry the political weight it had under Elizabeth, maternal symbolism had become especially problematic, because cultural ideals for virtuous motherhood were changing. During the early eighteenth century, privileged mothers began to be personally involved in their children's lives to a degree that would have been unimaginable just fifty years earlier; for a growing majority,

---

[62] For the power of Roman Catholic images before the reformation, cf. Aston, 20–34. For the continued power of Catholic dogma and iconography during the English Reformation, cf. Haigh. For the political power of Marian myth in Elizabeth's day, and for Elizabethan exploitations of that power, cf. Yates, *Astrea*, esp. 77–80; Strong, *The Cult of Elizabeth*, 114–16.

[63] Anon., *Sorrowes Joy*, 2. Thanks to Kevin Sharpe for bringing this poem to my attention.

successful motherhood was coming to mean retreat into a world apart not only from politics and large-scale economics, but also, for the first time, from productive work. *Production* and *reproduction* were being constructed as mutually exclusive activities.[64] Important material changes were brought about by the increasing demand for maternal breastfeeding and personal supervision of children. And the maternal was undergoing an ontological change as well: motherhood was being reimagined as a necessary absence, a symbolic activity without empirical significance in the public world. For all these reasons – in addition, of course, to her personal maternal history – Queen Anne was never able to inhabit symbolic maternal structures as Elizabeth had. Always, the effort to create political authority from symbolic maternal forms functioned in more complex and less positive ways than Anne apparently expected.

Finally, and most paradoxically, Anne's maternal representation failed to bring her political authority because it was actually *more* potent and threatening than Elizabeth's. As Louis Montrose has argued, what enabled Renaissance patriarchs to submit to Elizabeth's authority was the fact that Elizabeth was always represented, even in her own self-promotions, as essentially unlike other women. As the "royal exception," Elizabeth could "prove the patriarchal rule in society at large," reinforcing rather than undermining masculine prerogatives.[65] Indeed, Elizabeth inhabited a cultural space much like the Virgin Mary's in Roman Catholic tradition: her representation constituted an impossible fantasy of maternal power that rendered real-life mothers powerless. Though supposedly representative, she was as unlike other women as she could possibly be.[66] But as we have seen, Queen Anne (unlike Elizabeth) was always figured as exceptionally ordinary. She lacked Elizabeth's education, brilliance, and resistance to traditional female roles (sister, wife, mother); she was in many ways very much like other economically privileged women of her day. So Anne's matriarchal self-representation, ironically enough, was actually *more* threatening than Elizabeth's to patriarchal hegemony. Maternal power was all very well for the queen of heaven and the virginal Elizabeth, but not for Anne, with whom ordinary mothers might more readily identify.

Furthermore, as a childless mother (the oxymoron is important)

---

64 Cf. B. Hill, *Women, Work and Sexual Politics*, esp. 51; Part Three, below.
65 Montrose, *A Midsummer Night's Dream*, 81.
66 Cf. Warner, *Reading Clarissa*, 153; Kristeva, "Héréthique," 46.

Anne embodied a transgressive paradox. Her mere existence threatened to establish forms of authority outside, and potentially in opposition to, patriarchal systems of inheritance. Unlike Elizabeth (or, differently, Anne's sister Mary, who probably had at least one miscarriage), Anne had actually borne children. She was irreducibly a mother despite the fact that she did not leave an heir. In both her relative ordinariness and her paradoxical maternal childlessness, Anne constituted an alternative to patriarchal purposes for and definitions of both queenship and motherhood.

Queen Anne did not designedly pose these threats to patrilineal inheritance and patriarchal power. As we have seen, she passionately desired to bear a child and so perpetuate the Protestant Stuart line. Her repeated attempts to have children, her children's invariable deaths and her own failure to leave an heir broke her heart, ruined her health, and soured her spirit. Likewise, the necessarily acrimonious relationship between Anne and her father after 1689, together with possible ambivalence about having defied his authority and perhaps usurped his throne, seem to have rendered her position increasingly distasteful to the queen. It was only as a result of great pain and against her most ardent wishes that Anne came to the throne as a queen who threatened to rule in herself, not by virtue of her place as conduit in the chain of paternal inheritance, free of legitimating ties to father, husband, or son.

It might seem that Anne's elder sister Mary had preceded her as a childless queen whose right depended on her position as daughter of the unmentionable king, and therefore as a threat to patriarchal privilege. But the threat Mary might have posed was mitigated by her entire subordination to her husband William and by her clear proximity, as elder daughter, to James II. As is well known, William refused in 1688 to fill the place of consort; he insisted on being king regnant, and though he and Mary officially shared the throne during her lifetime, there was never any question about her subordination to his authority. But Anne's Prince George, as we have seen, was content to remain in his wife's shadow, supportive and decorous but not politically ambitious. Any desire Mary might have had to establish political authority in her own person was squelched beforehand by William's ambition; but Anne had to establish and define royal authority for herself, and she chose to define it as maternal authority. Furthermore, Mary's legitimacy was always more simply derived than Anne's. Unlike Anne, Mary had no sororal inheritance, and so did not present Anne's implicit challenge to patrilineal genealogy. Mary's notorious subordination to her husband and her more direct position in relation to her father prevented her from occupying the uniquely threatening position in which Anne undesignedly found herself.

Queen Anne, then, took the throne in her own person. A daughter without a father, a mother without a child, she was, first and foremost, a sister. And it was as a sister that she was greeted by the realm at her accession, as we saw in Sharp's sermon: "a Sister of our never to be forgotten QUEEN is yet left us."[67] Yet eventually, Anne's position as sister became a source of anxiety and distrust to her contemporaries. As her subjects were only too aware, the queen had the right to name her exiled brother as her successor, and until the day she died many feared (and some hoped) that she would do so.[68] Anne was entirely and dangerously anomalous, outside traditional categories of inheritance and legitimacy. She attempted to resolve this dilemma by styling herself as the symbolic mother of her people, but found the representation less empowering than debilitating. Perhaps in the last analysis this was because in her attempts to build authority from maternity, Anne never went beyond accepted patriarchal definitions, values and assumptions. Unlike Elizabeth who successfully manipulated the figure of motherhood for her own advantage, Anne declined to reconstruct maternal symbolism; instead, she hoped to be granted power by merely assuming a symbolic representation whose meanings lay in the hands of others, and which was being divested of political power even as she attempted to draw on it as a reservoir of public authority.

Anne's twelve-year reign was dominated by Britain's involvement in the War of the Spanish Succession, the war that sealed Britain's transformation from a remote backwater to an imperial power. Helpful as the war proved for the economy and for national prestige, it presented an inappropriate context for the representation of queenly authority in maternal terms. Anne's effort to build political authority was ambushed throughout the course of the war by patriarchal manipulations of the maternal self-representation she

[67] Sharp, "A Sermon," 18.
[68] The Duchess of Marlborough's friend Dr. Hare wrote in 1710 that if Anne were to support the Pretender's succession, she would "very probably succeed" (Marlborough, *Private Correspondence*, 2: 44). Cf. Rapin-Thoyras, *Histoire d'Angleterre*, 4: 372.

assumed, especially as these were used on behalf of her general-in-chief John Churchill (Sarah's husband), whom the queen created first Duke of Marlborough shortly after her coronation.

Anne's role as the war's presiding monarch was problematic to say the least. The decision to fight at all, and the scope and methods of British involvement, had been determined by William and his advisors (including Churchill) who did not consult Princess Anne or inform her of their decisions. When William died, English troops had not yet actually been deployed but it was too late to withdraw English commitments to allies. The new queen was forced to superintend the war's commencement and continuation despite her poor qualifications and almost entire ignorance of what had brought the nation to this point. So Queen Anne at once actively inaugurated and passively inherited William's war, standing in characteristically paradoxical relation to it, symbolically the war's enabler, but in practical terms, very much an outsider.

These difficulties were exacerbated, ironically enough, by Marlborough's dramatic abilities – the ability to proceed strategically, to negotiate diplomatically, to summon popular support, and, most of all, to win. An active campaigner, brave and resourceful on the field, cunning at the bargaining table, politically adept (even, many said, unscrupulous), gallant, handsome and charismatic, intimate with Anne's chief Whig minister Sidney Godolphin and with Anne herself through Sarah – Marlborough held all the cards. The situation was structured so as to minimize the authority of the reserved, obese, invalid queen and lend visibility and power to her charming and victorious hero.

Marlborough posed a threat almost from the start, although Anne was slow to recognize it. As early as 1703, contemporaries were revising Anne's maternal self-representation into a paternal image for Marlborough: in a letter consoling the Duke on the death of his only son in 1703, for instance, Robert Harley begs him "to consider that the nation are your children, [that] the publick needs all your care."[69] Almost immediately after the coronation – Anne's first and best attempt to derive authority from symbolic maternal self-representation – Marlborough already looms in this letter from a political rival as the nursing-father of the coronation text. The representation, moreover, was remarkably long-lived. As late as

---

[69] Marlborough, *Conduct*, 172.

1759, Thomas Marriott borrowed it to describe the lines of inheritance within the Duke's family: "When, in the *Marlbro-*Tree, one Branch is dead / Another golden rises in its Stead."[70] Forty-five years after Queen Anne's death, the images she chose to represent her authority to her realm at her coronation were still being usurped by Marlborough's eulogists.

For most of her reign, Anne was an enthusiastic supporter of the war effort and of Marlborough, the person most closely associated with its tedious campaigns and glorious victories. And especially during the early years of the war, Anne was consistently represented as the nation's symbolic mother and even sometimes as the embodied matrix of the war itself, which was widely seen as a positive and empowering undertaking. Even overseas allies perceived Anne's maternal relation to the war. Charles of Spain (one of the several rival claimants for the Spanish throne) wrote on July 27, 1705 to ask the Duchess of Marlborough "to inform her Majesty, that in her favours and her constant friendship I found all my hopes; that I deem myself to [sic] happy in the maternal affection of so great a Queen" (Marlborough, *Private Correspondence*, 1:9). More often, however, maternal imagery was reserved for Anne's relationship to her people. Samuel Wesley compared the "friendly Care" Anne extended to "Distant Regions" to the much greater blessing of her "Maternal Goodness" at home (*Marlborough*, 12).

As purported mother of a war waged exclusively on Continental soil, however, Anne was a peculiarly absent, abstract figure. While Marlborough campaigned gloriously abroad, the queen – always in poor health and now increasingly obese – remained at home. Contrasts were frequently drawn, to Anne's disadvantage, between Anne and her predecessor Elizabeth, who was still famous in the eighteenth century for having led her own troops on horseback. When Anne assumed the throne in 1702, Dunton's popular *Ladies Dictionary* had recently reminded readers of Elizabeth's exploit, reporting enthusiastically that she "led her Army into the Field *in* Person" (177) and even reproducing Elizabeth's famous speech on the occasion. In a poem devoted to drawing comparisons between Elizabeth and Anne, in which he emphasizes both queens' role as national "Mother" ("Eliza," 48), Richard Blackmore foregrounds

[70]   Marriott, *Female Conduct*, 39.

one important distinction: Elizabeth led her troops "in Person," giving them fresh courage, and Anne did not (167–68). Anne never visited the sites of even the most glorious battles; she left both active participation and inspirational presence to Marlborough.

So it is hardly surprising that even the most martial representations of Anne during the war suggest a stolid, remote figure, a female embodiment of the homeland for which men, epitomized by Marlborough, engage actively in risk and adventure. "In mighty *Anna*'s powerful Name," James Shute declared shamelessly in 1704, Marlborough "went, He saw, and overcame" (8). In the early years of her reign, Anne was occasionally represented as something approaching a martial figure in her own right. In 1705, for instance, just after the Blenheim victory, an unidentified poet laments William's "successless" martial ventures, and celebrates the "strange Female Force" of "*Imperial ANNE*" who "compleats the Work unfinisht by the Man."[71] But even in this poem, Anne's important maternal work is at home, among the "Enemies within":

> Them too with Art uncommon she subdues,
> And Mildness is the Weapon she doth use:
> Such Means to conquer Faction seldom fail,
> For where the Queen proves weak, the Mother does prevail.[72]

And in any case, such quasi-martial representations were soon abandoned. As the war wore on, Anne's status as an outsider to military affairs became increasingly obvious; by the war's end, she had long been represented as an absent, passive inspiration for male military activity. Defoe's "Hymn to Victory" imagines Anne as she was frequently pictured in visual art of the time: a monarch seated in the center of activity, herself passive. The queen is "*circl'd With* English Hearts *and* English Arms" and is "placed in ... a Seat" from which she inspires, by her "Glory" and "Victorious Charms," the "Valour" of the men who serve her. According to Defoe's preface, Anne is "*you that send us out*," but Marlborough is "him that leads."[73] And as if in extension of the emphasis on spiritual authority that we noted in the coronation sermon, the female monarch who prays at home while male agents campaign abroad became a frequent image in the poetry of Anne's reign. "If Empires mourn," Samuel Cobb wrote in 1705,

[71] Br., "Letter to ... Tallard," 47.   [72] Br., "Letter to ... Tallard," 47.
[73] Cf. Congreve, "A Pindarique Ode;" Pix, "A Poem."

Her *MARLBOROUGH* is sent
To stop their Tears, and calm the Continent ...
If we below Storm some important Fort,
She scales the Skies above, and shakes the Heav'nly Court;
Where'er the Wretched for Her Succour call,
The Equal Mother is alike to All.[74]

Elkanah Settle would put it most succinctly in the year of Anne's death: "whilst her HEROES *fought*, their *ANNA knelt*."[75]

The narrowing of Anne's representational options in relation to the war is made graphic in the medals cast over the course of her reign, all of which were reproduced in print by Abel Boyer in 1722 and again in 1735. The inaugural medal, designed by Kneller, was produced to commemorate Anne's coronation (figure 8). A bust of the crowned queen appears on what Boyer's explanatory caption calls "the right side" with a routine verbal inscription: "Anne by the Grace of GOD, Queen of Great Britain, France, and Ireland"; this would become the standard "right side" image for royal medals during Anne's reign. On the "reverse" side of the first medal is Pallas, the warrior goddess, actively engaged in warfare. As Boyer puts it in his accompanying description, Pallas is

holding her *Aegis* in her Left Hand, and a Thunderbolt in her Right, ready to strike at the *Hydra*, (the Emblem of Rebellion, Sedition, Schism, Heresy, Etc.) that lies beneath her; with this *Motto*, VICEM GERIT ILLA TONANTIS, that is, *she is the thunderer's vice-gerent* [sic]. (Boyer [1735], 718)

The legend at the bottom of the "reverse" side ("inaugurat. xxiii. Ap. MDCII" – crowned 23 April, 1702) conjures up the figure on the other side of the medal, conflating the new queen of the "front" side and the amazonian victor of the "reverse." Anne herself is an active warrior-queen, the agent of God's justice.

By the third medal, however (also cast in 1702) (figure 9), although the "right side" image is the same, the "reverse" is somewhat different. The medal pictures the siege of an unnamed Continental town. Only male figures are present, and the motto informs us that "Vires Animumque Ministrat" ("She gives strength and courage"). Between the first and third medals in 1702 Anne has changed from a latter-day Pallas engaged in active campaigning to the inspiration behind male military events, from which she is conspicuously absent.

This is the pattern of the medals that follow. Increasingly over the

---

[74] Cobb, "Honour Retrieved," 21–22.
[75] Settle, "Threnodia Britannica" (1714), 15.

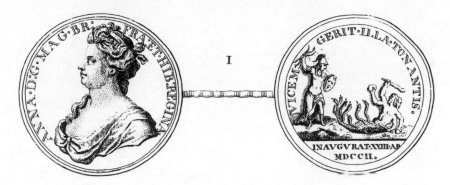

8   The inaugural medal of Queen Anne's reign, published in honor of her
coronation on April 23, 1702. After a design by Kneller.

9   "She gives strength and courage." The third medal cast during Queen Anne's
reign, depicting the seige of a Continental town. The coronation medal's representation of the queen (fig. 8) appears on the unpictured "front" side. 1702.

years, Anne's head on "the right side" becomes separate from the
events pictured on "the reverse," which admit female representations
only when these are allegorical, stationary, or heavenly figures,
separated from real-life victories. The military victories celebrated on
the medals (at Vigo, Blenheim, Gibraltar) are all-male events far
removed from the ponderous, impassive queen depicted on the front
of the coin. Indeed, the medals themselves physically repeat Anne's
removal from the scenes of action: one has to turn over and obliterate
the queen's face in order to see the battles and victories at all.

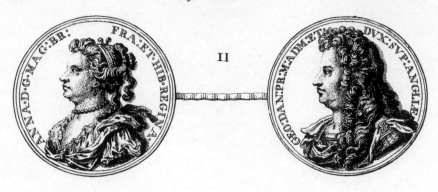

10   The second medal published during Queen Anne's reign. A relatively domesticated Queen Anne appears opposite her husband, Prince George of Denmark.
1702.

11   The fifth medal of Queen Anne's reign, cast in 1703. The domesticated Anne of
fig. 10 appears on the unpictured "front" side.

The second medal of the reign (1702; figure 10), was designed to
celebrate the royal couple; it presented Queen Anne on the right side
and Prince George on the reverse. It is a domesticated Anne who
appears on the second medal opposite her husband (who is rather
ludicrously extolled in the honorific titles Anne had insisted on giving
him – "High-Admiral and Generalissimo of England"). This second
image of Anne also appears on the "front" of the fifth medal (figure
11), struck in 1703, distinguishing it from most of the reign's other
medals. It is significant that this is the view of Anne chosen for the

fifth medal, because the reverse of the fifth coin represents Marlborough on horseback, and its motto ("Conqueror Without Slaughter") points directly to the Duke and only by implication, if at all, to the queen.[76] There is no suggestion of the queen on the reverse of the medal; she is off the scene of victory, and is subtly (by the reproduction of the second rather than the first bust) identified as a wife, not a warrior.[77]

Increasingly, then, Anne was represented as an inspirational figure who remained passively at home while male agents actively campaigned overseas.[78] Her role is oddly suggestive of the role of the domestic mother, which we shall examine in detail in Part Three. Matthew Prior's birthday poem to the queen, recited in her presence in February of 1704, makes the connection clear. The queen who just two years earlier had been pictured on the inaugural medal as Pallas, warlike and powerful, in Prior's poem has become a domesticated Minerva, contentedly teaching virtue and poetry while male representatives – particularly Perseus (Marlborough) – engage in battle.

> *Minerva* thus to *Perseus* lent her Shield,
> Secure of Conquest, sent him to the Field . . .
> Mean time the Deity in Temples sat,
> Fond of Her Native *Grecians* Future Fate;
> Taught 'em in Laws and Letters to Excel,
> In Acting justly, and in Writing well.
> Thus whilst the Goddess did Her Pow'r dispose,
> The World was freed from Tyrants, Wars, and Woes.[79]

The domestic queen, like the domestic mother of conduct literature, is responsible for teaching at home;[80] her "power" is "disposed" indirectly, while she remains invisible.[81] As Defoe put it in the same year,

---

[76] Defoe interpreted this medal as an insult to the queen (85, below).

[77] Only two of the medals cast during Queen Anne's reign, numbers six and twenty-two in Boyer's collection, picture the queen on both front and back. Both of these reproduce the "front" side of the coronation medal (figure 8). The reverse of medal six, which celebrates the queen's bounty to the clergy, pictures Anne seated on her throne, with a row of churchmen kneeling before her; and medal twenty-two shows her again seated on the throne, with the figure of Victory performing an action Marlborough had performed many times by 1710 when this medal was cast: appearing before the queen to claim praise and reward for his victories abroad.

[78] Cf. the representation of Queen Anne in Addison's "The campaign."

[79] Prior, "A prologue," 2.

[80] Cf. Part Three, 158.

[81] Among the meanings of "dispose" current during Anne's lifetime, according to the *OED*, most have to do with delegation: "to place [things] at proper distances," "to bestow or

Victorious Marl'bro' *conquers in your Name;*
His is the Conquest, Madam, Yours the Fame ...
Such Order must a suited End afford,
At home your Councils and Abroad their Sword.[82]

Representations of the maternal queen's passivity, however, were not always so complimentary. Poets often contrasted the victories achieved by English heroes abroad with Anne's maternal failure at home; sometimes they even blamed Anne's failed motherhood for devaluing the reign's military successes. In his "Ode to the Sun for the New Year" (1707), to note just one example, Elijah Fenton makes a military celebration into an occasion to remember Anne's failure to provide heirs. Calling on the sun to look down on Windsor and see Anne conferring well-deserved honors on the Duke of Marlborough, Fenton says

> O Phoebus! all thy saving Pow'r employ,
> Long let our Vows avert the destin'd Woe,
> E'er *GLORIANA* Re-ascends the Sky,
> And leaves a Land of Orphans here below!   (5)

Military conquest – however glorious – counts for little, Fenton implies, when it will be followed inevitably by the death of the queen whose childlessness will render her people orphans at last.

That Anne's role as at-home inspiration for the war was not as empowering as her propagandists liked to insist is most forcibly demonstrated by the degree to which Marlborough presented a threat to the queen's authority and even her position, especially after the all-important allied victory at Blenheim in 1704. In the sermon William Sherlock preached before the queen at the thanksgiving service for the Blenheim victory, he praised Marlborough in terms discomfitingly suggestive of the duke's superiority to the queen:

Certainly never was Man better fitted with Courage, Conduct, and unwearied Industry for so great an Enterprize ... This is true Nobility ... to defend their Prince and their Country by Arms; all the Titles and Ensigns of Honour originally came from the Field, and if they be not won there, but descend by Inheritance, or are conferr'd by the Favour of Princes, they seldom shine so bright in any other Sphere; for the People will admire a

---

hand over," "to distribute, assign or appoint." Also available was the denotation most familiar today, "to dispose of."

82 Defoe, "Hymn to Victory," preface. Cf. Edward Young's 1714 elegy on Queen Anne's death.

brave Captain, to whom they owe their Safety and defence, above some empty Images of Honour.[83]

The hint that Anne's self-representations are only "empty images of honour" compared to the "true nobility" Marlborough demonstrated on the battlefield (a source of legitimation not available to Anne) combines here with another reminder that the queen's claims to authority are tenuous: not only has she no bravery at arms to show, but she can't even claim that her powers "descend by Inheritance, or are conferr'd by the Favour of Princes" – neither her father nor William, after all, had endorsed Anne's accession. Sherlock goes on to wish Anne "a long and happy Reign" with continued successes by which she will "deliver the poor persecuted Protestants" and then be rewarded with "eternal Peace and Rest" (26). Marlborough's praise is sung at Anne's expense; maternal echoes ("deliver") are linked not with victory and life, but with anticipation of the queen's death.

Sherlock's implication that Marlborough possesses "true Nobility" and constitutes a threat to Anne's maternally represented authority is by no means an isolated example. The Blenheim victory was just one event that produced numerous comparisons of Anne and Marlborough; these were often presented as retellings of the biblical story of Deborah and Barak, and subtly disadvantageous to the queen. The title page to one such work uses as twin epigraphs two parallel verses from the book of Judges: "I Deborah *arose, I arose* a *Mother of* Israel"; and *"Arise* Barak, *lead thy Captivity Captive, thou Son of* Abinoam" (Shute). The rhetorical parallel between Deborah (Anne) and Barak (Marlborough) is obvious: both "arise." But all the mother-ruler does *is* arise; it is her captain, identified by his patrilineal descent, who actively leads troops and wins victories. The juxtaposition of these passages epitomizes the situation Anne found herself in *vis à vis* Marlborough: once "risen" to the throne and figured as symbolic mother, there was little more for Anne to do. The mother-queen was a necessary presence behind Marlborough's war, but not an active agent in it. Indeed, throughout the century Marlborough was remembered as the real force behind the reign's greatness. In 1759, Marriott expressed the common view that Anne's only contribution to the war had been to step in at the very end and ruin it.

> If *Anna* had not stopp'd, in full Career,
> Her Conquest, how we should her Name revere! . . .

[83] Sherlock, "A sermon," 25.

Battles, by *Marlbro'* won, in vain we boast,
Vain Battles, at pacific *Utrecht* lost![84]

Increasingly over the years, Marlborough's popularity, visibility, and authority encroached on the queen's. Congreve's "Pindarique Ode" of 1706 replicates this development textually: the poem starts out celebrating Anne, but ends up a hymn to her general. In an arresting transitional moment between praise of Anne and of Marlborough, Congreve insists on the impossibility of praising the Duke adequately:

> Attempt not to proceed, unwary Muse,
> For O! what Notes, what Numbers could'st thou chuse,
> Tho' in all Numbers skilled;
> To Sing the Hero's matchless Deed . . .
> What Verse such Worth can Raise?   (8–9)

Oddly, there had been no problem just before in finding adequate words to praise the queen; it is only when she gets to Marlborough that the poet's Muse cannot continue, because "Admiration stops her Song" (10). The moment is significant within the Pindaric structure of Congreve's poem. As Congreve and his classically educated contemporaries certainly knew, it was Pindar's practice to follow the invocation of a deity with the praise of a mortal hero, then to cut short the hero's praise to avoid arousing the envy of the deity. Congreve imitates Pindar exactly, casting Marlborough as the hero and Anne as the goddess in danger of becoming jealous of a mortal.[85] Likewise, Delarivier Manley has a quasi-fictional character note that after "Hippolito's [Marlborough] Return from a Glorious *Campaign* . . . *Hippolito*'s Health was observ'd to be oftner drunk, even than *Albania*'s [Anne]."[86]

By the second half of Anne's reign, literature accusing Marlborough of attempting to supplant the queen or praising him as the *de facto* king (depending on the writers' politics) proliferated. Marlborough himself clearly understood the situation, as he reveals in this letter to the Duchess dated September 7, 1709:[87]

It is not fitt that anybody but yourself should know that I have just reason to be convinced that 42 [the Queen] has been made jealous of the power of 39

---

[84]   Marriott, *Female Conduct*, 125–26.
[85]   My thanks to James McGlew for pointing this out.
[86]   Manley, *Queen Zarah*, 159.
[87]   Like most of Marlborough's correspondence, this letter was written in cipher and with orthography that we might charitably call idiosyncratic, even for an eighteenth-century writer. The identifications are by Snyder.

[Marlborough], so that 39 ... is resolved not only to convince 42 ... but all the world that he has no ambition, and at the same time be carefull not to be in the power of villains, nor even of 42.[88]

And in a pamphlet written (probably by Defoe) to justify Anne's removal of Marlborough from all offices in 1711, we are told that the people loved Marlborough so excessively that the Queen had to lower him "meerly in Defence of her own Safety, and in Vindication of Her Right to that Glory, which the Idolatrous Croud would rob Her Majesty of, and pay to Her Creature the Duke."[89] The author goes on to describe the extent to which Anne endured this humiliating threat before taking steps against Marlborough, focusing on a medal (probably medal five discussed above, figure 11) which he considers to have raised Marlborough iconographically to a position above the queen:

Her Majesty was pleased to admit Her Royal Head to be, as it were, but the Reverse of a Medal struck to his [i.e., Marlborough's] Glory ... the Queen on one Side of a Medal, and the Duke on the other, Her Majesty in Bust only, his Grace at full Length ... on Horseback, and the like Things. (9)

On this medal, the writer claims, "was represented more than any Subject ever was admitted to" (9) – and perhaps he was right. For the medal constitutes a kind of parody of the queen's Great Seal, where Anne is pictured enthroned on one side and mounted on horseback on the other. In the same year appeared the vitriolic *Fable of the Widow and her Cat*[90] in which a favorite cat who "so long with Tooth and Claw / Have kept Domestick Mice in awe, / And Foreign Foes defeated" begins to attack the childless Widow who cared for him, stealing "the Cream," tearing at her clothing, devouring all her other pets and sharing the spoils of her estate with his cronies. As in this violent fable, Anne's vulnerability to Marlborough was often discussed in gendered terms and with reminders of her widowed and childless condition. By the time of Sacheverall's trial in 1710, Swift tells us, Anne "looked upon the Duke with the same Displeasure as if he had been her Rival" (*Memoirs*, 78); and the threat Marlborough posed was especially great because of Anne's maternal failure – "the Queen was without Issue, a Widow, and of an infirm Constitution, and could do nothing to oppose him" (85).

---

[88] *MGC*, 3: 1356.
[89] Defoe [attrib.], "No Queen; Or, No General," 8.
[90] Rogers notes that the pamphlet may have been written by Swift (Swift, *Complete Poems*, 651).

As difficult as it is to sort out the layers of propaganda and interest in pamphlet tirades for and against Marlborough, it is certain that Anne herself came to believe the nation to be in danger of being "Rul'd by a John," as an anonymous anti-Whig drinking song put it in 1712.[91] The queen felt her autonomy being gradually limited and realized that she was excluded from the highest levels of decision-making concerning the war. As her prestige came to depend on foreign successes with which she had less and less to do, and as her once-ardent friendship with the volatile Duchess of Marlborough gradually cooled, Anne began keenly to resent Marlborough's great popularity and influence, and to understand that her metaphorical representation as matrix of the war was ironically reinforcing her removal from actual affairs both abroad and at home; her maternally imaged authority was becoming merely figurative. By the last days of 1711 Anne was dissatisfied enough to remove Marlborough from all his offices and turn for ministerial direction to the Tories, led by the first Earl of Oxford and Mortimer – that is, the same Robert Harley who eight years earlier had transformed the queen's "nursing-mother" imagery into a vision of Marlborough as the nation's nursing father. Under Oxford's influence, the queen supported the controversial Peace of Utrecht, a 1713 treaty that ended the long war but made concessions unacceptable to Marlborough's supporters, and experienced a dramatic loss in popularity. A major subject of debate in written discourse at the end of Anne's reign and for years after her death was the queen's (mis)management of the war's last years, and of the Peace in particular. And not surprisingly, vituperative pamphlets on sides of the quarrel employed the language of failed maternity to criticize the queen. An anonymous Tory pamphlet was entitled *The Miscarriages of the Whig-Ministry*; Povey called his Whiggish tirade *An Enquiry into the Miscarriages of the Four Last Years Reign.*[92]

In any case, the change of ministry came too late. Anne found that

91   Anon., "The Queen's ... New Toast" n.p.
92   Cf. Settle, *Distres'd Innocence*, (1722); Speck, "The Orangist conspiracy," 149; Holmes, *British politics*, 75–81. Salmon's defensive title (*The Life of Her Late Majesty ... Wherein her Conduct During the Last Four Years ... is ... Vindicated*) suggests the degree to which Anne's supporters felt called upon to justify the queen's role in the Peace. Settle speaks for her critics:

O'erpow'r'd by Councils, She whose Gracious Smile
Cou'd to such MERITS raise a BLENHEIM PILE;
The *Sovereign Goodness*, which so warm cou'd flow,
(Oh Betray'd Weakness!) sunk t'an Ebb so low"
("Threnodia Britannica" [1722], 12–14).

although the circumstances of her constraint were different with a Tory ministry, there was little alteration in her cipher-like position. In the final years of her reign, Anne was virtually excluded from practical governance, unable even to choose her own ministers or pay her personal attendants without Oxford's approval.[93] One chronicler quotes Anne calling herself a "royal slave";[94] and apparently her contemporaries would have supported that estimate with near unanimity. Abel Boyer acknowledged in 1722 that Anne "was not equal to the Weight of a Crown" (716). James Ralph insists that "The Queen was, on all Hands, considered and treated as a mere Property ... [by] State-Brokers" (259–60). He portrays Anne as "abject" and always in danger of being exposed as "a Royal Cipher in public as well as private," "neither Mistress of her own Power, nor at liberty to make Choice of her own Friends" (295, 253, 341). Even less charitably, Rapin-Thoyras argues that whatever "parts and abilities have been ascribed to her" in fact "belong[ed] only to her Ministers" (4: 371). The writer of the "Advertisement" to Millar's 1758 edition of Swift's *History of the Four Last Years of the Queen* concurs: "the best that has been said for her, shews no more than that she was *blindfolded* and *held in leading-strings* by her *ministers*" (x–xi).[95] Anne's physician, though speaking in her defense, made the same assumption when he noted in his diary on July 6, 1713,

It plainly appears Her Majestys forced, by Indisposition and returns of disquiet to trust others. She was kept not only from Persons of a Contrary Opinion, but from the Knowledge of things, and therefore her Ignorance, and progress suitable to that, is imputable to Others and not to Her.[96]

Every contemporary assessment of the degree of agency enjoyed by the queen is by definition partisan; still, Anne's status as outsider is

---

93 Gregg, *Queen Anne*, 370–74.
94 Rapin-Thoyras, *Histoire d'Angleterre*, 4: 371.
95 Historians have continued to present Anne as a weak monarch and the victim of ambitious subjects. Cf. Strickland, *Lives of the Queens of England*, 12: 236; B. Brown, *Letters and Diplomatic Instructions*, vii; *MGC*, xvi; Gallagher, "Embracing the absolute," 38. Anne's passivity is often seen as a result of her limited mental powers. "Queen Anne," Beatrice Brown announces in the first line of her book, "has the reputation of being a stupid woman"; Brown then goes on to argue that the real problem was Anne's "insufficient education" (vii). Gregg decorously sidesteps the question of the queen's "intelligence, or lack of it" and praises Anne for possessing a formidable memory, discretion, and common sense (*Queen Anne*, 138). The *DNB* suggests with stunning sexism that the queen's limitations were the result of her harrowing maternal experience, which "would have weakened the intellectual vigor of most women" (1: 471). For a different view, cf. Barash, *Augustan Women's Mythmaking*.
96 Hamilton, *Diary*, 56.

certain. It was lamented in 1709 by Delarivier Manley, whose gossiping Intelligence comments regretfully on Anne's vulnerability.

There you shall behold our graceful Empress, whose Heart is entirely upright. Were she but to judge all things by her own eyes and ears, all things would be administered with ... impartiality and justice ... But alas! what defence is there against the corruption of favourites, and the by-interests of ministers?[97]

And there is no doubt that Queen Anne herself felt she was being left out of power and had comparatively little share in many of her reign's finest moments. "Everybody," Anne complained to Oxford in 1713, is "too apt to encroach upon my right."[98]

Anne's decision to represent her political power by means of symbolic maternity, then, came at a most inopportune juncture. Against the backdrop of a distant war that kept the ailing queen removed from crucial scenes of political action, at a time when the empirical vitality of symbols was waning and when the social and ontological status of maternity was shifting from immediacy and physicality to immateriality and removal, Anne chose to build queenly authority on maternal symbolism. At such a moment, hers was a strategy doomed to failure.

Furthermore, Queen Anne's representational problems had important implications not only for her own political authority, but also for the developing institution of motherhood in her time. The paradigms for female/maternal authority that consolidated around her would throughout the century be used to circumscribe women's authority in the public realm; and reciprocally, norms limiting female public activity would be used to create specific varieties of normative maternal behavior. In this sense, the tragic irony of Anne's experience as queen is not simply, as is often said, her physical failure to produce heirs, but also, paradoxically, her success in delineating her increasingly limited authority in maternal terms. In the desperate need to bear a child that shaped her career until the turn of the century, and then in her problematic self-representation as symbolic national mother, Anne was unintentionally complicit in the construction of a normative definition of maternity as a kind of

---

[97] *New Atalantis*, 110. Cf. Rapin-Thoyras: "The Queen was deceived by her Ministry, and kept in total ignorance of affairs" (*Histoire d'Angleterre*, 4: 373).

[98] Queen Anne to Oxford, Tuesday, 21 July, 1713; quoted Gregg, *Queen Anne*, 350. Cf. the queen's speech to Parliament on March 2, 1714, where she complains of "attempts to weaken my authority or to render the possession of the Crown uneasy to me" (*PH*, 1258; Gregg, *Queen Anne*, 378).

failure, entailing a loss of position, voice and participation in the (male) public world.

The texts discussed in the following chapters dramatize this reduction in the public viability of the social institution of motherhood in the first half of the eighteenth century. But fortunately, they do something more: they demonstrate how historically particular experience exceeds generalized social rubrics and institutional codes. In popular representations of every kind from the first half of the eighteenth century, maternal bodies and voices redirect and subvert the reductive code of maternal excellence that was inaugurated during Queen Anne's reign.

PART TWO

Monstrous motherhood: violence, difference, and the subversion of maternal ideals

Typically, under patriarchy, the mother's life is exchanged for the child's; her autonomy as a separate being seems fated to conflict with the infant she will bear.

Adrienne Rich[1]

For a mother ... an other is inevitable.

Julia Kristeva[2]

[1] Rich, *Of Woman Born*, 166.
[2] Kristeva, "Héréthique," 48.

In July of 1659, a two-year-old London child drowned at home in a tub of water while in her grandmother's care. The news was immediately distributed in a hastily composed pamphlet titled *The Unnatural Grand Mother, Or a true Relation of a most barbarous Murther*. According to the pamphlet's anonymous author, the facts are these. An unnamed young mother sold fruit in Cheapside along with her mother, one Elizabeth Hazard. The young mother went away overnight, leaving her two-year-old in Hazard's care. Unfortunately, the devil stayed behind to whisper in the grandmother's ear.[3] At his suggestion, she

takes the poor innocent Babe in her armes, where after many Murthering and dissembling kisses they go to bed ... But the Devil that never sleeps, soon awakens her, lays before her the charge her daughter had of children, and a bad husband that would not endeavour to maintain them; and how that she was indebt [sic], and like to run her self more in debt towards the maintaining of them (with many such devilish and deceitfull suggestions which are apt to take with any that the Lord hath left, and given over to themselves). (6)

Spurred on by these "devilish" thoughts, and "more like an Infernal Hag, then the mother or grand-mother of children," Hazard "cacht the poor Childe by the heels, and thrust the head of it in the Tub of Water, and so held it under water while she had drowned it." (7)

Next, according to the story, the grandmother dresses in her best clothes and takes six pounds, "and as it is conjectured thought to make her escape" (7). Attracting attention by her unusual dress, she invites a neighbor upstairs to see "what I have done this morning." The neighbor cries "Murther!" and Hazard is carried off to the alderman. "What shall we think of this unnaturall Grand-Mother?" the author asks, "That in stead of nourishing, and cherishing that which come at first from her own Loines, she so unwoman like and unnaturally hath now destroyed?" (5)

There were no witnesses to the drowning. The account was composed and printed before Elizabeth Hazard's trial and admits to being speculative ("as it is conjectured"). One might wonder, then, why the possibility of an accidental death is never considered. True, murder sells more pamphlets than accident; but the specific details chosen for amplification suggest that something more may be at work. The pamphlet's author admits no doubt about Elizabeth Hazard's guilt because her "unnatural" behavior is explicitly con-

---

[3] The whispering devil is a common figure in infanticide narratives during the seventeenth century. Cf. MacDonald, *Mystical Bedlam*, 83.

nected to – even conflated with – an "unnatural" way of thinking about motherhood. The child's presumed murder is preceded causally by "devilish," unthinkable thoughts: that material circumstances can make motherhood untenable, that there are times when a mother will be forced to choose betweeen her own survival and the survival of her child. Elizabeth Hazard defines her daughter's motherhood as an economic problem; she presumes to place both financial and moral responsibility on her daughter's "bad husband." Only a depraved and abandoned mother with an ear open to the devil's suggestions, according to this text, would think such thoughts, thoughts that lead, inevitably and unsurprisingly, to infanticide.

We might pause to note that it is the grandmother, not the mother, who is the villain in this pamphlet. Why? The known facts hardly demand the innocence of the mother. It would have required little more than the considerable imagination already at work in *The Unnatural Grand Mother* for the author to have constructed the crime as a plot between the women. Yet the text takes pains to distinguish between "the greatest of horrors ... this unnaturall Grand-Mother" and her daughter, who is praised for being an "indulgent and careful" mother. This distinction becomes especially problematic when we observe that the daughter-mother was absent because she was taking her infant to a country nurse – an action beginning to become suspect in the late seventeenth century (5).[4] Why, then, is only the grandmother, not the mother, cast as villain?

We can find a possible explanation in the effect: isolated in her monstrosity, the grandmother becomes a scapegoat, an aberration proving the rule that her daughter upholds. For *The Unnatural Grand Mother*, despite its obvious function of relating juicy scandal, is less the story of a child's death than an outraged description of transgressive motherhood, an effort to define "natural" motherhood by displaying its perverse opposite. Elizabeth Hazard represents the worst and most threatening kind of mother, one who emphasizes economics over affect and who insists on recognizing the mother as separate from the child, with distinct and even competing needs. But the child's own mother, Elizabeth Hazard's daughter, provides reassurance. It is true that she works for a living and sends her children out to nurse; but, we are informed, she is "constrained" to do so, "forc't to take paines for her living" (6); we are invited to assume her reluctance. Unlike

[4] Cf. Part Three, 159–62, below. .

Elizabeth Hazard who speaks and acts with decision, the daughter-mother is shadowy, passive, victimized, absent at crucial moments, and – most important – anonymous. Less an individual woman than an extension of the murdered child, this paradigmatic "natural" mother serves as normative foil for the infanticidal Elizabeth Hazard, who "now hath almost destroyed her [the young mother], by Murthering the child" (5). Indeed, the pamphlet's final lines conflate the dead child and the young mother as the innocent objects of Hazard's inhumanity: "It is reported by several people that for this many years, she [Hazard] hath been tempted to kill the mother of this child before she was married, and had hid knives at severall times to that intent; but God did prevent it" (8).

For all its brevity and hasty construction, *The Unnatural Grand Mother* stands as an apt vehicle for displaying the mystifications and anxieties that surrounded motherhood at the brink of the Augustan age in Britain. The dense layers of maternal relation, the disturbing proximity of motherhood to death, the too-insistent denial of connection between maternal viability and economic circumstance – all combine to make this tale representative of an enormous and important body of writing in Augustan England, narratives of monstrous motherhood. Novels, pamphlets, broadside scandal sheets, drama and romance all dwell luridly on "unnatural" mothers – coldhearted, cruel, avaricious, cowardly, fraudulent, and lascivious – whose vices are measured against implicit norms of unwavering maternal tenderness and self-denial.

Defoe's *Moll Flanders* and *Roxana*, Smollett's *Roderick Random*, and Johnson's *Life of Savage* provide only the best-known examples of the kind.[5] Less-familiar examples include the luridly titled 1697 broadside *The Unnatural Mother: Being a Full and True Account of One Elizabeth Kennet, a Marry'd Woman, ... who, on Tuesday the 6th of April, 1697, privately Delivered herself, and afterwards flung her Infant in the Fire, and Burnt it all to Ashes, but a few of the Bones*; the scandalous revenge tragedy *The Unnatural Mother, The Scene in the Kingdom of Siam* (1698), where the mother depicted is a monster of greed and villainy without moral scruple or human feeling; *The Unnatural Mother and Ungrateful Wife*, where two mothers fail egregiously to provide financially and educationally for their children; *A Pittilesse Mother*, an anonymous seventeenth-century broadside in which an "unnaturall" mother's

[5] Cf. my "Critical complicities" for the function of the "monstrous mother" trope in Johnson's *Life of Savage*. Defoe's novels are discussed at length below.

wickedness is connected insistently to her Roman Catholic sympa-
thies;[6] and the long prose tale *The Unnatural Mother or Innocent Love
Persecuted* (1734), which we shall examine shortly, where an economically vulnerable mother is scapegoated for the death of her daughter.

There are many such tales. In *The Covetous Old Mother* (1720), a
mother who disapproves of her son's choice of a poor girl for his wife
secretly sells his fiancée into slavery. Martin Parker's *No naturall
Mother, but a Monster* (1634) narrates the tragic story of a young
servant girl who commits infanticide for fear of losing her position;
the girl is reviled as "more cruell ... than Savage creatures."
Elkanah Settle's *Distres'd Innocence* (1691) and Delarivier Manley's *The
New Atalantis* (1709) make much of the pernicious influence of evil
mothers, as does Eliza Haywood's *Female Spectator* (1744–46). Haywood's first volume, for instance, includes a common figure, the
mother turned pimp, who threatens, beats, and starves a daughter
who will not succumb to the sexual demands of a wealthy rake.[7]
These infamous, unloving mothers and scores more like them
represent one of early eighteenth-century British culture's most
fascinating terrors. Their stories were enormously important in
shaping Augustan attitudes toward motherhood, and inculcated
maternal mythologies that remain powerful even today.

Why should motherhood have constituted such an important and
troubled space in Augustan discourse? An explanation may lie in the
dissonance eighteenth-century culture increasingly perceived
between two uneasily reconciled values: unique, coherent personal
identity and sacrificial, self-effacing motherlove. In Augustan Britain,
motherhood and what we might call "personhood" began to be seen
as mutually exclusive alternatives. For the first time, it became
obviously difficult to reconcile developing norms of self-sacrificing
motherlove with increasingly powerful notions of individual subjectivity – what Lawrence Stone has called "affective individualism."[8]
Within Augustan structures of thought and action, a distinct,
coherent self figured increasingly as a crucial goal to be achieved;
and the means of its achievement was competition with other selves.

---

[6] Catholicism and infanticide frequently go together in seventeenth-century texts. By the
  eighteenth century, significantly, evil mothers are seldom inspired by Catholicism – they are
  just wicked individuals. Cf. Travitsky, "A pittilesse mother?" for a full examination of the
  case of Margaret Vincent, the so-called "pitiless mother."
[7] Representations of the mother-pimp abound. Cf. Anon., *The Cruel Mother*; Anon., *The Forced
  Virgin; or, The Unnatural Mother.*
[8] Stone, *Family, Sex and Marriage*, ch. 6.

That Augustan Britain put an increasing cultural premium on self construction is signalled by many of the age's most characteristic phenomena – the growing power of liberal dogma, the expectation that capitalist endeavour would make possible individual social mobility, the development of the myth of romantic love, redefinitions of monarch-subject and father-son authority relations, and the increasing cultural power of novels, to name a few. Furthermore, the all-important self was understood to be forged at the expense of other selves. Consider for example Defoe's *Robinson Crusoe* (1719), undoubtedly the century's most influential representation of isolated self-construction, where circumstances of extreme isolation mystify the assumption that the self is essentially a competitive achievement. Long alone in an inhospitable environment, almost entirely non-relational, Crusoe seems inevitably, even naturally, to survive and develop by leaving others behind, breaking faith, even engaging in violence and murder. But in the narratives of monstrous motherhood that Defoe produced in the 1720s, it is far more difficult for the protagonists' violently competitive and radically isolated self-con-structions to appear natural and unproblematic. Defoe's maternal protagonists, like Robinson Crusoe, abandon and defraud others who threaten their security; but those threatening others are, more often than not, their own children – irreducibly other, but also, strangely, themselves. *Moll Flanders* (1722) and *Roxana* (1724) pit mothers' needs to define autonomous selves and establish economic independence against the inexorable needs of their children; the psychic and material survival of the heroines comes to depend on the elimination of those competing needs. The result is a maternal fable – comic in *Moll Flanders* and tragic in *Roxana*[9] – that exposes as outrageous and "unnatural" not only the maternal behaviors of the protagonists but also, more significantly, the plot of competitive self-construction. In *Robinson Crusoe*, Defoe was able largely to deny the profound costs and limits of that plot; but *Moll Flanders* and *Roxana* relentlessly expose them. With increasing acuity and increasing despair, Defoe attempts to imagine motherhood and autonomy coexisting in a world where viable personal and social identity can be conceived only as the products of competition and opposition.

[9] That *Moll* is a comic version of *Roxana* has become a critical commonplace (e.g., Flynn, "Defoe's idea of conduct," 85, 88). We are concerned to define the matrix on which Defoe builds both Moll's comedy and Roxana's tragedy: the struggle to reconcile maternity with Enlightenment models for subjectivity.

"UNNATURAL" MOTHERHOOD
IN TWO NOVELS BY DANIEL DEFOE

Augustan maternal rhetoric granted the status of "natural" or "virtuous" maternity only to mothers who submitted to the developing code of domestic womanhood, abdicating both public intercourse and autonomous subjectivity.[10] But this kind of "natural" motherhood was not available to mothers without the leisure born of middle-class social privilege, or those who insisted on developing their own subjectivity according to the liberal, competitive and capitalistic models developing in Augustan England. For such mothers, infanticide – real or symbolic[11] – became the necessary condition of survival. In the "unnatural" maternal situations depicted in *Moll Flanders* and *Roxana* – as in analogous tales of monstrous motherhood like *The Unnatural Grand Mother* – a loosely-codified set of "natural" maternal behaviors gradually comes into focus: private, exclusively affective, self-sacrificing, anonymous. Maternal virtue is pitted against public and material success; the erasure of autonomous subjectivity becomes the price of maternal excellence. But although these maternal ideals constrain the behavior and attitudes of Defoe's mothers, they have little relevance to the material conditions of their lives. Defoe's narratives of maternal monstrosity foreground the experiences of mothers whose material circumstances, social positions, and needs for autonomous security make impossible the behaviors they themselves deem "natural."

Moll Flanders, for instance, – who is abandoned as an infant by her own mother – bears fifteen children between her first marriage and her old age; but notoriously, she raises none of these children herself, and most often abandons them during infancy. In an episode we shall consider in detail in a moment, Moll declares that "Affection was plac'd by Nature in the Hearts of Mothers to their Children" (173) and that to send a child to be raised by a hired caretaker is "to

---

[10] For the eighteenth century's development of new norms for virtuous womanhood, see especially Armstrong, *Desire and Domestic Fiction*.

[11] I define "infanticide" broadly as the elimination of children (especially one's own), however achieved. Infanticide in this sense is a pervasive theme in both *Moll Flanders* and *Roxana*; the construction and protection of the protagonists repeatedly requires the elimination of their children. Cf. Maddox, "On Defoe's Roxana," 686; Flynn, "Defoe's idea of conduct," 91.

It should be noted that "infanticide" was not a specific crime under English law until 1938, when it was defined in gendered terms as murder *by a mother* during the first postpartum year. Cf. Travitsky, "A pittilesse mother," 56; Walker, *Crime and Insanity*, 125–37.

be unnatural, and regardless of the Safety of my Child" (176); but immediately, Moll turns her own newborn child over to a wetnurse because the child's existence threatens her pending marriage (to a man who is not its father), her means of entry into middle-class respectability and security. Likewise, between the two marriages that frame the action of *Roxana*, the heroine bears at least eleven children but doesn't look after any of them for long.[12]

The apparently casual way in which Moll and Roxana abandon their children has scandalized critics. In an essay available to numberless students by virtue of its appearance in the Norton Critical Edition of *Moll Flanders*, for instance, Michael Shinagel argues that Moll's decision to leave the family in Virginia "is, as her husband charges, 'unkind' and 'unnatural';" Moll is "a mother totally devoid of ... 'honest affection'" ("Maternal Paradox," 406, 410). But it is important to see that Defoe's characters themselves express horror at their behavior. Roxana is convinced that as mother to the merchant's son "I had shown a general Neglect" (Defoe, *Roxana*, 263). She hears his affectionate words for the son with pain: "I was asham'd that he shou'd show that he had more real Affection for the Child, tho' he had never seen it in his Life, than I that bore it" (228). Likewise, Moll Flanders says that her decisions as a mother "did not at all satisfie my Mind" (*Moll Flanders*, 177). Whatever their material successes, Moll and Roxana see themselves as "unnatural" mothers who fail to practice the tender personal care and sacrificial love that both claim are the characteristics of "natural" motherhood.

The gap between what Moll and Roxana *say* about motherhood and what they actually *do* requires more explanation than it usually receives. Typically, critics have considered Moll Flanders's and Roxana's monstrous maternal behaviors as manifestations of individual aberrance, the isolated failures of psychologically immature women.[13] But while there is no question that *Moll Flanders* and *Roxana* are concerned with the difficulties of establishing individual psychological coherence, or that Defoe's representations invite

[12] Apparently Roxana has eleven children: five by the brewer, two by the landlord-jeweller, three by the prince, and one by the Dutch merchant. At one point, however, Roxana says she had six children by the brewer (73), which would take the total to twelve. Roxana also offers to act as foster-mother to Amy's child by the landlord.

[13] See for example Maddox, "On Defoe's *Roxana*," 674; Durant, "Roxana's fictions," 235; Stephanson, "Defoe's 'malade imaginaire',” 101; Shinagel, *Defoe and Middle-Class Gentility*, 413; Castle, "Amy," 90–91; Faller, *Crime and Defoe*, 224. Chaber provides a summary and critique of this strategy as it has applied to *Moll Flanders* ("Matriarchal mirror," 212–13).

readers to consider his heroines in psychological terms, still maternity
is not a purely psychological experience in *Moll Flanders* and *Roxana*.
It also constitutes a social and material trauma, and presents at least
as direct a threat to economic as to psychic autonomy. To argue that
Moll's or Roxana's rejection of motherhood is merely a manifestation of personal immaturity is to collude with the maternal
mythology that Defoe's novels helped to construct, particularly the
notion that motherhood may be reduced to an affective, individual
matter, separate from material, political, and social considerations.

So when critics assert that only late in her life can Moll "afford,
emotionally and fiscally, to become a *real mother* for the first time"
(Erickson, *Mother Midnight*, 67, my emphasis), or that it is "curious,"
considering her "casual" attitude toward childrearing, that Moll
should at all object to "abortion and incest" (Bell, "Crime and
comfort," 103), unstated but important assumptions about motherhood are at work. Virtually all existing readings of Moll's and
Roxana's motherhood employ an oddly companionate tone, as if
writers can freely assume that readers share their assumptions about
acceptable maternal behaviors (e.g. Starr, *Defoe and Casuistry*, 143–5).
Such reduction of possible differences among readers functions as an
ideological tool, *making* natural or unnatural maternal behaviors that
appear only to be *recognized* as such. Even otherwise revisionist and
sympathetic essays accept it as a matter "of course" that "one would
hardly want to claim that Moll is an exemplary mother" (Lerenbaum,
"A woman on her own account," 46). Exactly, we might ask, why not?
The question is less perverse than it may seem. For the point is not so
much to recommend Moll as a maternal model as to forestall her pre-
emptive disqualification, to step out of the circle of supposedly
universal, unchanging norms for virtuous motherhood. To do otherwise is to enforce the fiction that readers necessarily stand at a safe
distance from the alternative motherhoods Moll Flanders and Roxana
represent, and to simplify the complex agencies always at work in
maternal "choices." In *Moll Flanders* and *Roxana*, maternal relations
are "unnatural" not only because of the protagonists' peculiar
psychologies, but also, and not separately, because maternity is
imbedded in larger relations that create contradictions between ideals
for motherhood and the behaviors required for maternal survival.[14]

So the most interesting thing is not the aberrant psychology of a

[14] Cf. Chaber, "Matriarchal mirror," 212; Richetti, "The dialectic of power," 33. My
      argument is indebted to these fine studies, though I believe that *Moll Flanders* and *Roxana*

couple of fictional mothers, but the fact that Defoe's representations of their experiences suggest the practical impossibility of applying supposedly universal norms for "natural," virtuous motherhood to concrete experiences of mothering. This suggestion does not merely undermine the specific norms in question; more fundamentally, it challenges the very possibility of codified, universal maternal norms separate from, superior to, and regulative of actual experience. Despite their "abbreviated psychic development" (Castle, "Amy," 92–93), their marginal social positions, and the paradoxical fact that their experiences are at once devoid of and saturated by maternal connection, Moll Flanders and Roxana may not be nearly the monstrous mothers they have traditionally seemed to be. The exaggerated dissonance between the maternal norms Moll and Roxana subscribe to and the behaviors they engage in may turn out, surprisingly enough, to say more about the social functions of such notions as "natural" or "normal" maternity than about Moll's and Roxana's troubled psyches.

Incest and maternal identity in Moll Flanders

There is no possibility whatsoever, within the current logic of sociocultural operations, for a daughter to situate herself with respect to her mother: because strictly speaking, they make neither one nor two, neither has a name, meaning, sex of her own, neither can be "identified" with respect to the other ... How can the relationship between these two women be articulated?[15]

Halfway through *Moll Flanders*, the protagonist seems at last to have entered that supposedly secure haven for which she is always searching – middle-class domesticity.[16] Moll is living on a prosperous

challenge the fundamental distinction between "the personal" and "the social" on which both Richetti's and Chaber's arguments are based.

[15] Irigaray, *This Sex Which Is Not One*, 143.

[16] For my use of the term "middle-class," see the Introduction, notes 60 and 61. That Defoe recognized the existence of a middle station in his own society is demonstrated by the rubric he provides for distinguishing "the Conditions of all the People" during Anne's reign:

1. The Great, who live profusely.
2. The Rich, who live very plentifully.
3. The middle Sort, who live well.
4. The working Trades, who labour hard, but feel no Want.
5. The Country People, Farmers, Etc who fare indifferently.
6. The Poor, that fare hard.
7. The Miserable, that really pinch and suffer Want.

"The middle Sort of People," according to Defoe, "live the best and consume the most of plantation in Virginia, with a husband, two children and a friendly mother-in-law. "I thought my self," she says, "the happiest Creature alive" (85). In particular, Moll is pleasantly surprised with her husband's mother, "a mighty chearful good humour'd old Woman" who "us'd to entertain *me* . . . with abundance of Stories" (86). These stories, however, turn out to be the undoing of all Moll's respectable happiness. For as she listens to the narrative of the old woman's life, Moll learns a terrible secret.

> She went on with her own Story so long, and in so particular a manner, that I began to be very uneasy; but coming to one Particular that requir'd telling her Name, I thought I should have sunk down in the place; . . . I came to reflect that this was certainly no more or less *than my own Mother*, and I had now had two Children, and was big with another by my own Brother, and lay with him still every night. (87–88)

After considerable inner struggle, Moll decides to leave the now-monstrous family in Virginia and return alone to England. But she resolves not to tell her husband why she is leaving, fearing his power to incarcerate or destroy her. This reticence to explain, Moll tells us,

> provok'd him to the last degree, and he call'd me not only an unkind Wife, but an unnatural Mother, and ask'd me how I could entertain such a Thought without horror as that of leaving my two Children (for one was dead) without a Mother, and to be brought up by Strangers, and never to see them more? *It was true,* had things been right, I should not have done it, but now, *it was* my real desire never to see them, or him either any more; and as to the Charge of unnatural I could easily answer it to myself, while I knew that the whole Relation was Unnatural in the highest degree in the World. (91)

For Moll, the peculiar "relation" in which she stands in respect to her family eliminates the possibility of "natural" maternal behavior for her as a mother: her children are automatically alienated from her, as the offspring of an illegitimate union.

This straightforward reading of Moll's words, however, recognizes only a fraction of their resonance. For while Moll refers directly to her problematic "relation" to the Virginia family, she is also involved in the larger "relation" of her life story – "the whole Relation" of the novel's preface (3). At the moment when she realizes that her mother-in-law is also her mother, the narrative – hitherto Moll's own

---

any in the Nation . . . [and] are the most numerous also among us"; it is they "with whom the general Wealth of this Nation is found." (*Review,* 6: 36 (June 25, 1709) [Secord, 14: 142]; cf. 5: 129 (Jan. 22, 1709) [Secord, 13: 515]).

– becomes a tangle of confused "relations," a story where mothers and daughters cannot safely co-exist, and where there is no possibility for unequivocally satisfactory or "natural" choices. In Moll's narrative, motherhood itself is a kind of "unnatural relation" – "not a story," as she later puts it, "that would bear telling" (324).

Moll keeps her secret for three years, agonizing alone over whether and when to make her relation known, how much of it to tell and to whom. Finally she reveals "my own Story and my Name" to her mother(-in-law), providing identifying "Tokens" like a long-lost orphan in a romance or a reclaimed foundling at Coram's hospital (95). Not surprisingly, the mother resists Moll's story, which by establishing Moll as her daughter threatens the mother's hard-won identity as the respectable matriarch of a promising family. Faced with such a threat, Moll's mother tries to revise her relation. "As if she had been willing to forget the Story she had told me of herself, or to suppose that I had forgot some of the Particulars," Moll says, "she began to tell them with Alterations and Omissions." But Moll disallows such tampering with a narrative which after all is not only her mother's, but her own as well: "I refresh'd her Memory, and set her to rights in many things which I supposed she had forgot, and then came in so opportunely with the whole History, that it was impossible for her to go from it" (96).

Every thing concurr'd so exactly with the Stories she had told me of her self, and which if she had not told me, she would perhaps have been content to have denied, that she had stop'd her own Mouth. (95)

In response to the mother's story, Moll offers – indeed, insists on – a narrative that is too close a match; her "relation" comes too near, making it impossible for the mother to control the effects of her own story. *"Dreadful Girl!"* she cries at last, "... what will become of us? what is to be said? what is to be done?" (95–96).

As always in *Moll Flanders*, the apparently insoluble problem resolves with surprising ease. Moll does escape to England, and when she returns to Virginia years later she finds that her mother, now dead, has provided substantially for her and that one of her abandoned sons stands ready to welcome her with outstretched arms and open purse. Moll's first care is to determine that the mother is really dead ("I enquir'd then how long my Mother had been dead, and where she died"). This done, she can proceed in safety to replicate what her mother had done before: tell stories that unquestionably establish her maternal relation to young Humphrey: "[I] told so many particulars of the Family, that I left him no room to doubt the Truth of my being really and truly his Mother" (334). Thus, as Moll puts it with characteristic insouciance, "all these little Difficulties were made easy" (342). Moll finds prosperity and ease in Virginia in the form of a "maternal inheritance"[17] left her by the mother who once threatened her very life. Like so many of Moll Flanders's near-tragedies, her problems in Virginia evaporate in the balmy atmosphere of fortuitous coincidence and well-managed deceit. Her mother's threatening presence is eliminated, allowing Moll to reassert her social and domestic position by means of a maternal relation no longer subject to the disquieting echoes of the mother's story.

"For Decency sake": Moll Flanders *and the mystification of maternal economy*

Every woman is supposed to have the same set of motives, or else to be a monster. I am not a monster, but I ... was glad to be freed of you.[18]

The shocking discovery of her mother in Virginia constitutes one of many episodes in *Moll Flanders* where maternity emerges as a life-threatening crisis. Moll's decision to leave the monstrous family behind and begin again in another country is also typical: whenever her children threaten her survival, Moll abandons them, often with quite startling impunity. It is worth noting, however, that despite the coldheartedness critics often find in Moll Flanders, in fact she never leaves her children until she considers the impasse between their survival and her own to have become insurmountable. It is true that children are for Moll one more debit to be factored into the ever-updated balance sheet, a disproportionate item that threatens to unbalance the budget entirely; but they are not *merely* so. The complexity of Moll's responses to her children and the extent to which those responses are necessitated by economic stress have never been fully recognized; instead, critics tend to dismiss Moll as simply indifferent to her children and to concentrate instead on Roxana's (supposedly) more interesting maternal failure. Christopher Flint's comparative interpretation is representative: both Moll and Roxana, he says, "scatter progeny in many places"; but "unlike Moll, who feels much less compunction, ... Roxana ... only gives up her

17   *"Moll Flanders,"* 4.   18   Eliot, *Daniel Deronda*, 691.

children in the face of a convincing necessity" (Flint, "The anxiety of affluence," 407).

The contrast drawn between Moll and Roxana as mothers in such arguments is simply too stark to meet the facts. Moll records great "compunction" about each child not left with a father or grand-parent; more often than not, she leaves her children unwillingly, after considerable struggle, and in circumstances of economic desperation. Consider the language Moll uses to describe her feelings when she must part with the son of her Bath lover (who promises to "take due care of the Child" [124]):

And now I was greatly perplex'd about my little Boy; it was Death to me to part with the Child, and yet when I consider'd the Danger of being one time or other left with him to keep without a Maintenance to support him, I then resolv'd to leave him where he was; but then I concluded also to be near him my self too, that I might have the satisfaction of seeing him, without the Care of providing for him. (125)

It has proven easier for critics to deplore Moll's disinclination to assume "the Care of providing for" her children (as if she were merely lazy or indifferent) than to recognize these as the words of a woman straitened financially and socially (the child, we recall, is the product of an extramarital liaison). Moll cannot support her son, but finds the thought of leaving him tantamount to "Death." One wonders what, if not this, would qualify as Flint's "convincing necessity." Miriam Lerenbaum has rightly observed that "there is a world of difference between saying ... that Moll does not wish to be personally responsible for her children and saying ... that she does not care what happens to them" ("A woman on her own account," 44). But there is even more to it than Lerenbaum recognizes. For we cannot say that Moll does not "wish" to be responsible for her children; in periods of financial security she acts upon this wish unexceptionally. But more often the material conditions of her life make such a wish a kind of wishful thinking. For most of her life, it is not so much that Moll "does not wish" to care for her children as that she *cannot* do so and still survive.

Besides the terrible struggle in Virginia, Moll's most difficult maternal decision – and the one that has brought down the harshest judgments from critics – occurs when she is faced with the choice of parting with her newborn son (the child of the highwayman Jemy) or forfeiting proffered marriage with a respectable London banker. This marriage, like the incestuous one in Virginia, holds out the promise of entrance into the "safe Harbour" of middle-class security (188), Moll's best hope of escape from crime. Moll's ruminations at this crisis call attention to the difficulty she has in reconciling her notions of correct maternal feeling and behavior with material necessities and with her own desires. So great is that difficulty, in fact, that we are forced to consider the alternative Moll herself chooses: abandoning altogether the attempt to reconcile maternal theory and practice. At the same time, Moll's deliberations expose as fraudulent a notion of virtuous motherhood incompatible with the material circumstances of unmarried or impoverished mothers.

Moll considers the existence of Jemy's child to be "the great and main Difficulty" obstructing her acceptance of the banker.

I knew there was no Marrying without entirely concealing that I had had a Child, for he [the banker] would soon have discover'd by the Age of it, that it was born, nay and gotten too, since my Parly with him, and that would have destroy'd all the Affair. (173)

Mother Midnight, the midwife-pimp in whom Moll confides, hints darkly about how this "concealment" should take place: "the Child ... must be remov'd, and that so, as that it should never be possible for any one to discover it" (173). But Moll balks at the suggestion.

It touch'd my Heart so forcibly to think of Parting entirely with the Child, and for ought I knew, of having it murther'd, or starv'd by Neglect and Ill-usuage, (which was much the same) that I could not think of it, without Horror; I wish all those Women who consent to the disposing their Children out of the way, *as it is call'd* for Decency sake, would consider that 'tis only a contriv'd Method for Murther; that is to say, a killing their Children with safety. (173)

Moll's outrage is formulaic; many texts of the time decried the custom of "putting children out to nurse" in strikingly similar language.[19] But when it comes to the particulars of her own situation, Moll cannot maintain the stance she has adopted. Despite

---

[19] Cf. Haywood's *Female Spectator* (1: 6: 368–69), where it is "astonishing" that a woman who has sent an illegitimate child out to nurse "could act so contrary to Nature" as to "abandon" her child "to Miseries of she knew not what kind. – This was a Barbarity ... exceeded the Crime to which it owed its Birth." Cf. Cadogan, *Essay upon Nursing*, 27 for an echo of Moll's comparison between sending a child out to nurse and murdering it. Concerning the "Practice of sending Infants out" to be nursed "by another Woman," Cadogan sniffs, "the antient Custom of exposing them to wild Beasts, or drowning them, would certainly be a much quicker and more humane way of dispatching them" (27). According to the most influential works of Augustan conduct literature, nursing-out is morally reprehensible, against religion, and unnatural (cf. Part Three, below; Shinagel, "Maternal paradox," 408).

these fighting words, she realizes that personally to care for her child, even to be known as his mother, "would be Ruin and Destruction to me, as now my Case stands" (175). And so Moll does precisely what she expostulates against: she reluctantly gives her child away "with a heavy Heart and many a Tear." "And thus," she says, "my great Care was over, after a manner, which tho' it did not at all satisfie my Mind, yet was the most convenient for me, as my Affairs then stood" (177).

Obviously, there is comic irony in Moll's use of a superior moral tone to describe "those women" who pack off their children to nurses shortly before she does the same herself because it was "most convenient for me." But there are deeper ironies at work in Moll's moralizing, and tragedy as well as comedy in this scene. Take, for example, the word "convenient." In Defoe's day "convenient" meant not only "easy" or "handy"; more often, in a meaning now lost, to call something "convenient" meant that it was "suitable to the conditions or circumstances." The *OED* cites Wesley describing a group of paupers in 1741: "Many were destitute of convenient clothing." So Moll's decision to do what is *convenient* with her child encompasses not only lazy unconcern, but also dire need. The two denotations exist simultaneously, necessarily complicating our response to Moll's comment. Moll is quite right when she says that the child will probably die with the nurse; a great many infants sent to country nurses never came back. Fildes notes the "huge numbers" of deaths among country nurslings (*Wet Nursing*, 97), and cites the horrific case of the 16-month-old son of Sir John Bramston of Essex, who died in 1639 after coming down with "scabbies" at the home of his nurse. As Bramston wrote later, the nurse

to cure it hastilie that wee might not know it, aplied, as she sayd, burnt or fried butter, on brown paper, whereby grew a great soare on the brest, and a core came out (soe that one might see the very hart pant).[20]

Despite the intervention of "a very good surgeon," the baby died, leaving his father to mourn: "he was a very lovelie child." (95)

So Moll hardly exaggerates when she says that by sending her child to one of Mother Midnight's nurses, she engages in a kind of indirect infanticide. At the same time, Moll's outburst constitutes an act of self-alienation akin to suicide: she denigrates women like herself, whom she speaks of in a distanced, third-person voice. Much

[20] Fildes, *Wet-Nursing*, 94–95. Cf. *Tatler* 15 (May 14, 1709), a satiric narrative of the painful experiences of an infant sent to a careless country nurse.

more than a piece of unconscious hypocrisy, Moll's castigation of "those" women who would bury their children (literally or figuratively) "*as it is called* for Decency sake" is a means of erasing her own particularity, and so participates in the mystifications that make possible Moll's paradoxical and painful maternal "relation." Further, Defoe's locution mystifies the material basis of Moll's dilemma and allows "decency," an (apparently) economically neutral term, to cover over the complex, conflicting problems that motherhood poses for Moll. The description of mothers who put away their children "for decency sake" flattens social distinctions among those mothers and implies that they share similar motives and a single standard of "decency."

But Moll's moralizing rings hollow in the context of the material situation that elicits it. For it is only within "my present Circumstances" that Moll considers it an "inexpresible Misfortune ... to have a Child upon my Hands" (171). And these circumstances are certainly bad enough.

I wanted to be plac'd in a settled State of Living, and had I happen'd to meet with a sober good Husband, I should have been as faithful and true a Wife to him as Virtue it self could have form'd: If I had been otherwise, the Vice came in always at the Door of Necessity, not at the Door of Inclination; ... [but] I found no encouraging Prospect; I waited, I liv'd regularly, and with as much frugality as became my Circumstances, but nothing offer'd ... and the main Stock wasted apace ... the Terror of approaching Poverty lay hard upon my Spirits ... [my] case was almost desperate ... I found my self in great Distress. (128–130)

Despite her unquestionable desire for secure respectability, "Decency" is not the primary issue for Moll (nor, perhaps, for "all those Women" of whom she disapproves); her very survival is at stake.

So the problem ultimately exposed in this episode, though never addressed directly, is not that mothers put their children out to nurse; far worse are social norms that make marriage the only means to economic viability for women, while placing it permanently out of reach of women with sexual experience. That her marriage to the banker, and all that it represents in terms of social and material security, is contingent upon the disposal of the child points to the impossibility of the situation Moll finds herself in, the complex and compromised nature of the "choice" she is making, and the mythical status of the maternal "consent" she decries. The economic and sexual double standards that defined relations between the sexes in Augustan England make maternal "choices" like Moll's tragically inevitable; the murderous mothers she chastises hardly deserve the unilateral blame she assigns to them. In her castigation of mothers who send their children out to nurse, Moll colludes with a sexual politics that has little to offer her, one that polices and punishes female desire, recasts economic survival as social convention, and invalidates the forces most urgently at work in the experiences of impoverished mothers. The point is less to defend Moll's decision to abandon her child than to refuse to join in the reductive attack she stages against herself. Whether or not Moll will give up her son is not as crucial to our understanding of Augustan maternal mythology as the fact that Defoe, in Moll's voice, cannot frame the problem in terms that allow her to have both maternal virtue and social/material needs.[21]

This inability to square theory with practice produces instructive dissonances. Moll declares, for instance, that what children need is not necessarily personal maternal care but "an assisting Hand, whether of the Mother, or some Body else" (173). But then she says that only mothers (in whose hearts "Nature" has "placed" the "Affection ... without which they would never be able to give themselves up ... to the Care and waking Pains needful to the Support of their Children") can rightly care for their own offspring; mothers who relinquish children's care to a surrogate "neglect them in the highest Degree," and "to neglect them is to Murther them" (173–74). Well, we might ask, which is it? Are children as well cared for by surrogates as by mothers, or will only mothers do? By presenting apparently exclusive alternatives in such close proximity, Defoe's narrative suggests much more than that Moll's "maternal moralizing is specious and insincere."[22] In its contradictory assumptions and conclusions, and especially in the glaring incongruity it displays between maternal theory and practice, *Moll Flanders* exposes as inadequate the very idea of a definitive truth about motherhood.

---

[21]　For a different reading of this scene, cf. Starr, *Defoe and Casuistry*. Starr notes that Moll's "anticipatory denunciations of the very misdeeds she is about to commit ... serve to ... distinguish her essential self from the sinner whose past she is recounting" (144). This interpretation assumes a clear distinction between, as Starr puts it, "what Moll is" and "what she does." I argue that as a mother Moll cannot "be" *except* in the contradictory space between what she does and what she says about it. Simultaneously inhabiting both sides – what she "is" and what she "does" – Moll blurs the distinction Starr attempts to reinforce.

[22]　Shinagel, "Maternal paradox," 408.

When Moll damns women who send their children out to nurses and then sends her own son out, we witness a phenomenon that Augustan discourse on motherhood – with its emphasis on regulation, homogenization, and codification – all too often disallowed: the representation of two versions of motherhood that seem to demand each other's exclusion but that nevertheless remain simultaneously operative – differently true, and equally false.

When Moll Flanders the fictional character wrestles with the problem of whether to send her son to a hired nurse, *Moll Flanders* the novel is participating in a specific public debate, the debate over maternal breastfeeding. In the course of staging a scene of maternal "choice," Defoe situates his novel as a text to be reckoned into Augustan England's considerable and growing body of writing on the evils of nursing out, a body of writing that we shall consider in some detail in Part Three. But the debate over breastfeeding in the first half of the eighteenth century concerned the behaviors of women from the middle stations and above, not women in Moll's social orbit.[23] By transplanting familiar Augustan arguments for maternal breastfeeding to a lower-class scene, Defoe at once abets and exposes the denial of class difference in his society's efforts to define "natural" motherhood monolithically. The issue of maternal breastfeeding is the same, he implies, for criminal mothers as for leisured married women. But the importation of this debate into Moll Flanders's world also raises the disturbing contradictions we have noticed; under the circumstances, it seems odd that Moll should imagine that she might *not* part with her son. The flattening of social and economic distinctions backfires, drawing attention to precisely the class differences that are under denial, revealing the inadequacy of abstract rules for definitively "correct" and "incorrect" maternal behaviors and exposing the fiction that maternity can be defined apart from the particularities of economic and social difference.

That Moll's eloquent harangue against putting children out to nurse functions as an ironic prelude to her decision to put her own infant out, then, is not merely comic or psychologically revealing, though it is certainly both of those. And it does not merely provide a launching pad for Defoe's defense of maternal breastfeeding, though it does that, too. Most important, this resonant incident demonstrates enormous contradictions between the maternal norms Moll defines

---

[23]   Cf. Fildes, *Wet-Nursing*, 112.

herself by and the kinds of mothering she can hope to achieve, and exposes the class complicities behind arguments like those she makes in favor of maternal care. In *Moll Flanders*, virtuous motherhood begins to look impossible except for women with the leisure, means, and desire to "give themselves up" to the care of their children. Good motherhood and (economic) autonomy are pitted against each other as if they really were mutually exclusive possibilities –and so, increasingly, they become so.

"Dreadful Necessity": motherhood as death in Roxana

Women ... can *act* like men, but, unlike men, they cannot leave their children and get away with it: that plot does not exist.[24]

Two years after the publication of *Moll Flanders*, Defoe reconsidered that novel's most troubling dilemma, the conflict between motherhood and survival. In *Roxana*, Defoe once again tells the story of a mother who cannot care for her children and still survive, and of a daughter and mother who threaten each other's lives merely by existing. But here there is no fortuitous end to "all these little Difficulties." Roxana attempts, like Moll, to refuse motherhood; but she finds that there is no escape. Her agonized abandonment of her children, her subsequent failure to reclaim them, and the tragic results of her coincidental meeting with a long-lost daughter anxiously rewrite Moll's "unnatural relation." In *Roxana*, Defoe finally tells the story that does not "bear telling," the story of motherhood as death.

Like Moll Flanders, Roxana begins to mother from within marriage, economically well-off and respectable. But Roxana's brewer-husband proves incapable of sustaining the prosperous business he has inherited, and eventually abandons her, destitute, with five children, "none of them big enough to help one another" (15). In the face of such grievous economic distress, Roxana, like Moll at the birth of her son by Jemy, begins to feel trapped. But there are important differences in Defoe's representations of maternal desperation in the two novels. For one thing, the newly abandoned Roxana spends no time worrying about maternal imperatives not consistent with her own survival. From the very first, she dispenses with affective rhetoric and reckons the children as a material liability:

[24] Hirsch, *Mother-Daughter Plot*, 183.

I was dreadfully frighted ... and the more when I look'd into my own Circumstances, and consider'd the Condition in which I was left; with five children, and not one Farthing Subsistance for them ... if I had had but one Child, or two ... I would have ... work'd for them with my Needle ... but to think of one single Woman ... to get the Bread of five Children, that was not possible. (12, 15)

Over and over she reminds us of the economic facts: "I had five little Children ... and I had not one Shilling in the House to buy them Victuals ... They must inevitably be Starv'd, and I too, if I continued to keep them about me" (17, 19). So we are not terribly surprised when

the Misery of my own Circumstances hardned my Heart against my own Flesh and Blood ... [so] I began to be reconcil'd to parting with them all, any how, and any where, that I might be freed from the dreadful Necessity of seeing them all perish, and perishing with them myself. (19)

Roxana appeals to her well-off sister-in-law, whom she hopes will adopt the children. But the sister-in-law refuses unequivocally, using logic reminiscent of Moll's at the Sign of the Cradle. A mother, she insists, should care for her own children personally, regardless of whether she can afford to or not: "Let her that brought them into the World, look after them if she will; what does she send her Bratts to me for?" (20). Roxana's sister-in-law (whose behavior has almost exact contemporary analogues[25]) requires of Roxana maternal behaviors possible for women circumstanced like herself (she is "married, and liv'd very well" [13]), but no longer tenable for Roxana. The sister-in-law proceeds as if the power to assume responsibility for children were equally and universally available to all mothers. It does not occur to her that economic differences might engender differently valid maternal behaviors.

In *Moll Flanders*, Defoe assigned this kind of reductive thinking to Moll herself at the very moment of maternal abdication, and so created the dissonances we have noted. In *Roxana*, he places similar arguments about maternal responsibility in the mouth of an outsider, the sister-in-law. This shift provides Roxana with greater consistency

---

[25] For example, in the story of a child left in a basket at the door of a woman said to be his grandmother in 1709. The baby was accompanied by a letter from its mother, who addresses her mother-in-law in language very like Roxana's: "I am not able to support myselfe, haveing neither money, any calling, or friends, much less am I able to support them, and I cannot see them starve, and I thank God that he has given me the grace to overcome the temptation I lay under to make away with them" (Fildes, "Maternal feelings," 154). The grandmother, despite the mother's appeals to "your natural affection (which you ought to have)," turned the child over to the parish immediately.

as a character, leaves readers less room to dismiss her as merely hypocritical or ironic, and reduces the stark contradiction between theory and practice so evident in *Moll Flanders*. Yet *Roxana*'s notions of maternal virtue are not necessarily more forgiving or inclusive than those in *Moll Flanders*. Although Roxana attacks her sister-in-law as unfeeling ("her Heart was harden'd against all Pity, who was really and nearly related to the Children" [22]), the sister-in-law's rebuke simmers throughout the novel, and comes back at last to haunt and finally destroy Roxana. So despite the sister-in-law's personal heartlessness, the kind of thinking she represents is crucial to *Roxana*'s complicated defense of the same myth that Moll espoused – the myth that mothers are fully and individually responsible for choices made in constraining and even coercive social situations, choices so overdetermined as to be inevitable. In *Roxana*, as in *Moll Flanders*, motherhood always imposes choices; but in *Roxana*, all options are deadly. The apparent choice between the mother's survival and the survival of her relation to her children, the driving problem of Roxana's "relation" as of Moll's, is eventually exposed in *Roxana* as no choice at all. Whatever course Roxana takes, she risks her integrity, her identity, her social respectability, and her sanity.

"She does not own me": Roxana *and the economy of maternal denial*

For much of the novel, Roxana thinks of motherhood as a purely financial activity over which she can exercise control and from which she can remain emotionally independent. Even when she does turn back to her adult children, the care Roxana extends to them is entirely economic; she remains distant and anonymous, convinced that if she sends her children money, this fulfills her obligation to them. In a fascinating moment of reflection, Roxana distinguishes her relationships to two of her sons according to this reductive economic criterion:

I had shown a general Neglect of the [merchant's] Child, thro' all the gay Years of my *London* Revels; except that I sent *Amy* to look upon it now and then, and to pay for its Nursing; as for me, I scarce saw it four times in the first four Years of its Life ... whereas a Son which I had by the Jeweller, I took a different Care of, and shew'd a differing Concern for, tho' I did not let him know me; for I provided very well for him. (263)

It does not occur to Roxana that she may have shown similar neglect to these two sons, neither of whom would recognize her if they saw her. What matters is that one child is better "provided for" than the other. When Sir Robert Clayton asks her whether she has any children, she answers, "None, Sir *Robert . . . but what are provided for*" (168).

By insisting that she has "provided for" her children, furthermore, Roxana implicitly argues for her own innocence of their fates. For in Augustan England, "making provision" for one's children was a precise and legally operative term. It denoted an expectant mother's preparation of childbed linen before delivery, an action assumed to indicate maternal affection and often successfully cited in defense of mothers accused of infanticide. In Old Bailey sessions transcripts throughout the early eighteenth century we find juries relying heavily on the demonstration that accused mothers did (or did not) "make provision" before delivery, and handing down sentences accordingly.[26] Indeed, throughout the 1720s, when physical violence was not clearly in evidence, the so-called "benefit-of-linen" argument virtually guaranteed acquittal for mothers accused of the murders of newborns.[27]

The "benefit of linen" defense was not only likely to clear a woman of the charge of infanticide; it also helped to strengthen her defense against the related supposition of prostitution. Unmarried mothers accused of infanticide were routinely assumed to be prostitutes in Augustan England.[28] But the fact that an accused woman had "made provision" mitigated against this possibility: a whore, it was reasoned, would not lavish money on the rituals of lying in, and a woman who did lay aside linen was likely to have a husband somewhere paying the bill. So a woman who could demonstrate that she had "made provision" for a dead child had gone a long way toward establishing both her innocence of the child's fate and her own social legitimacy.

So convinced was Augustan society by the benefit-of-linen argument, in fact, that by 1728 Defoe was chastising his contemporaries for their gullibilty in this particular.

I wonder so many men of sense, as have been on the jury, have been so often imposed upon by the stale pretence of a scrap or two of child-bed linen being found in the murderer's box, etc., when alas! perhaps it was

---

[26] Cf. for example the Old Bailey *Proceedings* for 13–16 January, 1720 (2–3), 30 August–1 September 1721 (3), 11–14 October 1721 (3–4).

[27] Hoffer and Hull, *Murdering Mothers*, 69.

[28] E.g., Dunton, *The Ladies Dictionary*, 239, 261.

ne'er put there till after the murder was commited; or if it was, but with a view of saving themselves by that devilish precaution; for so many have been acquitted on that pretence, that 'tis but too common a thing to provide child-bed linen before hand for a poor innocent babe they are determined to murder.[29]

Defoe set the same critique into motion when, at the Sign of the Cradle, Moll Flanders lays aside linen for the child she subsequently abandons, fully expecting it to be misused or murdered: "making provision" does not *necessarily* indicate maternal virtue for Defoe, though he clearly felt himself to be in the minority in this opinion. So when Roxana claims sanctimoniously to have "provided for" her children, she exploits more than one reductive notion used in Augustan discourse to differentiate virtuous from monstrous motherhood.

Throughout *Roxana*, there is a close connection between the protagonist's increasing financial independence and her masculinization. The key turning point occurs after Roxana escapes prosecution for theft in Paris and sets up in Holland as "a Woman of Business" (131). From this point on, Roxana's wealth brings her a level of freedom usually reserved for men in the eighteenth century. As she explains to the Dutch merchant, a wealthy, unmarried woman is "Masculine in her politick Capacity"; she is "a Man in her separated Capacity ... in Subjection to none" (148–49). In the beginning of the novel Roxana had been a typical bourgeois wife and mother, "not bred to Work" and unable to provide for her children (15); but by the time of her marriage to the Dutch merchant, Roxana is what she calls "a *Man-Woman*" (171), in full control of financial matters. And as she moves from economic helplessness to complete independence, Roxana also changes her maternal style dramatically, revising anxiety and helpless responsibility into distance, anonymity, and calculation.

Because of the surprising connection it draws between motherhood and economics *Roxana* might seem to constitute a promising revision of *Moll*'s attempt to define "natural" and "unnatural" motherhood without reference to material circumstances. But Defoe takes the revision too far, and merely inverts *Moll Flanders*'s reductions: where Moll discounted maternal economy, Roxana denies maternal affect. Ironically, of course, this new reduction actually suggests the conventional code of affective maternity, which looms

---

[29] Defoe, *Augusta Triumphans*, 9–10. Cf. Malcolmson, "Infanticide," 199.

large throughout the novel by virtue of its nearly total absence. Overdoing the dependence of motherhood on economics, *Roxana* reveals that economics is only part of the truth about motherhood. For even Roxana must eventually confront her motherhood as a psychological, emotional, and affective relationship undertaken in a particular economic and social place – not affective *or* economic, but always both.

Perhaps the most significant difference between Roxana and Moll as failed mothers is the fact that in *Roxana*, the economic extremity that precludes bourgeois maternal behavior (and, to some extent, extenuates maternal abdication) is so short-lived. Like Moll's, Roxana's abandonment of the children is precipitated by urgent material need. But *Roxana* offers neither excuse nor forgiveness for its heroine's lack of concern about her children through many subsequent years of economic security – indeed, of extravagant prosperity. Not until Roxana is past fifty does she look up her "five little children" again, only to find that all have led hard and disadvantaged lives, and two have already died. For much of that time, their mother's most pressing problem was how best to protect her immense wealth. Moll's hard-won middle-class security, which she really comes into only in her old age, is here inflated into early, ill-gotten excess. The difference makes Roxana's continued maternal abdication far less justifiable than Moll's and denies Roxana both of the redemptive possibilities at work in *Moll Flanders*: the optimistic possibility that abdicated motherhood may be transformed into a saving relationship for both mother and child, and even the darker hope of successfully avoiding motherhood. Motherhood threatens Roxana's survival, but so does maternal abdication. There is no escape.

Roxana's response to the overpowering emotion she feels upon meeting her grown daughter Susan (who does not know her) is illustrative. Roxana records an orgasmic intensity of feeling when saluting Susan:

It was a secret inconceivable Pleasure to me when I kiss'd her, to know that I kiss'd my own Child; my own Flesh and Blood, born of my Body; and who I had never kiss'd since I took the fatal Farewel ... No Pen can describe, no Words can express, *I say*, the strange Impression which this thing made upon my Spirits; I felt something shoot thro' my Blood; my Heart flutter'd; my Head flash'd, and was dizzy, and all within me, *as I thought*, turn'd about, and much ado I had, not to abandon myself to an Excess of Passion at the first Sight of her, much more when my Lips touch'd her Face; I thought I must have taken her in my Arms, and kiss'd her again a thousand times, whether I wou'd or no. (277)

But Roxana is convinced that she must conceal her emotion, for "upon my concealing it, depended the whole of my Prosperity." So, she says, "I rous'd up my Judgment, and shook it off ... I us'd all manner of Violence with myself, to prevent the Mischief which was at the Door" (277). Maternal emotion figures here like an unwanted pregnancy, a slip to be concealed. Roxana in effect aborts her love for Susan ("I us'd all manner of violence with myself") in an effort to avoid the financial ruin that she is sure will be inherent in "discovery." But her insistence that maternity and financial prosperity are mutually exclusive is riddled with infanticidal language that betrays her, ironically, into a conflation of economics and affect, a confusion of the categories she works so hard to keep separate.

"O!" Susan cries, "She is my Mother; She is my Mother; and she does not own me" (304). In one sense, of course, Susan is quite wrong; Roxana is perfectly willing to "own" Susan economically. Indeed, by the time Susan makes this complaint, Roxana has already redeemed her from a life of labor and bought her entrance into refinement and respectability. But Susan insists on extending the connotations of "owning" to include not only economic control but also emotional recognition and acceptance. She wants to be able to call Roxana mother, and to hear Roxana name her as daughter. It is this larger, more encompassing "owning" that Roxana resists (of another of her children, she says she is "privately resolv'd that when it grew up, it shou'd not be able to call me Mother" [228]). Susan threatens Roxana because she refuses to observe the distance Roxana requires. She insists on interpreting her mother's financial support as an indication of an emotional connection that Roxana is afraid to feel. Susan embodies the fundamental threat maternity poses for Roxana, the specter of an "other" who is also, inevitably, an estranged self. Roxana does not want to hear her daughter name her because, as she says, "she was my own Name" (205).[30]

At the same time, Roxana is never at peace about her own maternal "choices," never quite sure that she *doesn't* want to "own" her children fully, despite the invasions and compromises this would entail. She maintains a precarious distance from her children, but

[30] Likewise the other surviving daughter is "the very counterpart of myself" (329).

finds it increasingly difficult to validate her own behavior internally or live contentedly with its consequences. She cannot "digest it very well" that all her goodness to her son must be "due, in his Opinion, to a Stranger" (204); she has great difficulty restraining the urge to visit Susan, and is only prevented from doing so by Amy – "lest indeed, as there was reason enough to question, I shou'd not be able to contain, or forbear discovering myself to her" (206). Roxana's attitude toward her motherhood is duplicitous and contradictory, dangerous and self-defeating. She cannot live with the guilt and ambivalence she feels about having abandoned her children, though at the time there seemed no other choice. She regrets the necessity of denying Susan, but cannot risk owning and being owned.

Ironically, then, Roxana's capitulation to *Crusoe*'s notion that the self is created and protected at the expense of other selves does not assure her survival after all. The novel's terrible end makes explicit the peculiar double-bind of the mother who attempts to protect her self by escaping from her children: as often as not she ends up finding that this desperate bid for life results in its own kind of death. Roxana once believed that *not* abandoning her five children would necessitate either death for them all, or infanticide ("unless like one of the pitiful Women of *Jerusalem*, I should eat up my very Children themselves" [18]). But leaving the children turned out to be scarcely better: Roxana remembers it as a "fatal Farewel . . . , with a Million of Tears, and a Heart almost dead with Grief" (277). For Moll Flanders too, it had felt like "Death to me, to part with the child"; but for Roxana, it is also "Death to me, but to think of" being reunited with her daughter (287), a possibility exactly parallel to Moll's fortuitous reclamation of her son Humphrey.[31] Even Susan's

---

[31] It is interesting to speculate about whether a comic ending is possible for *Moll Flanders* but not for *Roxana* at least partly because *Moll Flanders* focuses on maternal relationships with sons rather than daughters. For feminists' special interest in the peculiar dynamics between mothers and daughters, see Hirsch, *Mother-Daughter Plot*; Flax, "The conflict"; Rich, *Of Woman* (ch. 9); essays by Hirsch and Scharfman, among others, in *Yale French Studies*, 62; and Gallop's critique of that volume ("Monster," esp. 21). I know of no studies of relationships between mothers and sons in eighteenth-century novels.

There are several popular-psychology books on the subject of mother-son relations (e.g., Bassoff, *Between Mothers and Sons*; Klein, *Mothers and Sons*). Unfortunately, these tend to proceed from unexamined ideological assumptions. Bassoff, for instance, advises single mothers to forego sexual relationships until their children are grown lest the children be "forced to recognize their parents' sexuality" (144) – thus denigrating one of the many *advantages* that can accrue to the children of sexually expressive parents, single or not. The real threat for Bassoff, it seems, is not that "parents" have sexual lives, but that mothers might have sexual lives apart from husbands.

death does not make Roxana safe: when Amy offers to make away with "that Impertinent Girl," the very suggestion brings death-like symptoms on Roxana: "that Expression fill'd me with Horror," she says; "all my Blood ran chill in my Veins, and a Fit of trembling seiz'd me, that I cou'd not speak" (270). For Moll in Virginia, the coexistence of mother and child precipitated a crisis, but resolution was possible. Moll went away until the mother's eventual death of natural causes, and all was well. But in *Roxana*, even absence and avoidance are impossible; every chance that motherhood might be productive of anything other than death is systematically eliminated. The relationship between mother and child is necessarily a fatal, violent one for both parties – infanticide, suicide, and murder all in one. Roxana is denied even the grim alternative of choosing her own life at the expense of her children's; she is destroyed by Susan's destruction. Thus *Roxana* demonstrates the dark side of Moll Flanders's triumphant self-forging. For a mother, *Roxana* suggests, a coherent self cannot be constructed in competition with other selves; with no other model for self-construction available, Roxana's eventual disintegration is inevitable.

Roxana's agency in her own maternal choices remains an active question throughout the novel. When she describes the early abandonment of the children, the narrative is remarkable for its insistent denial of maternal volition. Roxana sobs helplessly in a heap of rags on the floor while her friends lay plans to leave the children on the doorstep of their aunt (the sister-in-law who had earlier refused to care for them). "This was what these good Women propos'd, and bade me leave the rest to them," Roxana says. "So I agreed [to] leave the Management of the whole Matter to my Maid *Amy*, and to them, and accordingly I did so" (18–19).

This early episode, in which Roxana allows others to define maternity for her, is structurally parallel to the novel's terrible conclusion, where Roxana is again passive and Amy is again writing the murderous maternal script. Roxana absents herself from the final, crucial act of abandonment and violence that ends her story, just as she did in the beginning, refusing again to be accountable for her own failed motherhood.[32] But the second (supposed) infanticide exposes more complicated relations of agency and accountability than Roxana is willing to admit, and retrospectively throws into

---

[32] For a different interpretation, cf. Castle, "Amy."

question her helplessness and innocence at the first abandonment of the children. For as the novel progresses, the distance between Roxana and Amy seems gradually to close; and the conflation of the two makes problematic Roxana's insistent denial of responsibility for Amy's actions, particularly when it comes to Susan's disappearance:

It is true, I wanted as much to be deliver'd from her, as ever a Sick-Man did from a Third-Day Ague ... But I was not arriv'd to such a Pitch of obstinate Wickedness, as to commit Murther, especially such, as to murther my own Child, or so much as to harbour a Thought so barbarous in my Mind: But, *as I said, Amy* effected all afterwards, without my Knowledge, for which I gave her my hearty Curse, tho' I cou'd do little more; for to have fall'n upon *Amy*, had been to have murther'd myself. (302)

So despite the fact that Roxana is not the direct agent of her children's abandonment or of Susan's presumed murder – the novel's two crucial scenes of infanticide – she is never absolved of accountability, either. Instead, she is devoured by a sense of responsibility – "eaten alive," as has been said of another mother, "by the children she has never fed."[33] Even when her choices are constrained to the degree that they are not choices at all ("they must inevitably be Starv'd, and I too, if I continued to keep them about me" [19]), and even when others are making the decisions and doing the acting ("I agreed to ... leave the Management of the whole Matter to ... them" [19]), Roxana's passivity is never simply absolving – she is always accountable, not only for what she *does* as a mother but also for what she *allows*. She is tormented by responsibility for actions over which she has uncertain control. The book's final words, referring to Susan's disappearance, demonstrate Roxana's complex entrapment.

the Blast of Heaven seem'd to follow the Injury done the poor Girl, *by us both*; and I was brought so low again, that my Repentance seem'd to be only the Consequence of my Misery, as my Misery was of *my Crime*. (330, my emphasis)

Shared agency ("by us both") is revised into individual guilt ("my Crime"), making explicit the duplicitous process at work all along, whereby the mother is at once denied autonomous agency and assigned unilateral responsibility.

So although Roxana attempts to evade responsibility by casting herself as a passive spectator rather than an active agent, the

[33] B. Johnson, "Apostrophe," 34. Johnson refers to the speaker in Gwendolyn Brooks's "The Mother."

narrative undercuts that effort and presents maternal agency in much more equivocal terms. Roxana consciously relinquishes decision-making authority; but this resignation does not free her. Instead, it puts her in the duplicitous position common to so many mothers in Augustan writing – she is not quite guilty, but not quite innocent, either. Moll was able to avoid maternity while she needed to, then to capitalize at last on culturally normative maternal sentiments (when she spots her grown son Humphrey, Moll gushes unconvincingly over "my one, and only Child" and claims "the Infirmities of a Mother in preserving a violent Affection for him, who had never been able to retain any thought of me one way or other" [332–33]). But Roxana is denied even the option of successful maternal abdication. In her story, the categories of personal identity and maternal identity are not to be made complementary, and confrontation with a lost child – an other who is also the same – precipitates not healing, but further loss.

For all *Moll Flanders*'s celebrated attention to material detail, there is something more realistic – relentlessly, unforgivingly realistic – about *Roxana*. In *Roxana*, others really are inevitable, not to be disposed of, erased, or silenced when they become inconvenient, not to be recalled when once rejected. There is in *Roxana* a new, overpowering closeness between mother and children, a sense of eerie doubleness not at all part of Moll's maternal experience that makes maintaining a stable distinction between maternal self and child-other exceedingly problematic. Susan's unwitting assault on her mother's carefully constructed and manipulated persona results in Susan's own presumed destruction, which circles back again to demolish Roxana, despite her desperate attempts to preserve herself, attempts which, first and last, take infanticidal forms.[34] "I wou'd not murder my child, tho' I was otherwise to be ruin'd by it," Roxana declares (313). Her words conjure up a host of Augustan infanticide narratives, where the murder of infants provides an apparent alternative to economic and social "ruin" for desperate women; but once discovered, infanticide was also a way of *being* ruined. Damned whether she does or does not, cornered by motherhood, Roxana punctures Moll's fantasy that competitive individuation can work for mothers and exposes the costs of imagining subjectivity as necessarily predicated upon the denial of others as subjects.

---

[34] Cf. Flynn, "Defoe's idea of conduct," 91.

Maternity and the necessity of infanticide in Moll Flanders *and* Roxana

The "unnatural" maternal "relations" in *Moll Flanders* and *Roxana*, then, finally encompass far more than Moll's incestuous union with her brother Humphrey or Roxana's desperate fear of Susan. And the uneasily absent relationships Moll and Roxana have with their children delineate more than personal immaturity or psychosis. On the contrary, the "whole relation" of maternity in both novels is marked by a bleak, repetitious pattern of abandonment and loss, helplessness and guilt. At the moment when Moll's long uphill odyssey to middle-class respectability seems finally to have been achieved, it is her mother who inexplicably appears and destroys her success merely by existing (and Moll's presence constitutes precisely the same kind of threat to the mother). *Roxana* likewise presents motherhood as a harbinger of social and economic destruction: the reappearance of her daughter signals the death of Roxana's dreams, and Susan's identification of Roxana seals the daughter's doom. In both novels, maternal relation figures as a social and economic catastrophe, a non-negotiable impasse that threatens the survival of both mother and child.

Against this dark background, Moll's and Roxana's theoretical subscription to a "natural" motherhood which neither of them ever actually practices, their investment in denying or mitigating the enormous gap between their culture's theories and their own practices as mothers, demonstrates one of the ways that ideology works, as individuals within societies come to define imaginary relations as "real" and "real relations" as fictional.[35] As maternal failures, Moll and Roxana embody implicit arguments for a specific kind of normative maternal success, a success to which they continue, however hopelessly, to aspire. At the same time, Defoe's bad mothers expose the inadequacy and injustice of the ideals that elude them, and the false choice between "natural" and "unnatural" relations.

The location of responsibility for deviant motherhood is a crucial

[35] I allude to Althusser's familiar description of ideology as that which represents "not the existing relations of production . . . but above all the (imaginary) relationship of individuals to the relations of production and the relations that derive from them" ("Ideology," 165). Cf. Flynn, "Defoe's idea of conduct," 76. I wish to keep provisional the distinction (itself ideologically produced) between "imaginary relations" and "real relations"; there can be no category of entirely unmediated "real relations." Yet there *is* tension between the particular material circumstances of actual mothers and the reductions of codified maternal norms.

project in both *Moll Flanders* and *Roxana*. Is "unnatural" motherhood the result of willful perversity and choice, or is "natural" motherhood impossible in certain circumstances? In both novels, the only viable answer is a revision of the question. For despite much rhetoric to the contrary, *Moll Flanders* and *Roxana* – like the sensational discourse on monstrous motherhood in which they are embedded – demonstrate that unnatural maternity is never entirely the responsibility of an individual mother, any more than it is unilaterally a result of forces beyond her control. As bad mothers, Moll and Roxana are at once both active and passive, both criminals and victims. Defoe attempts at the end of each novel to resolve this ambiguity. He relieves Moll of the consequences of her "unnatural" motherhood by rewarding her in explicitly maternal terms, through both her mother and her son; in *Roxana*, alternatively, he places the blame for maternal failure squarely on his heroine, denying credence to the arguments for her constraint and passivity that have punctuated the narrative all along. The particular resolution chosen for each novel may be less important, finally, than the fact that Defoe feels it necessary to reduce and control the cacophonous crowd of agents at work in the complex maternal stories he tells, and to assign maternal agency to a stable place outside of complicating historical conditions, the fictional place of the isolated, individual psyche. That readers have traditionally found both novels' endings disappointing, confusing, or unconvincing exposes as insufficient the effort to assign unilateral accountability for Moll's and Roxana's maternal failures – or even, as I have argued, to reduce their maternal behaviors to simple "failure" at all.

Both Moll Flanders and Roxana are locked into cultural assumptions and material relations that make infanticide, symbolic and actual, a necessary condition of maternal survival and the erasure of others a requirement for the establishment of the self. The inadequacy of those assumptions and the injustice of those material conditions are demonstrated especially by the endings of both books: the fantastic resolution of *Moll Flanders*, with its exaggerated, even parodic emphasis on the saving potential of relationships between mothers and children; and the agonized failure of resolution and relationship in *Roxana*. The figure of necessary infanticide implicitly reveals the dark side of Moll's and Roxana's efforts to construct autonomous selves, and exposes social formations that make a choice between autonomy and maternity seem inevitable.

DREAMS OF MATERNAL AUTONOMY: SCANDALOUS
MOTHERHOOD IN THREE TALES BY ELIZA HAYWOOD

Maternal metaphors have long haunted evaluations of the writings of
Eliza Haywood (c. 1693–1756), arguably eighteenth-century England's most prolific storyteller and one of its two bestselling novelists
before Richardson.[36] A much-remarked passage in Pope's *Dunciad*,
for instance, represents Haywood's near-incredible productivity as a
matter of monstrous motherhood, a spawning of numberless bastard
texts.[37] More recently, Haywood has begun to be recognized as a
mother-figure for the novel itself. But the important thematic role of
motherhood in Haywood's fiction has scarcely been noticed; indeed,
recent work on amatory writing tends explicitly to minimize it.[38] Yet
motherhood looms large in Haywood's tales of seduction and
betrayal, constituting a crucial *topos* where urgent questions about
the possibility of autonomous female authority are asked and surprisingly radical alternatives emerge.

Most often in Haywood's tales, maternity figures as an unwelcome
accident necessarily bringing with it eternal shame and regret. Like
Moll Flanders and Roxana, Haywood's scandalous mothers often
fear motherhood as the harbinger of isolation, dependence, and loss;
and far more than Defoe's heroines, they internalize the shame and
regret Augustan culture expected unmarried mothers to feel. But in
the three tales we shall consider, Haywood's heroines refuse to
choose between their children and their own survival: they insist on
both, and find that motherhood can actually engender economic
independence and social authority. Beginning with the same stereotype as Defoe, in other words – the abandoned young mother,
penniless and alone, forced to survive on her own efforts – Haywood
imagines an entirely different plot in which motherhood redefines
subjectivity and even provides authority in the public world. As we
shall see, however, Haywood's writing evinces considerable ambivalence about the viability of autonomous maternal authority in male-
dominated society, the central problem in the three texts of interest
here. Haywood's maternal subjects thrive, but only so long as they
are sequestered from patriarchal intrusion and influence. From one

---

[36]   The other is Defoe. Cf. Beasley, "Eliza Haywood," 255. McBurney adds Swift (250). Cf.
       Schofield, "Exposé," 93.
[37]   *Dunciad*, 2: 149–52. Cf. Reeve's contemporary assessment of Pope's motives for the attack
       (1: 120–21).
[38]   Cf. Ballaster, *Seductive Forms*, 203, n.15.

point of view, of course, this fact severely circumscribes the achievement of autonomous maternal authority in all three texts. But at the same time, Haywood's rejection of heterosexual relationships as sites where autonomous maternal authority can develop leads her to experiment with alternative and empowering relationships between her maternal heroines and other nurturant women, new sites for the construction of virtuous motherhood. Despite its ambivalence and limitations, hers is a radical vision of maternal possibility.

Maternal autonomy and patriarchal authority: The Rash Resolve

In the same year that Defoe published *Roxana*, Haywood also produced a work concerned with the experience of motherhood under the stress of abandonment and poverty. In her enormously popular *The Rash Resolve: Or, the Untimely Discovery* (1724),[39] as in Defoe, motherhood emerges as a serious threat to the heroine's survival. But the reaction of Haywood's Emanuella to this threat is very different from those of Moll and Roxana. Though penniless and unmarried, Emanuella manages to maintain her infant son by means of her own respectable labor, constructing a unique version of maternal virtue not inconsistent with economic independence. But the virtuous, loving, and authoritative motherhood Haywood imagines survives only as long as Emanuella and her son are careful to avoid the child's father. Their uniquely satisfying relationship, and Emanuella's position as self-sufficient matriarch, unravel instantly when confronted with the rival authority of the father, Emilius, and his new wife, who compete for Emanuella's place in the child's life. *The Rash Resolve* is thus both more hopeful and more tragic than Defoe's novels: Haywood offers a vision of successful, autonomous motherhood, but finds it impossible to imagine such motherhood remaining viable except in isolation.

Like many of Haywood's heroines, the wealthy and accomplished Emanuella, only child of the governor of Puerto Rico, "had the misfortune to lose her Mother very young" (2). When her father dies, her guardian defrauds her of her inheritance and tries to make her

---

[39] Of all Haywood's works, only *Love in Excess* (1719–20), one of the century's greatest bestsellers, was more widely read than *The Rash Resolve* (Beasley, "Eliza Haywood," 255). Two editions appeared in 1724, and the novel appeared again the same year in Haywood's collected *Works*. It was also reprinted in *Secret Histories, Novels, and Poems*, of which there were 3 editions in 1725.

marry his son; she escapes to Spain where she successfully sues to recover her fortune. But before the goods can arrive, Emanuella finds a fervent admirer in the dashing Count Emilius, and unwittingly makes a dangerous enemy of her cousin Berillia. Frequent nightly appointments and growing intimacy between Emanuella and Emilius have a predictable result: "from one Liberty they ventur'd on another, till rapacious, greedy Love, too conscious of his Power, encroached on all, and nothing left for Honour." (56)

At this point, Emanuella learns that her fortune has been lost at sea. Berillia takes advantage of the crisis to create misunderstanding between the lovers, and Emanuella, heartbroken, enters a monastery. There she discovers that she is pregnant. All her misfortunes so far, the narrator assures us excitedly, are nothing compared to this catastrophe.

Now the Hour was come which was to make her know, that all she had endur'd ... were trifling Woes in competition with those in store for her – She found she was now destined to go through all that can be conceived of Shame – of Misery – of Horror ... With Child without a Husband! ... and what was yet worse, by a Man whom she accounted the vilest, and most perfidious of his Sex! (84–85)

Her "superior Understanding," "Greatness of ... Spirit," and "Fortitude," all of which had assisted her in earlier trials, now combine to make Emanuella especially wretched, because she will not "stoop" to abortion (euphemized as "those Measures by which she alone could hope to secure her Reputation, and screen what had happen'd from the Knowledge of a censorious and unpitying World" [85]). Nor will she call on Emilius, who, the narrator says, would have been "obliged ... to protect and support her" out of "Honour and Gratitude"; had Emanuella once spoken with him, "all might have been well" (85). But Emanuella feels "Contempt" for the very idea of asking "a Favour" of Emilius. She insists that the coming child is entirely her own responsibility, though she also feels "Resentment" about this state of affairs (85–86). Her unhappy determination to go it alone reveals the text's uneasy engagement with issues of maternal autonomy and authority, and particularly with Augustan society's assumption that mothers are responsible for their children even though they may have little control over the conditions that will define their own and their children's existences.

Despite this bad beginning, Emanuella turns out to be an extraordinarily affectionate and attentive mother. "Never," the narrator declares, "did maternal Tenderness reach to a height more elevated than her's" (96). Moreover, Emanuella's maternal excellence is not diminished by her compromised status as an unmarried mother: if anything, her relationship with her son Victorinus is augmented by this apparent privation. Because of Victorinus, Emanuella develops a heterodox view of the norms for female virtue on which she once believed her happiness to depend.

All the ignominy which this Adventure, if divulg'd would bring upon her, was now no longer a Concern to her – Even Virtue was become less dear; and she could scarce repent she had been guilty of a Breach of it, so much she priz'd the Effect. (96)

Unfortunately for Emanuella, however, her malevolent cousin Berillia lurks close at hand. Pretending solidarity, she calls on Emanuella and suggests that they journey to a distant city and establish a home together "'till Death enforces a separation" (101). The echo of marriage vows in Berillia's proposal is unmistakable; it suggests an alternative relationship betweeen the two women that will substitute and atone for the failed heterosexual bond between Emanuella and Emilius. Encouraged by the prospect of "a Settlement for Life" (103) with Berillia – "my best, my only Friend!" (100) – Emanuella cashes in her assets and hires a wetnurse, and they set off. But on the first morning of travel Berillia disappears, taking Emanuella's money with her.

"What now," the narrator asks poignantly, "could this unhappy Lady do? ... No condition sure was ever so calamitous as her's" (107). Like Moll Flanders after the birth of Jemy's son and Roxana after her husband's disappearance, Emanuella finds herself alone and isolated with a young child, with "scarce any Money remaining" (107). Her first reaction is much like Moll's and Roxana's: "We must starve ... ! The little All we had, is lost – no means is left us for Support – no Hope but in the Grave" (105). But then Haywood's novel takes a new turn. Moll and Roxana saw their children as obstacles to their own survival, and saved themselves by relinquishing their motherhood. But Emanuella finds that at this crisis, her relationship with her child sustains her.

Her Spirits had doubtless sunk beneath the weight of Sorrow, which oppress'd her, if the Vigour of her Care for her dear Child had not kept them up. – Something must be thought on for the procuring for *him* the Necessaries of Life, whatever should become of herself. (107)

Because of her son, and with the support of the miraculously faithful nurse, Emanuella effects a complete self-transformation.

She threw off the fine Lady … She took a little Lodging in the cheapest part of the Town, and leaving her *Nurse* at home to take Care of that which was much dearer to her than all other Considerations, she went every day to a *Convent* in that City; where doing Services for the *Nuns* in the manner of an *Out* or *Lay-Sister*, she made a shift to get as much as maintain'd them. (107–8)

Emanuella, in other words, supports herself and her child without resorting to thievery or prostitution. It is impossible to imagine Moll Flanders or Roxana, shrewd and self-reliant as they are, exerting themselves in this way, or constructing anything approaching this kind of autonomy. Alone among the most-read novelists of the Augustan age, Haywood offers a vision of powerful, enabling, and independent motherhood.

Haywood does not sentimentalize Emanuella's labor. The "mean and servile" drudgery at the convent she must "endure … for it could not be call'd living" (107–8). She takes "little notice … of every thing but what concern'd her Business" (109), and changes so much that, she thinks, "a Person who had been … perfectly acquainted with her Face, should now not have any notion he had seen it before" (110). Her feelings for little Victorinus, however, are heavily romanticized – indeed, Haywood describes their relationship in language reserved in most of her other works for the satisfactions of heterosexual love.

What will not Love enable one to go through! … She condescended to every thing with Chearfulness, for the sake of Victorinus; and while she fed her longing Eyes with gazing on his Infant-Charms, and clasped the lovely Innocent in her Arms, she thought herself not wretched; and passing all the Night in that sweet Employment, forgot the Hardships of the Day … All the Passion she once had for the *Father*, was now transmitted to the Son; which join'd to the soft Care which all who are *Mothers* feel, rais'd her's to the most elevated Pitch that Humanity is capable of being inspir'd with. (108)

As her passion for Victorinus comes to substitute for – even to exceed – sexual passion, Emanuella finds pleasure and exercises true virtue in her motherhood.

The Rash Resolve exhibits two subversive aspects of Haywood's writing, both of which we shall observe again. First, Haywood insists that succumbing to seduction has not disqualified the heroine from virtuous maternity. On the contrary, Emanuella sets a new standard – "the most elevated Pitch that Humanity is capable of being inspir'd with" – *because of* her motherhood, the most visible result of her sexual lapse with Emilius. Still more radical, perhaps, Haywood represents motherhood as providing Emanuella with physical, as well as emotional, satisfactions.[40] Thus Haywood presents a vision of maternal possibility immeasurably more positive and powerful than Defoe's. Moll Flanders and Roxana were hopelessly encumbered by their children; but in *The Rash Resolve*, it is poverty, not motherhood, that is the unmarried mother's problem. Only "the Reflection how little it was in her power to do for him" sometimes gives "a check" to Emanuella's "Pleasure;" "she felt, indeed, all the Mother's *Joy*, but with it infinitely more *Care* than ordinarily attends that Title" (96). Emanuella lacks money, but she does not lack love, virtue, work, self-respect, physical pleasure, or hope, all of which she finds in mother-hood and outside of marriage.[41]

For all its courage, however, *The Rash Resolve* still partakes of a fundamental duplicity at work in Augustan England's developing maternal mythology, a duplicity that eventually results in the erasure of Emanuella's uniquely authoritative motherhood and even in her death. For the maternal autonomy Emanuella builds is viable only so long as it exists in a kind of quasi-monastic isolation, apart from the patriarchal social structures represented by Emilius. From the first, Emanuella had defined her motherhood as a matter of absolute and isolated responsibility. This vision of motherhood prevented her from seeking Emilius' assistance when she desperately needed it; but it also allowed her to transform motherhood from the greatest threat to her survival to the scene of autonomous self-creation. Unfortu-nately Emanuella, like Moll Flanders and Roxana, confronts a destabilizing figure from the past – not mother or child, this time, but the child's father. When Emilius re-enters the scene, there is no longer room for Emanuella's all-sufficient motherhood. But Haywood, it seems, cannot imagine any alternative.

At the time of the crucial meeting, Emanuella is living with a wealthy young widow, Donna Jacinta, and working as governess to

---

[40] For an eloquent argument against the separation of motherhood and sexuality, cf. I. Young, "Breasted experience," 196–200.

[41] For a very different interpretation of *The Rash Resolve*, see Schofield, *Quiet Rebellion* (75), *Eliza Haywood* (29–30), and "Exposé" (99). Schofield sees Emanuella as entirely "victimized."

Jacinta's children. Here Emanuella is relieved of her cares, and "the Amendment in her manner of living made ... so great a one in her Looks, that ... she now began to resume her former Charms, and appear again herself" (113). Her happiness depends, however, on complete isolation from the world; indeed, so fearful is Emanuella of meeting someone from her past among Jacinta's houseguests that she makes it an unexplained condition of her employment that she will not mingle with visitors (111). But by a chain of accidents, she is one day brought face to face with the visitors she least wants to see, Emilius and his new wife Julia.

A number of *éclaircissements* follow. Emilius reveals Berillia's hand in estranging him from Emanuella, and the lovers realize that they were duped. Upon this, Julia magnanimously declares that "*Emilius* first was yours, [and] is still yours," and, in a parodic reversal of the usual exchange of women, offers to give him back (124). Emanuella refuses this extraordinary offer, but Julia is not finished yet. She goes on to threaten the maternal autonomy Emanuella has so painfully fashioned, demanding that Emanuella allow her to regard Victorinus "with a Mother's Tenderness" (126), and to insist that there is "another Tye, ... which you have not the power to disengage" (126). That tie, of course, is between Victorinus and Emilius, whose status as the child's father authorizes Julia's demands. Emilius is the more threatening "rival" behind Julia's coercions: by asking for recognition as another "mother" to Victorinus, Julia also demands in effect that Emanuella submit to Emilius' claims as father. Indeed, we might say that the real intruding "rival" in Emanuella's relationship with her son is not Julia, nor even Emilius, but the system of heterosexual marriage and patriarchal privilege they represent.

"You must consent," Julia declares, and she is right. Emanuella is being pressured to abdicate; but if she should fail to comply, she can be sure that her maternal authority and autonomy will be usurped. There is no choice. Faced with the certainty of usurpation, Emanuella follows James II's royal precedent: she abdicates.

Over-press'd with Shame, with Gratitude, with Tenderness, and perhaps, a mixture of another Passion more difficult to be supported than all the rest; had no longer Strength to struggle with the differing Agitations, and sunk fainting in her Chair. (126–27)

Emanuella never stands or speaks again. In three days she is dead, "of no other Distemper than a broken Heart" (127).

On the surface, at least, it is an odd conclusion. Just when the losses and betrayals in Emanuella's experience seem to be reversing at last, we are told that "her Misfortunes were now arriv'd at their utmost height, and ... must know a Period with her Life" (127). What, we might reasonably ask, is so heartbreaking *now*?

A clue may lie in the "other passion more difficult to be supported than all the rest" that seizes Emanuella just before she faints. The fact that this mysterious passion remains unnamed reminds us of the only other place in the text where there is a missing word, also the name of a dangerous emotion. It occurs when Emilius is clearing up the details of his estrangement from Emanuella. Oddly enough, Emilius never mentions the birth of Victorinus in his detailed narrative.

That was a Subject he fear'd wou'd be too shocking to the well-known Niceness of *Emanuella*'s Modesty. – Besides, he knew not how his Wife might take a Repetition of what, by many Circumstances, she cou'd not but be sensible of without, —— ... that Mean Passion Wives are too liable to fall into. (123–24)

The key word – *jealousy* – is missing. In a text where suicide, murder, and adultery appear without apology, jealousy, it seems, is simply too shocking to mention. But the denied term suggests its presence again when Emanuella – who, as we have seen, "transmitted to the Son all the Passion she once had for the *Father*" – hears Julia say she regards Victorinus "with a Mother's Tenderness." Emanuella, it may be, is overcome not only with shame, gratitude and tenderness, but also with jealousy, "more difficult to be supported than all the rest." She loves Victorinus more than a mother ever loved a son or a wife loved a husband; but she will have to watch as he is absorbed into Emilius' family, grafted back into the lines of patrilineal inheritance, and loved by a rival mother. This is why the moment of restoration is so terrible for Emanuella, as it most emphatically would *not* be for the heroines of many another amatory tale. And ironically, Emanuella's lack of resistance – her muteness and eventual death – guarantees that Victorinus will be entirely absorbed into Emilius' family, empowered by his father at the expense of his mother.

Haywood's narrator provides one other hint as to why Emanuella dies.

Resentment was all which for a long time had kept the Lamp of Life awake, and that being now extinguish'd in a Flood of softer Passions, the other must of necessity expire. (127)

The idea that only "resentment" had been keeping Emanuella alive may come as a surprise to readers. What about "the Vigour of her Care for her dear Child" which we were told keeps up her spirits, the "Inclination" she feels to do everything with "Chearfulness, for the sake of *Victorinus*" (107, 108)? Indeed, resentment has until now hardly been mentioned as a motivation for Emanuella's exertions.

But it has not been entirely absent, either. There is one place where we have already heard about Emanuella's resentment. When she first learned that she was pregnant, it was "Resentment" that kept Emanuella from calling on Emilius for help – a mixture of "Haughtiness" of soul and "fatal Consciousness, how little she had deserved the Treatment she had found" (86). Emanuella's late "resentment," then, echoes her earlier feelings when she decided to go it alone as a mother – a choice she also felt as an unfair imposition. What Emanuella most eagerly pursued and jealously protected – complete, unrivaled, unrelieved intimacy with her son – was also what she most resented.

What she wanted, of course, was a friend who would share her maternal responsibility without threatening her authority. Berillia promised to be such a friend, and her betrayal was deeply disillusioning to Emanuella – "so shocking, so dreadful, as rendred all her Courage useless" (105). Unfortunately, Berillia's betrayal leads Emanuella to isolate herself not only from Emilius and other reminders of her past, but from potential female friends as well. Emilius destroyed Emanuella's faith in men ("In knowing one, I know the whole deceiving Sex!" she cries in typical amatory style [65]); Berillia makes it impossible for her ever really to trust other women. This is the real tragedy of Emanuella's story: faithful female friends surround her, but she consistently fails to trust and appreciate them.

Three women in particular stand out: a poor mother whom the pregnant Emanuella meets on the road just after leaving the monastery, Victorinus' faithful nurse, and Donna Jacinta. Each of these is described in maternal language, and each seems to offer Emanuella the sustaining friendship she needs. But the possibilities they embody are cut off as quickly as they arise. Saving connections among women remain partial, shadowy possibilities in *The Rash Resolve*.

Emanuella meets the first of her potential allies while fleeing the nunnery in Madrid. The journey, of course, is just as difficult as possible – "such as no Woman, but herself, perhaps, ever sustained with Life" – and involves violent rain, a windstorm, and even a

"Hurricane" (88). But just as Emanuella is giving up, lying along the road with "her tender Limbs exposed to all the Rage of the unpitying Elements, and pouring forth Tears almost as fast as the Sky did Rain; she perceiv'd, when she least expected it, a Light" (89). The light reveals "a little Cottage," where "a poor good Woman, sitting up tending a sick Child" extends her maternal care to Emanuella – clothing her, feeding her, and putting her to bed (89). But Emanuella is so "discontented" that she is "little capable of tasting" what the woman offers (89), and "would not consent" to rest (90). She keeps her pregnancy a secret, but "the Woman having had many Children herself, suspected [it] ... and pitied her extreamly" (90). In the morning Emanuella hurries on, after "transmographying herself" (90) by exchanging clothes with the poor mother, who is never seen again.

Her generosity and sympathy are repeated in large, however, in the person of Victorinus' nurse, the second of Emanuella's potential allies. The nurse remains a shadowy figure until Berillia's betrayal, when she emerges as another sympathetic comrade, at once a sister to Emanuella and a surrogate mother to Victorinus.

Never did any one bear a greater part in the Sufferings of another, than did this faithful Creature in those of *Emanuella*; the Affability and Kindness with which she had been treated by her, had gain'd as great an Interest in her Affections in the short time she had been with her, as tho' she had been bred up with her; and then her Tenderness for the young *Victorinus*, was more than equal to that which Mothers ordinarily feel for their own Children. (106)

This nurse (a happier Amy) becomes Emanuella's double, even at times her guide. She faithfully keeps Emanuella's secrets, cares for the baby while Emanuella works at the convent, and when Emanuella is offered the job at Jacinta's, "her poor *Nurse*" rejoices and goes along (113, 112). The nurse, in other words, makes possible Emanuella's achievement of self-sufficiency by redefining it as co-operation; she bolsters and augments Emanuella's motherhood without ever threatening it. But the nurse is forgotten once Emanuella gets to Jacinta's. Her absence is especially notable at the climactic scene of Emanuella's reunion with Emilius. She simply fades out of the story, her potential for solidarity forgotten.

The last of Emanuella's (potential) friends is the generous Donna Jacinta. Emanuella at first hesitates to accept the offer to live in Jacinta's family as governess, because she fears separation from

Victorinus, "whom as yet she had never been absent from one Night, and whom her very Soul was wrapt in" (111). Jacinta, however, sets this fear to rest.

She told her she commended the Love and Care she seem'd to have of her Child, and that she would be far from endeavouring to alienate an Affection so praiseworthy, or make her unhappy by taking her from that which she so dearly priz'd. You shall have your Child with you, *said she*, both that and a Nurse . . . shall be as welcome as your self. (112)

Jacinta even promises that if Emanuella should die, she herself will care for Victorinus as her own son (114). Like the nameless nurse, in other words, Jacinta is a second mother for Victorinus; she helps and supports Emanuella in her maternal role without undermining or usurping her authority. But still Emanuella is unwilling to confide in her. Though Jacinta "frequently solicited her to give the History of her Life" (113), Emanuella assumes a false name and makes up a fictonal past instead. And ironically, it is Emanuella's reticence and inability to trust Jacinta that finally betrays her: Jacinta introduces Emilius and Julia to Emanuella without knowing their connection to her, because Emanuella never told her.

   Even after she has heard the details of the tale and knows about Emanuella's deceptions, Jacinta continues to act on her behalf with faithfulness and solidarity, revising Berillia's lies into truth: Emanuella, she says, "must continue with me 'till Death inforces a Separation" (126). And "she was about to say something more" at the moment when Emanuella collapses. What might Jacinta have said? – it is tantalizing to imagine. Perhaps she would have made some response to Julia's demand for Victorinus, a demand attached – as Jacinta's and the nurse's maternal love for the child have not been – to a patriarchal figure, Emilius. But Jacinta is neutralized by Emanuella's despair, and becomes from this moment indistinguishable from Emilius and Julia. Their names henceforth are always mentioned together – "Donna *Julia*, Donna *Jacinta*, or *Emilius*"; "Donna *Julia*, . . . *Emilius*, and *Jacinta*" (127). They compete over Emanuella's care until her death, lament her passing "equally," then work to "out-vye" each other in doting on Victorinus, who at last inherits fortunes from all three (127). Originally powerful and independent of patriarchal authority (as a wealthy widow), Jacinta is finally, necessarily, absorbed by it, like motherhood itself in *The Rash Resolve*. Jacinta might have said something that would have preserved

Emanuella's maternal autonomy, allowing her to realize at last a saving connection to another woman. But Emanuella herself eliminates that possibility.

The Rash Resolve, then, does not leave Emanuella without opportunities for connection to other maternal women. The poor cottager, the nurse and Donna Jacinta all step forward as maternal figures willing to assist Emanuella in her struggle to unite autonomy and motherhood. But the cottager and the nurse are simply not noticed: as lower-class women, they are taken for granted, their subjectivities are overlooked, and they are not called upon to be present at climactic moments in which they might have taken an important part. And Emanuella fails sufficiently to trust Donna Jacinta, silencing her just when she might have turned the conversation either by rescuing Victorinus for Emanuella or by suggesting some compromise that could allow for continued maternal authority and satisfaction alongside Emilius' new paternal presence. The possibility of such a compromise remains the missing piece in *The Rash Resolve*: Haywood herself is unable, finally, to imagine what Jacinta might have said.

The Rash Resolve exposes a central contradiction in Augustan maternal ideology: mothers are at once fully responsible for children but largely without power, subordinated by the prerogatives of fathers. Having recognized this paradox, Haywood goes further and envisions an alternative: autonomous maternal authority, practiced cooperatively in all-female spaces. But when circumstances finally constrain Emanuella to confront Emilius's authority, the only option left is death. So the *Rash Resolve* is, finally, both radical and capitulatory. Emanuella's story rewrites the usual plot of female victimization and creates something really new: an unmarried maternal subject who achieves economic security, independence, and authority, and who demonstrates true virtue, *because of*, not *despite*, her motherhood. But the mechanism that could sustain this achievement – nurturant bonds between women – requires more trust than Emanuella is capable of. Autonomous maternity remains a dream that cannot survive in the waking world of patriarchal entitlement.

Imagining publicly authoritative motherhood: The Force of Nature

Haywood again attempted to imagine independent and publicly authoritative motherhood just a year after the appearance of *The*

Rash Resolve. In *The Force of Nature; Or the Lucky Disappointment* (1725),[42] she presents a uniquely authoritative mother, Berinthia, who enters the public, male-dominated space of a courtroom and commands a hearing by virtue of her maternal status. Once again, Haywood challenges her society's denigration of unmarried mothers and resists the reduction of female virtue to physical chastity. Furthermore, she presents – albeit with considerable ambivalence – a publicly powerful maternal voice. *The Force of Nature* eventually reduces its vocal matriarch to a silent, cloistered arranger of respectable marriages, and to that extent Haywood's revolutionary dream is once again incomplete. But the text also makes visible various residues of that containment, and allows space for imagining a public authority engendered specifically in maternity. *The Force of Nature* is enormously important because it imagines an alternative to the apparently inevitable absence of maternal voices from public discourse.

The story goes, very briefly, like this. A wealthy young Castilian named Felisinda, daughter of Alvario, turns down suitor after suitor, to her father's growing consternation. Finally she rejects even the rich and handsome Carlos, whom Alvario, parodically homosocial, "passionately desir'd to have ... for a Son-in-law" (6). At last Alvario discovers the reason for all this insensibility: Felisinda is carrying on a secret courtship with his penniless ward, Fernando. Enraged, Alvario demands that she marry Carlos the next day. But Carlos declares himself unwilling to cause Felisinda unhappiness and withdraws his suit. The loss of Carlos so upsets Felisinda's "remorseless Parent" that, like a heartbroken lover, he takes ill and shortly dies. First, however, Alvario makes two revisions to his will: he divides his estate between Felisinda and Fernando, on the condition that they never marry; and he instructs Felisinda to enter a convent run by his long-time friend, the Abbess Berinthia.

As soon as Felisinda enters the convent, she and Fernando begin to scheme for her escape. They are assisted by another young devotee, Alantha, who is secretly in love with Fernando. When Fernando's servant comes by secret arrangement to take Felisinda away, Alantha disguises herself as her friend and is carried off instead, cynically hoping that "Fernando wou'd in time be brought to prefer the present ... Fair, to one who was at a vast distance from

---

[42] *The Force of Nature* first appeared in Haywood's 1725 collection, *Secret Histories*. It was frequently reprinted in collections of her works, but did not appear separately during the eighteenth century.

him" (25). Alantha never reaches Fernando, however. The servant attempts to rape her along the way, and she is rescued (fortuitously, to say the least) by Carlos. Alantha confesses to having deceived Felisinda and Fernando, and she and Carlos set off to help the thwarted lovers. Fernando, meanwhile, is looking for Felisinda. After many disappointments and delays, he returns to Castile only to be immediately arrested, tried, and sentenced to death for the abduction and presumed murder of Alantha.

Until this point, the tale exhibits many familiar conventions of the amatory writing at which Haywood so excelled: exotic locations, forbidden and unrequited loves, blocking parents, clandestine escapes, disguises and impersonations, dangerous voyages, attempted rapes, impossible coincidences.[43] But here the plot takes an unusual turn as the Abbess Berinthia, Alvario's friend, takes center stage.

Donna Berinthia, who had sat all the Time of his Tryal in a Chair near the Bar, and with the greatest Anxiety of Mind imaginable, had listen'd to all that pass'd, no sooner heard the fatal Doom, than unable to contain herself, she cry'd out with a great Shriek; – Oh! my Son! – my Son! – My dear unhappy Son! and fell that Moment motionless at the Judges Feet. (40–41)

When the judges request an explanation ("there was scarcely one in presence, who would not have given almost any thing to have had the Mystery unfolded" [42]), Berinthia tells her story to the courtroom. She and Alvario had been youthful lovers, but were kept from marrying by Berinthia's greedy guardian, who wanted her to marry his son. The secret affair between Berinthia and Alvario resulted in the birth of a child, Fernando. But marriage was impossible, and Berinthia eventually entered the monastery, where she became "a Lady whose exemplary Piety, Goodness and Wisdom ... render'd her universally beloved and respected" (41). Alvario cared for Fernando as his ward, married elsewhere, and fathered Felisinda.

As Berinthia herself points out, her story "unravels" two apparent "riddles": why Alvario left an enormous inheritance to Fernando and why Alvario and Berinthia joined forces in opposing a marriage between Fernando and Felisinda (46). And the confession has a further practical result: Berinthia's "Agonies" prompt the judges to grant Fernando a one-month reprieve to produce Alantha. Otherwise, however, Berinthia's painful self-exposure accomplishes little: Fernando remains under sentence of death, Alantha is still missing,

---

[43] For the conventions and purposes of amatory writing, see Ballaster's indispensable study; cf. my "Sex, lies, and invisibility."

Felisinda still believes herself betrayed. Although Berinthia is "transported" at the news of the reprieve, Fernando's response is perhaps more realistic: he "seem'd little mov'd at it" (47).

What does finally redeem the situation, in fact, is not Berinthia's disclosure, but the dramatic eleventh-hour entrance of Carlos and Alantha into the courtroom. "Fernando is Innocent," Carlos announces; "Alantha only is to blame, and comes repentent to confess her Fault, and clear the injur'd Prisoner" (47). As it turns out, however, Alantha does no confessing; instead Carlos, like one of Defoe's "editors," tells her story "as he had receiv'd it from her own Mouth" (47). Alantha "spoke not ... her Presence and her Blushes sufficiently confess'd the Truth of what he said" (47–48). It is Alantha's (silent) testimony, ventriloquized by Carlos, that brings about the reversal Berinthia tried to achieve.

To a certain extent, Alantha's silence in the courtroom underscores the subversive quality of Berinthia's ringing testimony just before. Both women have pivotal stories to tell, but unlike Alantha, who is reduced to a mute, involuntary, and acceptably feminine language of "Blushes," Berinthia speaks for herself. Moreover, Berinthia has the audacity to speak as both the abbess of a monastery and a mother – a combination scandalous in itself. Yet her position does nothing to reduce her respectability. Instead, she actually receives "Compliments ... on her generous Manner of proceeding" and increases by her confession "the general Esteem her Behaviour had acquir'd" (47). By making Berinthia's confession of scandalous maternity powerful in the public space of the courtroom, and by retaining Berinthia's reputation for unspotted virtue even after her confession, Haywood implicitly disputes cherished Augustan myths about motherhood, as she had done before in *The Rash Resolve*. Once again, she attacks the maxim that any sexual lapse before marriage disqualifies a woman from virtuous motherhood; and here she even revises, to an extent, the idea so limiting to *The Rash Resolve*'s denouement – that maternal authority is only possible when separate from the public world. In *The Force of Nature*, unmarried motherhood is no barrier to social authority and respect; motherhood is not the epitome of female withdrawal, but an alternative that can engender public authority and practical power.

In other ways, Alantha's silence and Berinthia's speech have much in common. Neither, after all, can bring about Fernando's liberation alone – both depend on Carlos's authorizing male voice. And

Berinthia's bravery is mitigated by the many apologies, denials, faintings and tears with which her tale is punctuated, and especially by her insistence that she would prefer not to speak at all. After her initial cries of grief at Fernando's sentence, for instance, Berinthia faints several times, then apologizes abjectly to the assembled justices: "Pardon, my Lords ... my Woman's Weakness ... if a Mother's Love cou'd not permit her only Son to go to Death unknowing of her Grief, it ought not have been this August Assembly my Complaints shou'd have disturb'd" (4). She tells her tale only after "those whose Privilege it was to speak" request it; and she concludes by denying to other women the kind of public speech she has just engaged in: "Methinks I wonder all my Sex are not Monasticks, or how they can be so far infatuated, as to prefer the bitter Sweets and Troubles of a noisy World, to that happy Tranquility a Cloyster affords ... I shall return contented to my Cell, and have no more to do with Care or Fear" (46). Once "done speaking," moreover, Berinthia finds herself "little in a Condition of answering" her auditors, and like Alantha can only communicate "by her Looks and Gestures" (47). So Haywood's representation of publicly powerful maternity is by no means unequivocal. Webs of denial reveal deep ambivalence about the possibility of a publicly efficacious maternal voice.

Berinthia's story in *The Force of Nature* rewrites the main events of Emanuella's story in *The Rash Resolve*. Both women start out wealthy, but are defrauded by unscrupulous guardians. Both become pregnant by men they love; though they wish to marry, they are prevented from doing so when their guardians usurp their inheritances. Both enter convents, and watch as their former lovers marry other women and raise their children. And both tales display ambivalence about the possibility of maternal authority. But there are also important differences between Haywood's representation of autonomous maternal authority in each story. Berinthia's story is distinguished from Emanuella's by the fact that Alvario cares for their child from the beginning and so helps Berinthia to preserve her reputation. The price of this protection, however, is social withdrawal and maternal abdication: Berinthia enters a monastery, puts Fernando entirely into Alvario's care, and allows her son to believe that his mother is dead. What makes it possible for Berinthia to take refuge in the cloister also traps her there, unable to enjoy the maternal satisfactions that Emanuella's story so eloquently described.

Only at Alvario's death is Berinthia free to "exert that Authority, which Alvario had transferr'd to her," a parental authority that had once been hers by right (18). Although in the courtroom Haywood does briefly imagine Berinthia's maternity as publicly authoritative, motherhood still demands withdrawal and isolation, and Haywood is still unable to imagine the father as a solution that does not require the erasure of the mother.

Nevertheless, echoes of Berinthia's powerful maternal voice remain, disturbing and subverting her desire to "return contented to my Cell" (46). Berinthia is not the same person when she goes back to the cloister as before she left it: she has been publicly recognized as Fernando's mother, and must now join her maternal role to her established (and traditionally incompatible) identity as abbess. And paradoxically, her first act as mother-abbess undermines her claim to "wonder all my Sex are not Monasticks": she releases both Felisinda and Alantha from their pending vows and unites the couples in marriage: Felisinda marries Carlos (thus fulfilling Alvario's wish) and Fernando marries Alantha.

The narrator wants to insist that these marriages signal the end of all disequilibrium in the tale: "Thus happily ended an Affair, which at first promised only a lasting Series of Misfortunes" (49). But in fact, Berinthia's machinations are by no means entirely satisfactory either to readers or to the fictional parties concerned, and the inadequacy of the hurried ending opens the way for further transgressions. For though Carlos and Alantha are delighted to learn that Felisinda and Fernando are brother and sister and therefore cannot marry, Fernando and Felisinda, not surprisingly, "cou'd not presently [i.e., immediately] fashion themselves to forget the Passion they had regarded each other with" (49). It is perhaps credible that Felisinda might agree to make Carlos "Reparation" by giving "herself as a Reward of his Fidelity"; but it is hard to imagine why Fernando would "follow her Example" and marry Alantha. The recalcitrant lovers are eventually won over by Berinthia's "Persuasions"; nevertheless, as the narrator hints, "remains of Perplexity" persist. Rather than neatly sewing up loose ends, Berinthia's matchmaking further tangles the complicated strands of incestuous relation in *The Force of Nature*, providing a ripe setting for a sequel featuring an adulterous affair between Fernando and Felisinda. The arrangement of the double marriage is the first act Berinthia engages in from her unorthodox new position as both scandalous mother and pious abbess; and despite her best intentions, it is as disruptive of conventional norms as she herself has become, providing neither the social isolation she advocates for all women, nor a strong chance for heterosexual monogamy.

In both *The Rash Resolve* and *The Force of Nature*, then, Haywood represents strong and independent mothers, but has difficulty imagining them taking a permanent place in society. *The Rash Resolve* presents in Emanuella a uniquely resourceful and capable mother who finds satisfaction – even delight – in autonomous maternity. But when the relation between Emanuella and Victorinus is complicated by the re-emergence of the father, the mother-heroine quite literally fades away. Emanuella's maternal identity depends on the absence of Emilius and the cultural systems he represents – heterosexual marriage, patrilineal inheritance, female subordination. In the *Force of Nature* Haywood again has difficulty imagining simultaneous places for both maternal and paternal authority; they can only exist sequentially. The sounding of Berinthia's maternal voice – publicly authoritative, famously virtuous, and scandalous all at once – constitutes an unheard-of departure from virtually all other Augustan representations of maternal possibility. But still Haywood cannot imagine powerful motherhood subsisting for long in the public world, a world constructed by and for the authority of fathers.

Maternity, community, and subversion in The Female Spectator

More than twenty years after *The Force of Nature*, Haywood was still wrestling with the same questions, this time in an interpolated tale from the twenty-second (1746) volume of her monthly *The Female Spectator* – "the first magazine by and for women" (Koon 44).[44] Supposedly penned by a correspondent named Elismonda, *The Triumph of Fortitude*[45] and *Patience over Barbarity and Deceit* once again features a young mother who faces abandonment and poverty. The echoes in this story of Haywood's two earlier considerations of

[44] In all, there were twenty-four issues ("books") of *The Female Spectator* produced between 1744 and 1746, most written by Haywood herself. With characteristic energy, she took on an enormous range of topics – from dissertations on wit and women's education to discussions of astrology, lying, marital relations, magic, the possibility of flying machines, filial duty, suicide, and caterpillars. Often her arguments appear in interpolated stories like *The Triumph of Fortitude*. For a detailed discussion of the purposes and history of *The Female Spectator* cf. Koon, "Eliza Haywood," 44ff.

[45] By "fortitude," Haywood seems to mean not only courage, but also resignation. Cf. *Female Spectator* 4: 373–76 (book 24).

maternal possibility are striking, to say the least, as is its evocation at particular points of key maternal cruxes from *Moll Flanders* and *Roxana*. Furthermore, a product of Haywood's later years, *The Triumph of Fortitude* constitutes a challenge to the critical axiom, inaugurated as early as 1785 in Clara Reeve's *The Progress of Romance*, that Haywood's work became ever more conventional as she grew older.[46] The truism is not, of course, entirely devoid of truth. Haywood is often moralistic in her late writings: she insists in *The Female Spectator*, for instance, that young women must obey their parents, ignore "Overtures of Love," and be content with their lot (4: 358, 376–84). But re-enforcing conventional pieties is hardly a one-dimensional project for Haywood; on the contrary, as *The Triumph of Fortitude* demonstrates, didacticism itself can function as a technique of subversion. Always a skilled reader of her audience, Haywood did not suddenly abandon decades of resistance to the social and domestic systems that empower fathers at the expense of mothers; instead, she devised new, more subtle, and arguably more successful strategies for resistance.[47]

When the story begins, the orphaned Jemima is being taken in by her father's sister Dalinda, a perfect replica of Roxana's sister-in-law: Dalinda "did not take her little Niece through any Motive of Compassion or Affection ... but meerly to avoid the Shame of having it said, that one so near to her in Blood should wear the Livery of the Parish" (193). Eventually Jemima is desired by Lothario, a rich and handsome rake. But to his surprise, she resists his sexual advances and refuses to see him unless he speaks to her aunt about marriage. Her virtuous determinations, however, are no match for Lothario's deceit. He stages a sham wedding which he says must be kept secret from his avaricious mother. Supposedly in the interests of this secrecy, he arranges for Jemima to live alone in rented rooms. There she becomes pregnant, and – predictably enough – Lothario moves on to new amours. Though alone and running out of money, Jemima continues to trust him and believes herself legally married.

[46] Reeve's critics hesitate to reject Haywood along with Behn and Manley as a writer of "amorous novels in her youth," since Haywood "had the singular good fortune to recover a lost reputation" with late works devoted to "the service of virtue" (1: 120–21). Cf. Schofield, "Exposé," 101; Koon, "Eliza Haywood," 44.

[47] Cf. Koon, who notes with some discomfort the dialectical relationship between orthodoxy and subversion ("unconventional" and "very nearly radical" moments) in *The Female Spectator*, the text she holds up as the epitome of Haywood's "moral" and "didactic" later work (49, 44).

Evicted from her rooms, Jemima moves in with a midwife recommended by her landlords, "with whom, they told her, she might live till delivered of her Burthen, and if she thought fit for a Sum of Money leave it behind her, to be disposed of so as never to be troublesome to her" (222). So Jemima finds herself in a situation much like Moll Flanders's at the Sign of the Cradle. And like Moll, she is scandalized at the suggestion that she dispose of her child. It "shocked her Soul," we are told, "to think there could be Women in the World capable of such a Barbarity to their Children, as to leave them to the Mercy of those mercenary Creatures" (222). Unlike Moll, however, Jemima does not capitulate, not even when she gives birth to twins and her problems (like her offspring) multiply. A maid steals all her possessions; the midwife demands most of her clothing in payment; appeals to Lothario go unanswered; her aunt will have nothing to do with her. Eventually, Jemima finds herself and the two infants on the street, walking to Lothario's distant country seat. Haywood excels at the melodramatic scene.

She became so weak that she rather crept than walked, and sometimes was near falling: – Unable to support the Weight of the two Children at once, she would lay one down, and carry the other a little further, – then place that in the same Manner, and go back and fetch him she had left behind. (240)

Jemima's fortunes begin to turn when a wealthy couple spot her toiling along and take pity on her. They make possible Jemima's eventual restoration to a sick and repentant Lothario, who has just enough time before dying to leave everything to Jemima and the children. His mother welcomes her "with the extremest Tenderness," turning out to be "in every thing, except her maternal Tenderness, the very reverse of what her Son, to carry out his base Designs, had represented her" (232). Most surprising, the fake marriage is ratified as legitimate after all. After Lothario's death, Jemima and his mother set up their own household, where they live together in "entire Harmony" (249). Jemima, a model mother, devotes herself to educating the children[48] and shows "the old Lady ... all the Respect of a Daughter." For her part, Lothario's mother "treat[s] her in the same Manner as if she had been her own" (249).

Though based on similar plot matrixes as the *The Rash Resolve* and *The Force of Nature*, then, *The Triumph of Fortitude* reaches a very

48 For the importance of pedagogy to the ideal of virtuous domestic motherhood, see Part Three, below.

different conclusion. The earlier tales ended with the death or
withdrawal of their maternal heroines, but *The Triumph of Fortitude*
ends with a pair of victorious, mutually supportive mothers. Jemima's
story breaks the pattern of maternal isolation. She recognizes other
maternal figures as allies and forges crucial connections with them.
She finds alternative emotional satisfactions in these female companions as well as in her children. And she figures with Emanuella and
Berinthia as a new kind of maternal exemplar, virtuous and scandalous at once.

All this despite the appearance of greater conventionality in
Jemima's story than in Haywood's earlier tales. Haywood's Emanuella and Berinthia were consciously heterodox, even defiant; both
of them engaged in pre-marital sexual affairs. Jemima, by contrast,
could hardly be a more conventional representative of seduced-and-
abandoned Augustan maidens: trusting and innocent, faithful to a
fault, suffering endlessly for the sake of a treacherous man who has
long forgotten her. Yet hers is, arguably, the most subversive tale.
What makes possible the unprecedented combination of complicity
and resistance in *The Triumph of Fortitude* seems to be a matter of what
The Female Spectator calls "Motives" (252). Jemima's adherence to
conventional codes for female virtue takes place within the same
conditions as Emanuella's and Berinthia's resistance – all three are
scandalous mothers. But only Jemima is represented as an unwitting
victim of trickery: unlike Emanuella and Berinthia, she lacks complicity in her own sexual transgression. Jemima believes herself to be
legally married – and at the end, her faith seems to make it so, when
a bevy of lawyers retroactively proves the validity of the wedding that
the narrator had explicitly held up as a "mock Ceremony" (248, 215).
Haywood goes to pains, in other words, to make clear Jemima's
essential innocence: "I could find nothing," the Spectator concludes,
"to condemn in what she did" (252).

From one point of view, of course, the construction of Emanuella
as virtuous after all marks a capitulation to Augustan social norms.
This scandalous mother can be rewarded, we might say, because she
is not really scandalous. But Jemima's story also demonstrates
another, more subversive, thesis: that virtue resides not in women's
sexual relationships with men, but in their behavior as mothers and
daughters. Jemima's *chastity* may be lost, but her *virtue* remains intact.
Virtue here is not a matter of having resisted seduction – which, as
Haywood shows, is often so well orchestrated as to be beyond the

resistance of the inexperienced young women at whom it is directed. Instead, Jemima's virtue resides in her *response to* having been seduced and betrayed, and this response is worked out in her motherhood. The powerful Augustan mythology that conflated female virtue with physical chastity[49] – exemplified most famously in Richardson's *Pamela* – is unseated in Jemima's tale, as in *The Rash Resolve* and *The Force of Nature*. And so is the related insistence that maternal virtue is only possible for married women who retained their virginity before marriage – a fundamental assumption in *Pamela*, Part 2, as we shall see. In *The Female Spectator* Haywood speaks in direct opposition to Richardson's influential voice, making virtue available to Jemima despite her sexual fall and her pariah status as scandalous mother – indeed, making virtue available precisely *in* its apparent lapses.

Despite all this, however, Haywood still grants Lothario power to ratify Jemima's virtue and legitimate her socially. Both the tale and *The Female Spectator*'s comments on it assume Jemima's entire dependence on the goodwill of Lothario. "I can but die with my Little-Ones for Want," Jemima tells herself at one point, "and Life would be a Misfortune to us without the Affection and Support of him from whom alone we can expect it" (229). To an extent, of course, she is correct: the story's happy ending does seem to turn on Lothario's last-minute repentence, without which, as *The Female Spectator* asks, "what must have become of the undone *Jemima*!" (251).

By what Means could she have proved herself his Wife! – Would not the whole World have laughed at her for asserting such a Thing? And with all that Stock of Honour [and] Fidelity ... would she have been look'd upon as any better than a Prostitute? (251)

Like Berinthia's confession without Carlos' authorizing narrative, Jemima's virtue would have counted for little without Lothario's concurrence.

Yet in fact, Jemima is not quite so dependent on Lothario for social validation as the Spectator suggests. For when it looks as if Lothario will die before Jemima and the children can be found, his mother promises to "share all her Tenderness" with them even after his death (236). Despite the dismal picture painted by *The Female Spectator*, Jemima's fate is not entirely in the hands of her husband after all. And equally important, her survival and the survival of her

---

[49]   Cf. Kern, "The fallen woman," 46; Koon, "Eliza Haywood," 46.

children are not left entirely up to Jemima herself. In the last analysis, though Jemima does depend on Lothario's word, she depends much more heavily on her own "fortitude and virtue" and on the "Support" of other women, particularly Lothario's mother. In *The Triumph of Fortitude* maternal "tenderness" intervenes between stark patriarchal authority on one hand and isolated maternal autonomy on the other, and creates an alternative: mothers may themselves be relieved and sustained by maternal care, as women of different generations define themselves in terms of their relations to one another, rather than in terms of their relations to men.

And what of the seemingly intractable problem that had troubled the earlier two tales – the relation between maternal autonomy and patriarchal authority? At the time she wrote *The Triumph of Fortitude*, Haywood seems no more sanguine than ever about the possibility that mothers and fathers could hope to share autonomy and authority in Augustan society. To be sure, in *The Triumph of Fortitude* the impossibility of heterosexual cooperation does not necessitate the erasure of the mother; this time it is the *father* who dies, leaving his two sons to grow up in a new, matriarchal family, a family neither wholly reclusive nor entirely part of the outside world. On the last pages of volume twenty-two, we are told that "an entire Harmony" characterizes the home Jemima and Lothario's mother have established; no "great Lovers of the Town," they remain at home except to visit the Lady who assisted Jemima on her journey, with whom they are "perfectly united" (249, 250). The arrangement seems private and sequestered, rather like Berinthia's withdrawal from public life or Emanuella's safe but isolated working existence; but the contented, carefully limited female circle Jemima shares with her mother-in-law and their friend is hardly a cloister. For Jemima's "Story" becomes "public" very soon after Lothario's death (249). Even Dalinda hears of it, and attempts to soil Jemima's reputation. But nothing can disturb Jemima's tranquility or diminish the social respect that she enjoys. Jemima, in other words, establishes herself as a private mother independent of male influence, but still enjoys a secure public identity as well. Her retreat to female society is a choice, not a requirement, and it does not entirely eliminate her place in a larger social world.

The possibility that Jemima might have lived in "harmony" and "unity" with Lothario is never considered in *The Triumph of Fortitude*. That is a choice Haywood could not make available to Jemima, a story she could not write, even as late as 1746 in *The Female Spectator*, a work often held up as exemplifying Haywood's late conventionality. In this light, we might complicate the traditional estimate of Haywood's later work. Much of that work is indeed more conservative and didactic in nature than Haywood's novels of the 1720s. But as *The Triumph of Fortitude* demonstrates, even Haywood's most conventional writing is riddled with radical suggestion. In *The Triumph of Fortitude*, Haywood revisits the plots of *The Rash Resolve* and *The Force of Nature* and writes a new, far more subversive ending featuring maternal survival, power, and community. Furthermore, *The Triumph of Fortitude* requires that we expand not only literary history's simplistic narrative of Haywood's moral "progress," but also the estimate of her maternal influence with which we began this chapter. Haywood, we noted, has long been considered a metaphorical "mother" of the English novel; and as we have seen, she struggled to represent motherhood independent of patriarchal prerogatives and to redefine maternal virtue, freeing it from dependence on sexual chastity. *The Triumph of Fortitude* further invites us to understand Haywood as an early progenitrix of all those who reject the dream that heterosexual marriage will one day incorporate autonomous maternal authority, and who choose instead to dream of maternal empowerment through female community.

MATERNAL FAILURE AND SOCIOECONOMIC DIFFERENCE: *THE UNNATURAL MOTHER*

Many less-memorable Augustan narratives feature "unnatural" relations between mothers and children; typically, such works assign to the mothers unilateral responsibility for those failed relations. Mothers become ideal scapegoats, and the rehearsal of their transgressions absorbs attention and pre-empts any suggestion of shared agency or reciprocal accountability. Or at least that's the idea. In reality, few writers were as skillful as Defoe and Haywood, and logical gaps and obvious interestedness tend to pervade Augustan tales of monstrous motherhood, unwittingly inviting resistance on the part of readers.

We might consider just one example, the anonymous tale *The Unnatural Mother or Innocent Love Persecuted* (1734). Set in Paris, the story concerns the seduction and eventual death in childbirth of a young woman, Mary-Magdalen de L'Epine. Mary-Magdalen's mother, recently widowed, has several children and is in financial distress. She anxiously pursues a lawsuit left on her hands by her dead husband, and depends on the help of a judge, Desprez, a powerful figure in a corrupt legal world where corruption and accessibility to personal manipulation are taken for granted. The judge's son, who narrates the tale, takes advantage of Mme. de L'Epine's vulnerability to insert himself into her family circle; once trusted, he seduces and secretly marries her eldest daughter, Mary-Magdalen, against his father's express commands.

Mary-Magdalen becomes pregnant, and finally tells her mother about the secret marriage shortly before giving birth. Initially Mme. de L'Epine raves, fearing that the judge will be angry, in which case she would be "reduced to Beggary" (84); shortly, however, she relents and arranges to assist her daughter. The Elder Desprez behaves quite differently when he learns of the secret marriage. He incarcerates his son, then accuses Mme. de L'Epine of trapping young Desprez in a marriage to a social and economic inferior. In the son's words, the judge uses

such language, and such a Rage, that Passion only could excuse: He even used her like the worst of Women. In vain did she swear to him that she was innocent of our Marriage; and that if she had her Daughter at Home, she would punish her; He would not hear her Excuses, but used her like a Suborner. (99)

By unfortunate coincidence, Desprez is attacking the widow just as Mary-Magdalen, whose baby is about to be born, arrives at her mother's house. Terrified by the scene before her, she falls down a flight of stairs. The mother calls for a chair and has her daughter removed to a hospital for indigent unwed mothers where Mary-Magdalen gives birth to a dead baby and then dies herself "in the midst of her Pains, and weltring in her Blood" (103). Only her mother is present.

Amazingly, young Desprez pins all the blame for the tragedy on the mother's single act of sending Mary-Magdalen to the hospital. Mme. de L'Epine, he says,

in whom such a Sight ought to have awaken'd all her Tenderness, treated her … with more Hard-heartedness than the most savage Beast; and far from giving her any of the Assistance that was necessary, she refused to acknowledge her for her daughter: See, Sir, said she, speaking to my Father, whether I was the Cause of their Marriage. This said, she sent immediately for another Chair, and in a Swoon, and streaming with Blood, as my Wife then was, she ... sent her to the *Hotel-Dieu*. What Cruelty! What Barbarity! Cou'd any one sacrifice her own Blood more inhumanly, to the Fear of losing an Estate? (100)

The judge, not surprisingly, receives no criticism for *his* merciless and vindictive behavior; neither does young Desprez assume responsibility for his wife's vulnerability. No notice is taken of a legal system so corrupt that a defrauded widow would have to court the personal favor of a judge in order to receive justice. Instead, Mary-Magdalen's death is entirely the fault of her "unnatural" mother.

Some responsibility certainly does attach to Mme. de L'Epine. But it is impossible to read the account and not feel the injustice of placing *all* the blame on her, just as we can hardly accept the title's characterization of the clandestine lovers as entirely "innocent." Young Desprez's narrative is patently self-serving: he writes at all, we learn, only because "all the World" is accusing him of having abandoned Mary-Magdalen (1). And although he intends the narrative as a defense of his own virtue, he comes across as a man willing to deceive his father and defraud his lover, then to place the blame for his own treachery on the most vulnerable person available, the impecunious widowed mother. Never at risk himself, young Desprez places Mary-Magdalen in danger of losing her reputation, her relationship with her family, and, finally, her life; yet even as he finishes the story, he still has not publicly acknowledged the marriage because "the Place where she died, would be no Honour" to him (106).

In short, no one in this crude little tale is "innocent"; everyone is, to some extent, "unnatural." Young Desprez's insistence on scapegoating Mme. de L'Epine sounds shrill and unconvincing; what comes to matter is not straightforward guilt or innocence, but the workings of complicity and coercion, the possibility of measuring relative accountability, and the status of personal agency. By such comparative standards, Mme. de L'Epine is resoundingly less guilty than any of the other principals in the story, and is considerably more pressed financially and socially. The "unnatural mother" turns out to be yet another mother hopelessly tangled in "unnatural relations."

What purposes are served by construing Mary-Magdalen's mother as the sole guilty party? The narrator's furious and unreasoning passion, so overcharged for the scope of the offense – "I live now only with Design to be revenged of this Mother-in-Law ... notwithstanding the Submissions she has made to me, the Pardons she has ask'd me, and the Sorrow she expresses for the Death of her Daughter" (105) – begins to suggest depths of interest behind maternal scapegoating that far exceed the circumstances narrated in the tale. Young Desprez's language reveals that he is outraged not only because his mother-in-law failed to care for Mary-Magdalen, but also because she acted in the interests of her lawsuit and with an eye on her own economic survival ("Cou'd any one sacrifice her own Blood more inhumanly, to the Fear of losing an Estate?"). Like the "unnatural Grand Mother" nearly a century earlier, Mme. de L'Epine dared to put her own survival first: this is where her most profound maternal transgression lies.

The representation of monstrous motherhood in *The Unnatural Mother* – as in *The Unnatural Grand Mother* and Defoe's and Haywood's tales – is important because of what it teaches us about Augustan efforts to assign blame for maternal failure simply and singly, to hold mothers uniformly accountable apart from historical particularities, complicating agencies, and patriarchal complicities. This reduction of agency contributes to the delimitation, in Augustan England, of motherhood itself to a single, stable place supposedly beyond history and change. But in the process of reducing maternal heterogeneity to a fantasy of similitude, the possibilities most anxiously denied tend insistently to reappear: the possibility that the binary, exclusionary thinking that defines "natural" and "unnatural" motherhood according to rubrics that deny their own embeddedness in class privilege *creates* the conditions necessary for maternal failure; the possibility that virtuous maternity may be a multiple, changing phenomenon, with many (also multiple) agents, causes and functions; and the possibility that there may be no such thing as uniform, reliable measures for virtuous or monstrous motherhood after all.

PART THREE

Domestic motherhood: constraint, complicity, and the failure of maternal authority

It is he who ... shows us how to discern the subtle, dishonest motives that hide and conceal themselves within other, more honest motives that hasten to show themselves first.

Denis Diderot[1]

Complicity in the not-said, connivance of the unsayable, of an eye's wink, of a tone of voice, of a gesture.

Julia Kristeva[2]

[1] Diderot, "Eloge de Richardson," 195.
[2] Kristeva, "Héréthique," 45.

If centuries of critical contempt and neglect provide any barometer of literary quality, then Samuel Richardson's 1741 continuation of his phenomenally popular *Pamela* (Part 1, 1740) is a failure of resounding proportions. According to Terry Castle's recent and representative estimate, *Pamela*, Part 2 "is more than a disappointment. At times it seems almost to insult us, to affront our expectations" (*Masquerade*, 135).[3] The problem, according to Castle, is that the "baleful sequel" lacks a unifying plot; nothing " 'happens' in it" (131). No one grows or develops, no suspense is built and then relieved. Except for the curious non-event of Mr. B.'s suspected affair with a Countess, even sexual pursuit is absent. The book is occupied instead with domestic details – weddings, births, adoptions, family squabbles, illnesses, household management, relationships between spouses. *Pamela*, Part 2's narrative structure reflects the diffuse, disjointed world of daily routine, not the linear structure we have been trained to think must define a good novel.

But perhaps the problem is not that *nothing* happens so much as that *what* happens does not conform to traditional critical standards and is not legible to traditional reading methods. In fact, *Pamela*, Part 2 functions less like a novel (traditionally defined) than like a novelized conduct book, a generic anomaly that we might call a "conduct novel."[4] The book *looks* like a novel – it deploys plot, character, and incident, for example – but it doesn't *work* like one. Instead, the novelistic elements in *Pamela*, Part 2 dramatize a set of norms for female virtue, norms much like those being more directly inculcated in Augustan conduct literature. Part of our purpose here will be to see how *Pamela*, Part 2 challenges conduct literature's cultural authority; but first it is important to note that in his sequel, Richardson seems to be offering a new kind of conduct book,

---

[3] Castle reviews the surprisingly unanimous critical appraisals of *Pamela*, Part 2 (*Masquerade*, 131–32); Cf. Chaber, "Moral Man," 213–14; Yeazell, *Fictions of Modesty*, 266. Schellenberg is virtually alone among modern critics in her attempt to defend *Pamela*, Part 2, arguing that it exemplifies a narrative model in which "conflict" between individuals "becomes consensus" within a social group (37). The thesis is attractive, but Schellenberg's arguments remain unconvincing. See note 35 below.

    Significantly, Richardson himself apparently held Part 2 "in much higher estimation" than Part 1, and sales were brisk enough to call for two more editions within a year after the first (Eaves and Kimpel, *Samuel Richardson*, 149, 146–47).

[4] Ball calls *Pamela*, Part 2 "a narrative conduct book" (334); Cf. Kinkead-Weekes, *Samuel Richardson*, 59.

improved in aesthetic as well as ideological ways. The generic ambidexterity traditionally so dismaying to critics, in other words, is potentially the locus of *Pamela*, Part 2's most important cultural functions. As a conduct book, *Pamela* 2 prescribes; as a novel, it fantasizes. Both activities are at work in its central representation, virtuous motherhood under trial. And the collision between the two exposes the difficulty of maintaining in practice Augustan culture's increasingly demanding standards for maternal virtue, standards that throughout the sequel have an unsettling way of coming into conflict with other measures of female virtue.

Pamela, Part 2's representation of class is as complex as its generic participations, and appears, initially at least, to universalize Pamela's experience. Pamela herself, like Part 2, is a kind of "hodge-podge" (Castle, *Masquerade*, 171) at once a member of all social classes and of none.[5] She was born into what we might today call the lower-middle class (her parents, we recall, once ran a small village school); but by the time *Pamela*, Part 1 opens, her family has fallen on hard times and her father is an impoverished ditch-digger. We first meet Pamela in Part 1 as a household servant who has been oddly also a companion, a kind of daughter, and even a double to her mistress. Eventually raised to the status of a "Lady" (3: 6), wife to a wealthy and almost-aristocratic husband, throughout the sequel Pamela remains ever humble, mindful of her inferior origins, and obsessed with bourgeois values and duties. But although Pamela seems to inhabit and represent a broad range of socioeconomic positions, the very strong middle-class aspects of her existence and thinking work to subsume other class associations under developing bourgeois rubrics.[6] Her apparent representativeness turns out to be far less inclusive than it seems.

Like the Virgin Mary, Queen Elizabeth I, or the maidenly Pamela of Part 1 who performs incredible feats of chastity and textuality, Pamela stands in Part 2 "alone of all her sex," at once an example to all women and a standard to which they can never hope to measure up. "What a bewitching Girl art thou!" Lady Davers cries early in the sequel; "What an Exemplar to Wives now, as well as thou wast before to Maidens!" (3: 104). The "matchless" Pamela of Part 1 becomes the "inimitable Mother" of Part 2 – worthy, as Richardson

[5] Cf. Flint, "The anxiety of affluence," 490.
[6] Cf., for example, the rubric of country-house domesticity that Pamela embodies. See Armstrong, *Desire*, 69–75 for the shifting valences of this ideal.

put it, "of the Imitation of her Sex, from low to high life," but beyond any real-life mother's powers of emulation. Indeed, Richardson's representation of Pamela as model of maternal virtue works to exclude *all* other women; the final irony of Richardson's ardent depiction of Pamela's virtuous motherhood is that the standards he sets are attainable only for his heroine – who, after all, does not really exist.

Still, the sequel's Pamela is of great interest to us, because she demonstrates the attributes of an influential vision of a perfect wife and mother. The two duties are, of course, intimately connected. Early in Part 2, Lady Davers lists for Pamela the behaviors that will be expected of her as Mr. B.'s wife. Pamela must, she says, "give Orders" to servants; "endeavour to please your Sovereign Lord and Master"; receive visitors, and visit in return; write often to Lady Davers (!); and produce "a Succession of brave Boys, to perpetuate a Family ... which ... *expects* it from you" (3: 41–42). Without this last, Lady Davers declares, all the rest means nothing, and Mr. B. will "want one Apology" for "descending to the wholesome Cot" (3: 42). Pamela's maternity is the *sine qua non* upon which depend all the rest – her social position, her marital happiness, the continued recognition of her virtue, and its concomitant rewards.

The possibility of virtuous maternity for the matronly Pamela of Part 2 depends, in turn, on the disturbing, reductively physical virtue on which Part 1 placed so much value. In Part 2, motherhood becomes the crucible that virginity had been before: the contested object, the authority Pamela and B. compete to define and claim, the site where violent struggles over autonomy and agency are waged. And once again, the weapons of warfare are letters. In *Pamela*, Part 2, as in Part 1, the power of Richardson's mythologizing depends to a great extent on the form through which he makes Pamela's voice heard, a form that is above all duplicitous, vulnerable to misappropriation, and ostentatiously private – like maternal authority itself in Part 2, as we shall see. What makes the second part's epistolarity different from the first part's, however, is that by 1741, Richardson's formal duplicities were beginning to be recognized as such. The authenticity claimed for the first edition of Part 1 (and accepted by many of the novel's original readers) had been undercut by an influx of spurious "continuations" and by Richardson's own efforts to control his inherently uncontrollable text, until for many readers, suspicion about (even complicity with) the fundamental falseness that defined and enabled epistolary fiction had become part of the experience of reading *Pamela*. The disingenuous, ventriloquized voice of Richardson's virtuous mother in Part 2 harks back to, and complicates, the problematic representation of female virtue in Part 1.

In representing and deploying an ideal mother, Richardson uses language and ideas around which there was already considerable consensus, thanks to conduct books – the increasingly popular handbooks designed to teach correct female behavior. But Richardson also brings forward some of the most delicate and vulnerable aspects of conduct literature's treatment of motherhood, particularly the problem of the relative authorities of mothers and fathers. In *Pamela*, Part 2, in fact, he at once contributes to the genre of conduct writing and assaults its central tenets, especially as these concern motherhood. Before we can understand how and why *Pamela*, Part 2 undertakes such a project, a review of those tenets is in order.

Maternal virtue in Augustan conduct literature

First, some clarifications. For our purposes, Augustan conduct books are those published in Britain between approximately 1680 and 1760, excluding manuals devoted to specific household tasks (cookery books, for example). Conduct books written after the 1750s tended to devote more direct attention to mothers and to what we might call "child management" than did the earlier works we are interested in. For this reason, late-century manuals are often assumed to have inaugurated a new British obsession with maternal behavior. In fact, however, late-century texts entered an established tradition, and relied on assumptions and positions already current. We are looking at the texts that formed and shaped the assumptions behind late eighteenth-century conduct writing.

Any reader of Augustan conduct books will be immediately struck by how alike they sound. The reason is simple. The majority of such works are simply reproductions, abridgements, or conflations – almost always without attribution – of two supremely influential works: Richard Allestree's *The Ladies Calling* (1673) and the Marquess of Halifax's *Advice to a Daughter* (1688) (sometimes, though less often, we may also detect echoes of Locke [*Education*], Fleetwood, or Fenelon). Allestree's work, in paticular, was frequently reprinted: it reappears under many titles and in fragmentary forms in countless other works throughout the century.[7] To cite Allestree and Halifax on maternal virtue, in other words, is to quote maxims that achieved ubiquitous authority during the Augustan period.[8] They outlined standards for maternal behavior that would become part of eighteenth-century Britain's cultural unconscious, and that continue even today to influence Anglo-American maternal ideals.

Outlining "the office and duty of a Mother," Allestree first requires that mothers feel "Tenderness" toward their children. "A Mother is a title of so much Tenderness," Allestree writes, that it "is often set as the highest Example our weakness can comprehend of the Divine Compassions" (201). Halifax would give the same prominence to maternal tenderness, albeit with characteristic cynicism: "A Woman's tenderness to her Children," he wrote, "is one of the least deceitful Evidences of her Vertue" (22). Further, Allestree requires mothers to care for, educate and breastfeed their children (201–13). Mothers should be "as much with [their children] as they can," and make "personal Inspection of them ... frequently themselves to examine how they proceed in the Speculative part of Knowledg [sic]; and no less frequently exhort them to the Practice" (213).

What was most important – and innovative – was the insistence that the *mother herself* should perform these duties. Augustan mothers were the first in English history to be insistently enjoined in print to constant attendance on their children. The necessity of personal attendance was emphasized especially in texts directed to economically privileged mothers, who traditionally did not perform the daily care of their own children.[9] When in 1697 Timothy Rogers preached a laudatory sermon at the funeral of Elizabeth Dunton, he portrayed her as an exemplary mother who best served her children by "being ever with them" (24). Raising a child, in the words of a derivative compendium of conduct maxims called *The Ladies Library* (1714),[10] requires "no less

---

[7]   Cf. Yeazell, *Fictions of Modesty*, 5; 240; 242, n.27.

[8]   J. Paul Hunter objects that Halifax's *Advice* is not "typical" of eighteenth-century conduct writing and therefore should be disqualified as a representative text. "Halifax looked back to an older tradition of courtesy books," he observes, "whereas the new Guides that became popular after the Restoration were aimed at a wide range of social classes" and have "far more 'progressive'" attitudes (394, n. 28). Professor Hunter is certainly right that Halifax worked from earlier generic models and wrote for elite readers; the *Advice*, as is well known, was composed as a gift for the Marquess's own daughter. But this does not disqualify Halifax as representative or influential. Instead, it makes even more significant the fact that his work was eagerly consumed and imitated by all classes of writers and readers.

[9]   B. Harris, "Property, power and personal relations," 612.

[10] The British Library Catalog lists only one 1714 edition of *The Ladies Library*, but two slightly

than a *Parents* Care and Watchfulness, and therefore ought undoubtedly to be the Mother's Business ... An Exemption from which, Quality (even of the highest Degree) cannot give" (2: 206).

A crucial part of the care required of mothers – indeed, mothers' "Principle Care" – was the education of their children (2: 134). By 1759, the mother's pedagogical role was familiar enough to be sentimentalized:

> The Females, the first Rudiments of Speech,
> The brightest Orators, and Poets, teach;
> The wisest, greatest, of what-e'er Degree,
> Were first instructed, on a Mother's Knee ...
> These first Impressions, who can e'er forget?
> No filial Duty can repay the Debt.   (Marriott, 209–11)

Of course, it was only children's *earliest* educations – the all-important first impressions – over which mothers, with their newly discovered domestic "leisure," had so much authority. Boys were routinely removed from maternal tutelage and placed under male supervision before they were ten years old; girls more often stayed under the influence of their mothers (though not always; cf. Wilkes 9–10). Allestree simply assumes this state of affairs: "When the sons are removed from under the mothers tuition and sent to more public places of Erudition," he writes, "her Providence is still the same as to her Daughters" (213).

In any case, standards for maternal success were unprecedentedly high; so it is not surprising that Augustan conduct writers developed whole rubrics for maternal failure. Allestree seems to have coined the truism that mothers can fail either by loving their children too much, or by loving them too little. This idea held up well throughout the eighteenth century; it was reformulated with a vengeance as late as 1792 by Mary Wollstonecraft, for whom maternal failure seems virtually inevitable: "Woman," Wollstonecraft says, "seldom exerts enlightened maternal affection; for she either neglects her children, or spoils them by improper indulgence" (*Vindication*, 222).

different editions bear that year's imprint, one "Printed for *J. T.* and Sold by *W. Mears* at the *Lamb*" (now at the Huntington Library), and one "Printed for *Jacob Tonson*, at *Shakespear's* Head" (available on microfilm from Research Publications). My citations are to the latter edition.

That *The Ladies Library* is largely plagiarized was noted with warmth in 1714 by one Royston Meredith, who observed that "the Second Volume ... is almost wholly Collected out of Bishop *Fleetwood*'s Sermons, *Locke* of Education, and *Hallifax's Advice to a Daughter* ... the whole Three Volumes are intirely a Collection out of Books" (18).

Allestree deals swiftly with those mothers who overdo their love, and with their children in the bargain. "The doting affection of the Mother," he informs us, "is frequently punish'd with the untimely death of her Children";

or if not with that ... they live ... *to grieve her eies* [sic], *and to consume her heart* ... and to force their unhappy mothers to that sad exclamation ... "*Blessed are the wombs which bare not.*" (205–06)

And not surprisingly, the too-indulgent mother makes frequent appearances in eighteenth-century writing in many genres. Mary Davys's *Ladies Tales* (1714) includes praise for a mother whose "Tenderness" is free from "that faulty Fondness, that is often of so fatal a Consequence" (8). Abel Boyer scolds, "'Tis well to be Tender, but to set the Heart too much upon any thing, is what we cannot justify ... there's no such Fop ... as my Young Master, that has the Honour to be a Fool of his Lady Mother's making" (*English Theophrastus*, 273–74). Richardson's Lovelace blames his indulgent mother for his own villainy (*Clarissa*, 8: 132 [1431]), and fools the Hampstead landlord into letting him hunt Clarissa down by explaining that she is "Mother-spoilt, landlord! – Mother-spoilt! that's the thing!" (5: 71 [765]). Likewise, Clarissa's father peevishly reminds her mother that "the fond Mother ever made a hardened child!" (1: 287 [191]). The physician William Cadogan draws a vivid picture of "the puny Insect, the Heir and Hope of a rich Family," who "dies a Victim to the mistaken Care and Tenderness of his fond Mother" (*Essay upon Nursing*, 7); the apothecary James Nelson criticizes the "tender (simply tender) Mother" (*Government of Children*, 10) who interferes out of "blind Fondness" when fathers try to exert their authority (32–33). By 1779, advice books were advocating that sons be kept away from their "dangerous," too-indulgent mothers (Barker-Benfield, *Culture of Sensibility*, 278).

The other kind of bad mother, the one who loves too little, Allestree demarcates by her failure to practice what emerged in the first half of the eighteenth century as the most important touchstone for maternal virtue: breastfeeding. In an enormously influential passage, Allestree argues against "the Mothers transferring the Nursing her Child to another" as an instance of maternal pride (203), a pride nowhere more clearly seen than among upper-class women, who fail to breastfeed their own children because of a vain belief in their own "State and Greatness." "No other motive, but what is founded in their Quality," Allestree says, "could so universally prevail with all that are of it" not to follow "the impulses of Nature" (203).

Such arguments resonated throughout the eighteenth century, when the desire to breastfeed attained status as one of the attributes of "natural" motherhood and a central part of virtuous womanhood itself. In eighteenth-century conduct books, as in Allestree, aristocratic mothers tended to be denigrated as unloving pleasure-seekers who refuse to be inconvenienced by breastfeeding – a characterization that reflects a general tendency among the nascent bourgeoisie to "see the aristocracy as deficient in maternal feeling" (Kunzle, "William Hogarth," 127). According to conduct writing, women who don't breastfeed become unloving mothers. As Jane Sharp argued in 1671, "if the mother do not Nurse her own child, it is a question whether she will ever love it so well as she doth that proves the Nurse to it as well as Mother" (361). "Mothers by suckling their Children," Nelson agrees eighty years later, "cherish that Tenderness which Nature has implanted in them towards their Offspring. For Experience shews, that the Office of suckling considerably augments in them the Affection from whence that Tenderness flows" (44). In 1714, *The Ladies Library* repeated what was already a well-worn argument: maternal breastfeeding is evidence of proper "Affection and Tenderness" which have been "implanted" in mothers by "Nature"; the only "restraint" breastfeeding places on women is restraint from the vices of vanity, excessive spending, theatre and gambling, all popularly associated with upper-class women (2: 221, 225–26).

As the language of *The Ladies Library* suggests, mothers who failed to breastfeed (most notably, upper-class mothers) were not merely faulty: they were *unnatural*.[11] "It is a thing against Nature," wrote "Gaius" in 1702,

for a Mother to bring forth a Child, and presently to cast it from her; to nourish in her Womb with her own Blood, I know not what, which she saw not, and not Nurse with her milk, that, which she seeth already living, a Man, and imploring the duties of a Mother. (9)

The finessing of maternal volition here is significant: the writer pretends that Augustan mothers chose pregnancy in the same way they chose whether or not to breastfeed. Equally striking (and typical), the baby being spurned is a little "Man," pathetically

---

11   For the cultural and political functions of the idea of "natural" motherhood in the eighteenth century, see esp. Nussbaum, "'Savage' mothers"; Perry, "Colonizing the breast."

dependent on the whims of a heartless mother. Breastfeeding emerges as a matter of (male) life and death, an act of terrifying female power, the sign of "natural" maternal virtue, and the class act *par excellence.*

Now of course, maternal breastfeeding had always been the practice of working women, and male authorities had long been pointing out its benefits. Furthermore, tracts like Elizabeth Clinton, Countess of Lincoln's *Nursurie* (1628) demonstrate that even a few aristocratic mothers breastfed early in the seventeenth century, when it was anything but fashionable to do so. But from the late seventeenth century on, breastfeeding was not just enjoined upon mothers of comfortable means or attempted by a few nonconformists among them; it was actually being practiced with increasing frequency. Maternal behavior began to change on a wide scale, and by the second half of the eighteenth century a dramatic transformation had taken place. Whereas in 1700 most babies of the upper classes and gentry were sent out to wetnurses for at least the first year of life, by the 1740s (when Richardson published *Pamela* and *Clarissa*), it was becoming increasingly common for women in easy economic circumstances to nurse their own children. Aristocratic mothers were less likely to follow the trend than were women of the developing middle classes; and conduct writing continued to use maternal breastfeeding to distinguish the selfless, virtuous, and "natural" domestic mother from the idle, selfish, "unnatural" aristocrat. But as a group, privileged women were breastfeeding far more, by 1750, than they had been a generation earlier.[12]

The increased popularity of maternal breastfeeding was part of a complex of changes in the dominant cultural definition of maternal virtue during the Augustan period. During the first half of the century, middle- and upper-strata husbands often disapproved of maternal breastfeeding and vetoed mothers' deeply felt desires to nurse their infants. In 1695, Newcome laments on his title page that more often than not, "Mothers ... are reproach'd for doing their Duty"; even as late as 1753, Nelson sighs that "many a tender Mother, has her Heart yearning to suckle her Child, and is prevented by the misplac'd Authority of a Husband" (43). Such husbandly recalcitrance was by no means limited to very wealthy families. One famous middle-class case involves the infant Samuel Johnson

---

[12]   Cf. Gelpi, *Goddess*, 44; Shorter, *Modern Family*, 182; Fildes, *Wet-Nursing*, 111, 116; Nussbaum, "'Savage' mothers," 134.

(b.1709), whose father, like a real-life Mr. B., overruled the wishes of his wife in the matter of breastfeeding.[13]

Despite such cases of persistent resistance, though, it is clear that by the 1750s many fathers with the means to send their children out to nurse had been convinced not to do so. Some saw maternal breastfeeding as the best option because it entailed a thoroughly respectable occupation for an idle wife at home and an alternative to more expensive feminine pursuits. Even those who resisted the trend often compromised by hiring a nurse at home. By mid-century, reluctant mothers were as likely to be pressured *to* breastfeed as formerly they had been forbidden *from* it.[14]

The paradoxes involved in this state of affairs are evidenced in Nelson's oddly ambivalent declaration: "I cannot help advising in the strongest Terms, that every Father consent, and even promote, that the Child be suckled by it's [sic] Mother" (45). Nelson, we might notice, fails to recognize differences among mothers and reinforces the notion that virtuous mothers are necessarily breastfeeding mothers.[15] But more important at the moment is his elision of difference between paternal "consenting" and "promoting." The fact is that mid-century fathers continued, like their fathers before them, to exert their prerogative in determining the method of infant feeding; they did not, as a group, consent to their wives' wishes when those were in conflict with their own. But constructions like Nelson's allowed husbands to imagine that when they required maternal breastfeeding, they were capitulating to the desires of their wives – or to desires their wives *ought* to have felt. The tyrannical exercise of paternal authority did not necessarily change, but it began to look more like consensual practice.

---

13 Cf. Fildes, *Wet-Nursing*, 84, 114; McLaren, "Marital fertility," 27–28; J. Perkins, "Changing concepts of motherhood." For the disagreement between Samuel Johnson's parents, see my "Critical complicities."

14 Fildes, *Wet-Nursing*, 118.

15 Nelson further suggests that the virtuous mother will find her sexual desire satisfied in the act of breastfeeding. "There is an inexpresible Pleasure in giving Suck, which none but Mothers know," he writes; "the Sensation ... is said to be mighty pleasing" (44). Cf. Gelpi, "The nursery cave," 45. Drawing on an ancient image of self-sacrificial love, Marriott summarizes more typical Augustan arguments for maternal breastfeeding, arguments that assume self-immolation, not satisfaction.

> The Phoenix builds her spicy Net, and dies,
> Pleas'd, that an Heir will, from her Ashes rise; ...
> By Nature, and by these Examples led,
> Fond Mothers, with their Milk, their Babes will feed.

(Marriott, *Female Conduct*, 264–65)

Nelson laments that there is "little Probability ... that my Advice herein will be follow'd by Persons in high Life" (45). Such concern was well founded. Though the prevailing trend was toward maternal breastfeeding (especially among those we now recognize as middle class), there were exceptions, as we have seen, and change was slowest among those of the highest social standing. Conduct writers continued throughout the century to complain that aristocratic mothers did not breastfeed, and novelists to portray wealthy mothers who withhold the breast as paradigms of maternal failure.[16] Though breastfeeding was strongly advocated in conduct writing and seems to have been the preference of an increasing majority of women and men, husbands still had final authority, and not every husband's opinion had changed.

What matters most, however, may well be this: that privileged women who did wish to breastfeed could find an alternate source of authorization in the unanimous counsel of conduct literature. Augustan conduct literature's authority was most often used in the service of patriarchal privilege; but because it taught objectively correct female behaviors – including maternal breastfeeding – conduct writing also constituted a potential rival authority on which wives might build resistance to their husbands' commands. When disputes about infant feeding arose between husbands and wives, conduct literature may well have functioned as an incendiary challenge to the authority of the father, a voice that spoke for maternal desire from within the sanction of an established (and largely male-authored) genre. Depending on the particular organization of desire in specific households, conduct literature could function either as a tool of male dominance or as a challenge to it.

Throughout the seventeenth and early eighteenth centuries, conduct writers further assumed that virtuous mothers love their children more than do equally virtuous fathers. The difference was usually attributed to men's purportedly greater rationality and to what Allestree called the greater "strength of feminine passion" (205). "The love of a Mother to her children," wrote Dorothy Leigh, "is hardly contained within the bounds of reason" (*The Mothers Blessing*, 11). Judith Drake contends that women are by nature "over and above enrich'd with a peculiar Tenderness and Care requisite to the Cherishing their poor helpless Off-spring" (*Defence of the Female Sex*, 18–19). And Chudleigh paints a comparative portrait

[16]   Cf. Greenfield, "The maternal bosom."

of the grief of Prince George and Princess Anne on the death of the young Duke of Gloucester in 1700: George thinks about his loss and decides it will do no good to express grief; but Anne "could not thus controul / The tender Motions of her troubled Soul." After all, Chudleigh informs us,

> Maternal Kindness still does preference claim,
> And always burns with a more ardent Flame.
>
> ("On the Death," 7)[17]

Perhaps it was because of the widespread belief in mothers' unique tenderness for children that early Augustan conduct literature granted to mothers a degree of authority greater than that granted to mere wives, and occasionally even resembling that enjoyed by husbands. To be sure, conduct writing shares with virtually all other forms of Augustan discourse the belief that women are by nature inferior, and rightly subordinate, to men. But motherhood was understood in some seventeenth-century texts to grant a special dispensation, as it were, from the usual sexual hierarchy. Halifax makes the inequity of women's situation painfully clear, but then goes on to suggest that women may offset this state of affairs by means of their extraordinary influence as mothers. "You must first lay it down for a Foundation in general," he informs his daughter, "that there is *Inequality* in the *Sexes*, and that for the better Oeconomy of the World, the *Men* ... had the larger share of *Reason* bestow'd upon them; by which means your Sex is the better prepar'd for the *Compliance* that is necessary"; nevertheless, "in the *Nursery*" women can expect to "Reign without Competition" (8).

Halifax characterizes the mother's reign as peculiarly duplicitous, an affective rule much like that employed by Elizabeth and Anne as symbolic mother-rulers.

You must begin early to make them [your children] *love* you, that they may *obey* you ... You must deny them as seldom as you can, and when there is no avoiding it, you must do it *gently*; you must flatter away their ill Humour ... This will strengthen your *Authority*, by making it soft to them; and confirm their *Obedience*, by making it their Interest ... Let them be more in awe of your *Kindness* than of your *Power* ... *Love*, rather than *Fear*, may be the Root of their *Obedience*. (22–23)

17　Cf. *The Ladies Library*, 2: 33; Rousseau, *Emile*, 37–38. It is interesting to note that when searching for a precedent for Anne's maternal anguish, Chudleigh finds only Andromache, whose story, as we shall see, is central to *Pamela*, Part 2's representation of virtuous motherhood.

"You are," Halifax advises his daughter, "to have as strict a Guard upon your self amongst your *Children*, as if you were amongst your Enemies" (23). Writing in the immediate context of the Glorious Revolution, Halifax renders the nursery a politically charged realm of female authority, an authority that he considers most successful when it proceeds with caution reminiscent of that practiced by the famous "trimmer" himself when negotiating the treacherous worlds of late seventeenth-century public politics.

Even the heavily coded and self-deprecating maternal "reign" Halifax imagined, however, was short-lived. Although subsequent works of conduct literature continued to insist that "there is a real Superiority in the Husband"[18] and that mothers should build their authority over children on love rather than fear,[19] later writers tend to shun Halifax's explicit identification of maternal affect as a political tool and his suggestion that motherhood might constitute a locus of unique, incontestable authority. The *Ladies Library* follows Halifax in recommending that mothers use "indirect" and "insinuating" methods for their children's "Instruction and Government" (2: 179, 214), and parrots his lessons on the superiority of men. But as if in direct rebuke to Halifax it also takes pains to distinguish such subtly manipulative procedures from the "winding and crooked Methods" of outright "Craft." "Persons of a crafty Temper, can never avoid those very Inconveniencies which they labour to shun," we are told; mothers should demonstrate to their daughters "that without Deceitfulness we may be Discreet, Cautious, and Diligent in the lawful ways of gaining our Point."[20] Furthermore, *The Ladies Library* denies that women-as-mothers enjoy special authority.

The *Father* is ... Superior to the *Mother*, both in Natural Strength, in Wisdom, and by God's Appointment ... if it happens, that the Inclinations

---

[18]   John Hill, *The Conduct of a Married Life*, 172. Posing as a woman, Hill declares, "the Law of God ordains it. We are weak and useless to the World, they [husbands] are our Support and our Defence"; this is the case not for "one Country or one Time" only, but for "all the World, and ... all Ages ... in all Places" (173).

[19]   In Cooper's *The Exemplary Mother* (1769), the mother's "empire" over the "inclinations" of her children (17) is attributed to the fact that she breastfed each of them and to a combination of Halifaxian tactics (diverting children's attention rather than denying them anything, not contradicting them too much, and so on). She continually begs her children to think of her as a "friend" more than as one with "the authority of a parent" (27).

[20]   *The Ladies Library*, 2: 172–3. The apparent difference is one of degree rather than of kind. Always *The Ladies Library* employs gentle, equivocal language where Halifax was directly political, but advocates the same maternal strategies. In effect, *The Ladies Library* uses on readers the kinds of insidious tactics both texts are advocating for mothers.

or Desires of the *Mother* should differ from those of the *Father* ... the Father
is the Superior Authority, and must be obey'd ... [The mother] is not
presum'd to have a Will contrary to her Husband's. (2: 33–34)

No longer, by 1714, could women expect to "Reign without Competition" even in the nursery.

On the whole, then, Augustan conduct literature privileged
motherhood *per se* in new ways. It represented mothers as uniquely
suited (indeed, obligated) to be their children's first teachers and
constant companions. It dictated maternal behavior across class lines
(though according to an invisible middle-class rubric). And it used
breastfeeding not only as a measure of maternal virtue but also as an
indicator of broader personal and class virtues. The trend to extol
virtuous maternal influence continued as the century progressed, as
did the tendency unilaterally to blame mothers for how children
turned out: "It will be owing to her Care," John Hill declared in
1754, that children's "Conduct ... is good, or to her Neglect that it
will be otherwise" (11–12).[21]

But at the same time, Augustan conduct literature increasingly
subordinated the power of mothers to that of fathers. The new
emphasis on paternal attention even to very young children is clearly
apparent by the middle of the century. Cadogan (1748) calls on
"every Father to have his Child nursed under his own Eye" and to
do away with traditional attitudes that made infant care "one of the
Mysteries of the *Bona Dea*, from which Men are to be excluded" (25).
Nelson (1753) goes to pains not to privilege mothers as his chosen
audience, insisting that he addresses "every Parent" (4). And writing
in 1769, William Buchan extols the great "importance" of mothers,
but is quick to add a revealing caveat: "The mother is not the only
person concerned in the management of children. The father has an
equal interest in their welfare, and ought to assist in every thing that
respects either the improvement of the body or mind" (5–6). So by
mid-century conduct books routinely taught that mothers love their
children more than fathers and are specially equipped to care for
them. But the suggestion implicit in late seventeenth-century handbooks that motherhood might therefore constitute a place where
wives' authority is actually greater than (or even exclusive of)
husbands' was being explicitly discredited. Mid-eighteenth-century
mothers were elevated as moral and religious exemplars and instruc-

21   Cf. 218, below.

tors, but fathers were directed to exert supervisory authority over even the smallest of nurslings.

Pamela, *Part 2 as conduct literature*

When Lady Davers insists that Pamela's first duty as a wife is to have children, her words echo contemporary conduct literature, which unanimously insists that motherhood is compulsory for all wives not physically disabled. *The Ladies Dictionary* (1694) follows long tradition in declaring that "*Generation* is the chief end of Marriage" (177) and castigates women "who from preapprehensions of their own pains" or from too-eager pursuit of "frolicks, and fancies ... deprive themselves, and their Husbands, of those blessings [i.e., children]" (144). Women resistant to motherhood were unquestionably lazy and selfish; sometimes they were downright evil, as in this barely allegorical flight from a sermon of the 1640s.

Every good Soul is a Mother, her Issue, Knowledge and Virtues and Graces, conceiv'd from those Seeds wherewith Nature and God's Spirit hath quickened her. Would our Soul, as she ought to retain, to cherish, to ripen, to exalt these, she might, with Joy, behold Children ... But now she is so taken with her own Beauty, that she cares not to be a Mother ... As we see commonly in Bodies ... so in Souls, those generous Principles ... being check'd and forbidden to display themselves into legitimate Births, break out into Monsters, Vanity and Vice. (Master, "The Virgin Mary," 114–15)

Having children, in short, was enormously important. And tractable as always, Pamela is exemplary in the sheer quantity of childbearing she undergoes. She is pregnant virtually throughout Part 2, seven times in all. Pamela herself refers to pregnancy as "A Circumstance I am, I think, *always* in" (4: 408). But it is not only in the heroine's commitment to what approaches full-time childbearing that *Pamela*, Part 2 exemplifies the precepts of conduct literature. The language used to specify Pamela's motherhood, and the conflicts raised by her double position as mother and wife, would have sounded familiar chords for Richardson's female readers, many of whom, we may assume, were also reading conduct books.

Throughout *Pamela*, Part 2, for instance, – as always in early eighteenth-century conduct literature's discourse on motherhood – "tenderness" is the key word for describing virtuous maternal sentiment and behavior. The book constantly makes much of Pamela's maternal tenderness, contrasting it to Mr. B.'s acceptably gruff attitude toward his son and heir. In a letter to Lady Davers, Pamela gushes about how "after every little Absence" from her new baby she is filled with "a true maternal Tenderness, every Step I move toward the dear little Blessing!" But unfortunately, "your dear Brother is not so fond of him as I wish him to be."

[He said] that if I gave myself so much Uneasiness every Time the Child ailed any thing, he would hire the Nurse to over-lay him. Bless me, Madam! what hard-hearted, what shocking Things are these Men capable of saying – The farthest from their Hearts, indeed! (4: 150, 175)

Mr. B. blames his infatuation with the Countess on Pamela's excessive devotion to little Billy – "why, my Dear, you are *so* ingag'd in your Nursery!" (4: 169) – and Pamela herself realizes that her love for Billy surpasses what she feels for her husband: the loss of B. to the Countess, she insists, would be tolerable, but she could not survive Billy's loss (4: 172, 194). Indeed, Pamela's maternal passion is even capable of overshadowing her faith in God. She finds consolation for B.'s presumed unfaithfulness in "my Nursery and my Reliance on God," only belatedly realizing that her statement needs revision: "I should have said the latter first" (4: 161). Pamela's maternal tenderness consumes all other passions, fills her time, and claims virtually all her energies.

In her love for her children, then, Pamela treads a narrow line, always in danger of being Allestree's too-loving mother. Indeed, when Billy becomes gravely ill, Pamela believes that she is being punished for maternal doting: "My dear Baby is taken with the Small-pox!" she cries. "I fear ... I had ... too much Pride, and too much Pleasure" (4: 252). Fortunately, Billy survives and so validates his mother's virtue. But throughout the novel, there is always the suggestion that Pamela's maternal virtues might really be covert vices, that her strengths as a mother might turn out to be fatal weaknesses.

As paradigmatic bourgeois mother, Pamela is also responsible for the early education of the children. "What Delights," she exclaims, "have those Mamma's, (which some fashionable Ladies are quite unacquainted with) who can make their dear Babies, and their first Educations, their Entertainment and Diversion!" (4: 365). Pamela and Mr. B. agree that their children's first educations will be entrusted to her, and for this purpose B. gives her a copy of Locke's *Some Thoughts Concerning Education* about which she writes at great length, composing what amounts to an embedded treatise – what Pamela calls "my little Book" (4: 413).[22] Just as he demanded permission to read Pamela's letters in Part 1, now Mr. B. demands access to this book: "I want to know the Sentiments of a young Mother, as well as of a learned Gentleman, upon the Subject of Education" (4: 314). Later, when Pamela fears that Mr. B. is thinking of taking Billy away from her, she begs for permission to continue as his teacher even if they must live apart (4: 194).

So Pamela demonstrates her "tenderness" by caring personally for her children, loving them above all things (but not too much!), and carrying out their early educations herself. All these duties became normative maternal behaviors during Richardson's generation, as did Pamela's other distinguishing trait as a mother: her self-consciousness about mothering itself. Like no fictional character before her, Pamela reads, writes, and worries about her motherhood, which emerges as a full-time occupation, absorbing her attention and excluding her from participation in virtually anything else. Motherhood provides Pamela with an acceptable excuse for failing to perform that most important duty of the privileged wife – the social visit – and even threatens (in vain, of course) to keep her from writing letters (4: 185, 148).

There is one maternal virtue, however, that Pamela does *not* practice – the most telling of all according to conduct literature. Pamela does not breastfeed her own children. The reasons for this lapse are important enough to occupy us for some time. They reveal that for Richardson, at least, specific maternal behaviors were less important than the context of wifely subordination in which they should take place. In this sense, Richardson's "conduct novel" works to contain the potential subversiveness of Augustan conduct literature, which by identifying universally virtuous female behaviors provided a rival authority whereby wives could, conceivably, resist their husbands' commands.[23]

---

22 The importance of Pamela's book, and of the maternal pedagogy it represents, is signaled by its reappearance in Richardson's "Conclusion" to *Pamela*, Part 2, a summary of Pamela's achievements as a mother: "She made him [B.] the Father of Seven fine Children, ... all ... educated, in every respect, by the Rules of their inimitable Mother, in that Book ... upon Mr. *Locke's* Treatise of Education" [4: 470].

　　For the enormous influence of Locke's *Thoughts Concerning Education* on eighteenth-century Anglo-American culture, see Fliegelman. Chaber discusses Pamela's critique of Locke ("Moral man").

23 By Richardson's day, some conduct writers were beginning to see and pre-empt this danger. *The Mother's Looking-Glass*, a 1702 defense of maternal breastfeeding, had argued

"He will have his way":
breastfeeding and patriarchal prerogative

Could you ever have thought, Miss, that Husbands have a Dispensing
Power over their Wives, which Kings are not allowed over the Laws? ...
Can you believe, that if a Wife thinks a Thing her Duty to do, and her
Husband does not approve of her doing it, he can dispense with her
performing it, and no Sin shall lie at her Door? ... Did you ever hear of
such a Notion before, Miss? Of such a Prerogative in a Husband? Would
you care to subscribe to it? (Pamela to Miss Darnford)[24]

Pamela's outraged description of her husband's domestic tyranny
signals the onset of the first conflict in her married life and her only
moment of direct resistance to Mr. B.'s authority. The conflict is
occasioned by her motherhood: Pamela and Mr. B. have disagreed
over whether Pamela should breastfeed their first child herself, as she
believes is her Christian duty, or hire a wetnurse, as Mr. B. insists.
The quarrel carries significant narrative weight. Pamela recounts
each debate between herself and Mr. B. in detail, adding her own
ruminations and soliciting the advice of various correspondents.
According to Pamela, her self-respect, her marriage to B., and her
soul's salvation all depend on the outcome of this disagreement.
More obliquely, the episode constitutes a test of the relative autono-
mies of the new husband and wife, and a defining moment for their
coming roles as mother and father.

Despite all the palaver the conflict elicits, it will be hardly
surprising to readers familiar with Part 1 to learn that Mr. B.'s
"prerogative" eventually wins the day, and baby Billy is placed in
the hands of a hired nurse. (Billy is not "put out," however; the nurse
lives in.) What does seem odd, though, is the dissonance between the
inevitable subordination of Pamela's desires and the language the
text uses to represent it. For despite the fact that Mr. B. eventually
prevails, Pamela's arguments for maternal breastfeeding are far
more powerful and persuasive. Every correspondent except Mr. B.
agrees that maternal breastfeeding is much to be preferred over
wetnursing, all things being equal; and Mr. B.'s arguments seem to
be deliberately cast as unconvincing and poorly motivated. So

---

that only "Sickness, Disability, Danger, publique necessity" or "Death" (!) can excuse a
woman from nursing her children "with her own Breasts" (Gaius, *Mother's Looking Glass*, 11,
17); *The Ladies Library*, published twelve years later, reproduces the same list of acceptable
excuses, but adds "the *Interposition* of the *Father's Authority*" (2: 221).

[24] *Pamela*, 3: 389–90.

clearly does the text valorize Pamela's position, in fact, that the dispute over maternal breastfeeding comes to seem only superficially about the matter ostensibly being debated. Instead, the struggle to determine whether Pamela should breastfeed is a struggle to define the relative authority of husband and wife over maternal behavior and the status of maternal subjectivity within marriage. Most fundamentally, what is being contested between Pamela and Mr. B. is the location of authority over a mother's body.

As we have seen, the vigorous arguments of a generation of conduct books and the increasing enclosure of women in domestic space were by the third and fourth decades of the eighteenth century convincing large numbers of comfortably off parents that maternal breastfeeding was preferable to hiring the services of a nurse.[25] In Pamela's central voice, *Pamela*, Part 2 powerfully repeats arguments already familiar to Richardson's audience, presenting a compelling case for maternal nursing. Mr. B., on the other hand, mouths stereotypical aristocratic attitudes toward breastfeeding, attitudes that Augustan conduct books unanimously disparaged. So the novel provides a kind of case study for readers' considerations: an encounter between traditional, patriarchal authority – represented by Mr. B. – and the authority of conduct literature to regulate female behavior.

By eventually privileging Mr. B.'s authority, Richardson reasserts the rights of individual fathers over the growing influence of conduct literature. But because at the same time it represents B.'s commands as logically flawed and politically suspect, *Pamela*, Part 2 undercuts its own efforts to contain the potential subversiveness of Augustan conduct writing's advice to mothers. When the patently incorrect Mr. B. is obeyed against reason and religion, merely because he flexes his patriarchal muscles, the enforcement of wifely obedience is exposed as totalitarian. As Pamela tells Miss Darnford, B.'s behavior looks very like the abuse of royal authority that England had rejected half a century before.

When she argues with Mr. B., Pamela rehearses the arguments, the tone and sometimes even the language of conduct books. She considers breastfeeding to be an "indispensable Duty" for all healthy mothers (4: 34). It is "most natural" to breastfeed, she says, and "unnatural," even "sinful," not to do so (4: 34–35). Pamela's

[25]   For the enclosure of women in domestic space, see especially Armstrong, *Desire and Domestic Fiction*; cf. B. Hill, *Women, Work, and Sexual Politics*.

dramatic rhetoric is by no means inflated when compared to that of conduct books, which routinely made a religious duty of maternal nursing, and traced a direct connection between the failure to breastfeed and infanticide.[26] And Pamela goes on to draw the conclusion obvious to Protestant readers: if breastfeeding is a spiritual duty for which she will be held individually accountable to God, then it supersedes all lesser duties, including her duty to obey Mr. B. For "as great as a Wife's Obligation is to obey her Husband ... even a Husband's Will is not sufficient to excuse one from a natural or divine Obligation" (4: 34, 36).

Mr. B.'s arguments, on the other hand, echo those that conduct literature assigned disapprovingly to the aristocracy: he wants Pamela to keep her figure; he wants to have her body at his disposal, not the baby's;[27] he wants her to continue her education (she is studying French and Latin); nursing is "beneath" her, as his wife; the child would disturb her sleep; he wants to take Pamela abroad. B. hints that if Pamela insists on breastfeeding he may take recourse in polygamy, a subject about which he has already made his wife "often somewhat uneasy" (4: 39).[28] And he even threatens to stop loving Pamela if she insists on nursing the baby herself:

I advise you, my dearest Love, not to weaken, or, to speak in a Phrase proper to the present Subject, *wean* me from that Love *to* you ... which hitherto has been rather increasing than otherwise, as your Merit, and Regard for me, have increased. (4: 43)

A problem of conscience emerges for Pamela: ought she to obey what she sees as a divine imperative to breastfeed her own children, or the unequivocal edict of her husband, to whom she owes obedience as the "one Indispensable of the Marriage Contract" (4: 34)? "If I think it a *Sin* to submit to the Dispensation he insists upon

---

26   Cf. Gaius, *Mother's Looking Glass*, 17; *The Ladies Library*, 2: 222.
      Halifax had also used the language of abandonment to discuss his version of maternal failure. But significantly, the worst maternal behavior Halifax can imagine is not failure to breastfeed, but letting motherly tenderness "break out [in] Company, or exposing your self by turning your Discourse that way; which is a kind of *Laying Children* to the *Parish*" (22). By exercising restraint, upper-class women may "distinguish" themselves from "Women of a lower size" (22). These pronouncements, not surprisingly, are among the few in Halifax not to be readily found in later writers of conduct literature.
27   B.'s reasoning draws on the notion, commonly believed in Augustan Britain, that sexual intercourse and breastfeeding were physiologically incompatible. Cf. Gaius, *The Mother's Looking Glass*, 13; Pollock, "Embarking on a rough passage," 50; Perry, "Colonizing the breast," 226–27.
28   Cf. Nussbaum, "The other woman," for a valuable discussion of Mr. B.'s use of polygamy in this argument, and of the ideological functions of polygamy in Augustan discourse.

as in his Power to grant," Pamela asks anxiously, "and yet *do* submit to it, what will become of my Peace of Mind?" (4: 44). The dilemma is a serious one. Pamela believes that she will be accountable to God for the decision she makes ("how can a Husband have Power to discharge a Divine Duty?" [4: 34]), while at the same time it is not really her own decision. After all, as conduct books were also insisting, a wife's duty is compliance. Pamela is irreducibly responsible for whatever action she chooses, yet autonomy and agency are also, paradoxically, denied her.[29] She agonizes over the compromised nature of her overdetermined choice: "Must not one be one's own Judge of Actions, by which we must stand or fall?" (4: 34).

Pamela, Part 2's answer to this crucial question is a resounding "no." Pamela's parents outline the text's rationalization for the necessity of Pamela's capitulation:

We think, besides the Obedience you have vowed to him, and is the Duty of every good Wife, you ought to give up the Point, and acquiesce; for this seemeth to us to be the lesser Evil; and God Almighty, if it should be your Duty will ... excuse a Wife, when she is faulty by the Command of the Husband ... So e'en resolve my dearest Child, to submit to it, and with Cheerfulness too. (4: 45–46)

Mr. B.'s version of the same reasoning is brutally explicit. He cites the Old Testament to demonstrate "of how little Force even the *Vows* of your Sex are, and how much you are under the Controul of ours" (4: 40).

Even in such a strong Point as a *solemn Vow to the Lord*, the Wife may be absolv'd by the Husband, from the Performance of it ... an Husband may take upon himself to dispense with such a supposed Obligation, as that which you seem so loth to give up, even although you had made a Vow, that you would nurse your own Child. (4: 41)

The husband's will takes precedence over "natural" and "divine" aspects of motherhood, and makes it excusable – indeed, necessary – or her to commit what she understands to be "sin." Even if a husband is wrong or disqualified to judge ("my dear Mr. B.," Pamela notes archly, "was never yet thought so intirely fit to fill up the Character of a Casuistical Divine, as that one may absolutely rely upon his Decisions in these serious Points" [4: 44]), his opinions have virtually divine authority.

---

[29]   Cf. Eagleton, *Rape of Clarissa*, 35.

The episode is disturbingly reminiscent of a story from Defoe's influential conduct book *The Family Instructor* (1715), in which a six-year-old boy has worries much like Pamela's. "Sometimes my Mother won't let me go to Church, if it be but a little ill Weather," the boy tells his father; "and if God requires me to go, and my Mother won't let me, *what must I do*? Won't God be angry with me for not going to hear his Word preached?" No, the father replies: "if your Mother won't let you go, then Child, it is none of your Fault" (1: 36–37). Echoes between Defoe's tale and the resolution of Pamela's uncertainty about breastfeeding signal the profound infantilization of the married Pamela. By worrying about her own responsibility, Pamela wrongly presumes that she, like B., can claim adult subjectivity and spirituality. *Pamela*, Part 1 had validated the lower-class heroine's claim to have a "soul equal to the soul of a princess"; but the breastfeeding debate in Part 2 explicitly denies Pamela's claim to have a soul equal to her husband's.

Though hardly one to capitulate easily, Pamela finds the combined weight of all these arguments and threats to be too much, even for her. "Recollecting every thing, [I] *sacrificed to my Sex*, as Mr. B. calls it," she writes (4: 52). After a good cry, finding that "my Heart was relieved by my Eye" and feeling "lighter and easier" (4: 52), she proceeds immediately to hire a wetnurse. "We are quite reconciled," Pamela reports to her relieved parents, "altho', as I said, upon his own Terms" (4: 54).

And so, we are to believe, the breastfeeding crisis is resolved. Never mind that immense questions about power relations between spouses, individual responsibility and agency, and maternal authority have been raised – a few tears and a toss of the head presumably make everything right. Although Pamela does regret the decision at one other point, when Billy seems to be dying of smallpox ("Had *I* been permitted – But, hush! all my repining *Ifs!*" [4: 252]), her faltering proves unjustified when Billy pulls through. And apart from this brief qualm, the text refuses to acknowledge that the disturbing problems raised in the breastfeeding crisis are not addressed, only deferred, by the decision to hire a wetnurse.

Nevertheless, much that follows complicates this ostensibly neat resolution. In fact, no sooner has Pamela acquiesced to B.'s demands than his authority begins to unravel. The exchange between Mr. and Mrs. B. at this delicate juncture – both what is said and what is left unsaid – shows how *Pamela*, Part 2 subverts its ostensible purposes, challenging the doctrines of patriarchal prerogative and wifely obedience in the very process of defending them.

Mr. B. begins by complaining that Pamela's resistance forced him to "a hated, because an ungenerous, Necessity of pleading my Prerogative. And if this was not like my *Pamela*, excuse me ... that I could not help being a little unlike myself."[30] B.'s complaint is consistent with the demands he outlined for his wife-to-be in Part 1:

She should not have given Cause for any Part of my Conduct to her, to wear the least Aspect of Compulsion or Force. The Word *Command*, on my Side, or *Obedience* on hers, I would have blotted from my Vocabulary ... she should ... have shewn no Reluctance, Uneasiness, or Doubt, to oblige me, even at half a Word. (2: 317)[31]

So Pamela can hardly contradict him. Accordingly, her response takes place on two levels – a largely acquiescent speech, and privately rebellious thoughts expressed only in a letter to her parents. Out loud, her response is laced with a rich mixture of irony and obsequiousness: "You know, Sir, I never had any Will but yours in common Points ... I had no Intention to invade your Province, or go out of my own. Yet I thought I had a Right to a little Free-will, a very little; especially on some greater Occasions" (4: 49–50). But silently, Pamela constructs a different response, astutely linking Mr. B.'s deployment of his "prerogative" in the breastfeeding crisis with his attempts at crude sexual force before they were married. "Ah! thought I," she writes later, "this is not so very unlike your dear Self, were I to give the least Shadow of an Occasion; for it is of a Piece with your Lessons formerly" (4: 49).

At stake in those former "lessons," of course, was the crucial

---

[30] It is amusing to compare Mr. B.'s self-righteous complaints to the pronouncements of Chudleigh's hilariously chauvinistic male speakers in *The Ladies Defence* (1701). Chudleigh's parodic Parson, for instance, instructs wives that:

> A blind Obedience you from Guilt secures,
> And if you err, the Fault is his, not yours.   (11)

And Mr. B.'s threats of abuse sound only too like the Parson's justification of unkind husbands:

> If we are cruel, they have made us so;
> What e'er they suffer, to themselves they owe:
> Our Love on their Obedience does depend,
> We will be kind, when they no more offend.   (Chudleigh, 8)

[31] Richardson's final revisions (published in 1801) introduce a prescient response on Pamela's part to B.'s demands for entire wifely submission: "If she would overcome, he says, it must be by sweetness and complaisance – *A hard lesson, I doubt, where one's judgment is not convinced. We all dearly love to be thought in the right, in any debated point. I am afraid this doctrine, if enforced, would tend to make an honest wife a hypocrite!*" (*Pamela*, Ed. Sabor, 469; cf. note 337, p. 537).

question of whether Pamela or Mr. B. had the authority to dispose of Pamela's virginity, to deploy her female body and its sexual desire. Now, power over Pamela's maternal body and the extent of her authority to determine her child's best interests are at stake. In other words, Pamela finds herself once again in the predicament she faced in Part 1: pressure to choose is brought to bear, but choice is not really offered – the only alternative to compliance is force. The issue now is breastfeeding, not sexual intercourse; and as Ruth Perry has argued, the text does much to enforce the notion that motherhood and sexuality are unrelated.[32] But we can resist this lesson, and observe instead that *Pamela*, Part 2 presents us with a new version of the old power struggle, in effect rewriting maternal virtue as an elaboration of the sexual virtue defined in Part 1 – namely, a virtue that requires the immolation of female desire and volition. The virtuous mother, like the virtuous maiden, is at once required to say no and denied any response but yes.

One might argue that the second part of *Pamela* does not so much *reinforce* as *revise* the first part on the issue of the relative authorities of Pamela and Mr. B. In Part 1, we might say, Pamela was right to resist; in Part 2 she is required to capitulate. But Pamela managed to come safely through the harrowing situations of Part 1 only because Mr. B. chose, at crucial moments, not to rape her after all. Choice, like desire, is B.'s peculiar privilege in Part 1 just as in Part 2; the difference is that in the breastfeeding crisis, B. makes a different choice than he did in Part 1. Forcing his desire on Pamela against her will, silencing her protests, usurping control of her body, keeping up the pretense of her consent, B. becomes at last, in the breastfeeding crisis, the rapist Pamela feared in Part 1. And crucially, it is the fact of their marriage that allows B. to perform this violence on Pamela *without seeming to violate her*, since as his wife she is permitted no desires apart from his anyway.[33] When Pamela pleads for "a Right to a little Free-will, a very little," Mr. B. responds with characteristic obduracy: "Why so you have, my Dear; but ... I must have your whole *Will*" (4: 51–52). As in *The Ladies Library*, the mother (who of course is only legitimately visible as a wife) "is not presum'd to have a Will contrary to her Husband's."

32 Perry, "Colonizing the breast," *passim*, esp. 226.
33 For the importance of the marriage in changing the social, political, and stylistic agenda of *Pamela* between Parts 1 and 2, cf. Schellenberg, "Enclosing the immovable," 30.

To her credit, Pamela recognizes these strategies for what they are: manifestations of tyranny.

> He is pleased to entertain very high Notions ... of the Prerogative of a Husband. Upon my Word, he sometimes ... makes a body think a Wife should not have the least Will of her own. He sets up a dispensing Power, in short, altho' he knows, that that Doctrine once cost a Prince his Crown. (4: 39–40)

The "doctrine" of patriarchal absolutism, like that of passive obedience, had long been rejected in the context of public relations between monarch and subject; yet as the breastfeeding crisis demonstrates, such ideas remained in force in the realm of domestic politics. Chudleigh scorned the passive obedience demanded of Augustan wives:

> Passive Obedience you've to us transferr'd,
> And we must drudge in Paths where you have err'd:
> That antiquated Doctrine you disown;
> 'Tis now your Scorn, and fit for us alone.   (*Ladies Defence*, 3)

But Pamela's parents advise capitulation: "it will signify nothing, after all [to resist]; for he will have his Way, that's sure enough" (4: 47). As Pamela complained to Miss Darnford at the start of all the trouble, Mr. B. enjoys "a Dispensing Power ... which Kings are not allowed over the Laws" (3: 389).

Still, B.'s victory over Pamela's claims to maternal authority and personal autonomy is not without cost. In order explicitly to subordinate Pamela's will to her husband's, Richardson must necessarily give her arguments a voice, permitting dissonance to sound in his otherwise well-tempered text.[34] Though ventriloquized, contradicted and finally neutralized, Pamela's subversive maternal voice sounds clearly in the breastfeeding episode, disrupting the presentation of virtuous maternity as unproblematically submissive to patriarchal authority. And Pamela's eloquent descriptions of her struggles continue to resonate subversively even when the breastfeeding debate is apparently resolved, threatening to spill over into

---

[34] Cf. Roxana's famous "Amazonian" speeches (155–61; 169–71). Like Pamela's insistence on her own responsibility, of course, Roxana's defiance is finally neutralized, and she comes to lament her radical opinions. But despite their eventual containment, Roxana's fighting words, like Pamela's, are never fully absent from the capitulations that follow.

Such proto-feminist speeches strike me as only more resonant by virtue of being spoken by an impersonating male. For a recent treatment of the phenomenon of "narrative transvestism," cf. Kahn, *Narrative Transvestism*.

readers' interpretations of later, ostensibly unrelated episodes, as we shall see. The issues raised in the breastfeeding crisis, in other words, continue throughout Part 2 to disrupt the apparent harmony of the B. home, and to expose that harmony's dependence on the denial of maternal authority, subjectivity and desire.[35]

As at the conclusion of the breastfeeding crisis, Pamela seems throughout the sequel to acquiesce cheerfully enough to her own powerlessness as domestic mother, and indeed to collude in calling it power. But at the same time, she develops in response indirect, manipulative strategies built on the subtle objectification and erasure of others, particularly – and most tragically – other mothers. In all circumstances Pamela slyly makes her own motherhood centrally important, the signifier of female virtue as her virginity had been before. But the duplicitous methods she uses to construct and preserve her own priority reveal that Pamela's maternal virtue is characterized by craft and compromise, deceit and dissimulation.[36] As in Halifax's *Advice*, maternal behavior in *Pamela*, Part 2 looks a great deal like political intrigue, and the domestic space that circumscribes Pamela's activities comes to seem indistinguishable from the public world from which she is supposedly set apart.

Pamela, Part 2's impossible maternal ideals – and the contradictions and duplicities inherent in those ideals – are especially apparent in three definitive incidents in the text: Pamela's attendance at and reaction to a performance of Ambrose Philips's *The Distrest Mother*; her adoption of Miss Goodwin, Mr. B.'s illegitimate daughter; and the nursery tales she tells her children at the end of the book. Each of these incidents includes a failed mother against whom Pamela models maternal success. But in each case, Pamela may also be seen as a version of that failed mother, a sharer in maternal inadequacy rather than an alternative to it. Consideration of these three incidents can give us important clues about the limits of Augustan maternal ideology and of Richardson's efforts to refine it in the interests of a particular domestic-political ideal.

[35] In a very different interpretation, Schellenberg approves of the "consensus" achieved in *Pamela* 2. Significantly, she devotes only one sentence to the breastfeeding episode: "while Pamela acquiesces in this issue, it is made clear that even the social authority of a husband would be superseded in a case of divine imperative" ("Enclosing the immovable," 36). I argue precisely the opposite: that according to *Pamela*, Part 2, the preeminence of husbandly authority is recognized by a virtuous wife *even in* a case of divine imperative. Conflict ends not in consensus but in an *apparent consensus* that disguises maternal capitulation.

[36] Cf. Castle, "*Masquerade and Civilization*," 143–44. For a different view, cf. Schellenberg, "Enclosing the immovable," 32.

Making a virtue of duplicity:
Pamela *and* The Distrest Mother

Shortly after the resolution of the breastfeeding problem, Mr. B. takes Pamela to London, where they attend several dramatic performances. The first of these is Ambrose Philips's *The Distrest Mother*, an adaptation of Racine's *Andromaque* (1675). First performed in 1712, *The Distrest Mother* remained popular throughout the Augustan period. Its virtues were sung in several numbers of the *Spectator*, its excesses were exposed in Fielding's hilarious *Covent-Garden Tragedy* (1732), and well-known actors vied for parts.[37] So Pamela's remarks on the play enter a larger discussion of considerable contemporary interest, and touch on several recurring topics of debate.

The action is set after the fall of Troy, when the victorious Pyrrhus has turned defender of Hector's widow Andromache and her son Astyanax, the last remaining Trojan male. Pyrrhus stands between Astyanax and the Greek states, who fear the child and want him executed. But this protection comes at a price: Pyrrhus demands that Andromache marry him in return for her son's safety, although it was Pyrrhus who murdered her family and destroyed her city, and although he is already betrothed to Helen's daughter Hermione. If Andromache refuses him, Pyrrhus promises, he will turn Astyanax over to the Greeks; only "the Mother's Beauty guards the helpless Son" (4).

What is fascinating about this situation of brute coercion is that everyone in the play – not only Pyrrhus, but also Andromache's companion Cephisa and even Andromache herself – constructs Astyanax's fate as Andromache's responsibility, as if it were she and not Pyrrhus who threatens the child's destruction. Pyrrhus is particularly adept at usurping Andromache's role as victim and putting her in the position of the cruel tyrant who wills the child's death. "Why will you force me to desert your Cause?" Pyrrhus demands (31); "let me intreat you to secure his Life!" (32). He sues

---

[37]   For the *Spectator*'s comments on the play, see especially 3: 31–34, 3: 239–42, 3: 250–54, 3: 265–9, 4: 493 and 5: 99–100. Bond cites William Egerton's *Faithful Memoirs of ... Mrs. Anne Oldfield* (1731) for the disturbance at the play's first performance, when "Mrs. Rogers, disappointed at not being given the part of Andromache, 'raised a Posse of Profligates, fond of Tumult and Riot, who made such a Commotion in the House, that the Court hearing of it sent four of the Royal Messengers, and a strong Guard, to suppress all Disorders'" (*Spectator* 3: 351, n.3). Cibber also refers to the disturbance in his *Apology* (2: 166).

for her "consent," as if she really had a choice or the outcome were
in her control. Likewise Cephisa urges her mistress to look favorably
on Pyrrhus as on a courting wooer who "invites you to a Throne"
(32). But Andromache is not to be fooled by force masquerading as
supplication.

> Hast thou forgot that dreadful Night, *Cephisa*,
> When a whole People fell! Methinks I see
> *Pyrrhus*, enrag'd and breathing Vengeance, enter
> Amidst the Glare of burning Palaces:
> I see him hew his Passage through my Brothers;
> And, bath'd in Blood, lay all my Kindred waste . . .
> This is the Courtship I receiv'd from *Pyrrhus*;
> And this the Husband thou would'st give me! – No;
> We both will perish first! I'll ne'er consent.   (33)

Recognizing the so-called choice Pyrrhus offers as only another
manifestation of violence, Andromache constructs a daring response
to his demands. She agrees to marry the king, but secretly resolves to
kill herself immediately after the wedding ceremony, thus obliging
Pyrrhus to care for Astyanax as stepson and heir while escaping the
necessity of being sexually unfaithful to the dead Hector (45). With
this plan, Andromache attempts to manipulate Pyrrhus's coercions to
her own advantage (or, more precisely, to the advantage of her son).
She takes her position as distressed mother and remakes it into a
position of power insofar as she, not Pyrrhus, defines the marriage
and controls her own sexuality. Of course, Andromache's power is
tragically undercut by her inability to exercise it except through her
own death; nevertheless, she manages by means of deceit to turn her
vulnerability as a mother into resistance.

As it turns out, Andromache's suicide is prevented by the oppor-
tune assassination of Pyrrhus by the Greeks immediately after the
wedding. Andromache finds herself once again a widow, but now
also queen of the Greeks and mother of Pyrrhus's new heir, her son
Astyanax. The play ends with her waiting solicitously for her son and
intoning a moral strikingly *à propos* to Pamela, whose courtship by
Mr. B. in Part 1, like Pyrrhus's brutal wooing, had been a dangerous
game of wits and timing.

> Though plung'd in Ills, and exercis'd in Care,
> Yet never let the noble Mind despair.
> When press'd by Dangers and beset with Foes,
> The Gods their timely Succour interpose;

And when our Vertue sinks, o'erwhelm'd with Grief,
By unforeseen Expedients brings Relief.   (57)

During B.'s pursuit, Pamela, like Andromache, had reached the point of suicidal despair; like Andromache, Pamela also triumphed at last. These are obvious points of similarity between Andromache's story and Pamela's. But more pertinent to the action of *Pamela*, Part 2 is the similarity between Andromache's poignant situation as "distressed mother" and Pamela's struggle with Mr. B. over breast-feeding. In both instances mothers are confronted with pseudo-choices; coercive situations are disguised as matters calling for their consent. And both mothers are represented as responsible for outcomes over which they have little control. Andromache's plight vividly re-presents the pressure Pamela faces as a mother: she is responsible for her maternal "choices," but she is not free to choose for herself.

Situations of forced consent thus begin to emerge as definitive maternal situations in *Pamela*, Part 2. And we can discern as well a pattern of maternal response to the veiled brutality behind such situations: the coerced mother appears to acquiesce, but continues in fact to exert opposition deviously. Andromache submits to Pyrrhus's demands, but secretly schemes to defraud him of her body while coercing his faithfulness to her son; Pamela agrees not to breastfeed her child, but inwardly despises her husband and, as we shall see, develops indirect discursive strategies for imposing her own agenda and reinforcing her maternal authority. Slyness, deviousness, and hypocrisy come to characterize the mother struggling to survive – and to protect her children – against brutality disguised as entreaty. Pamela's responses as mother repeat and intensify the cunning she learned to practice when, as a younger woman, she was courted with the promise of rape.[38]

It is hardly surprising that one of the two places in *The Distrest Mother* most commented on by eighteenth-century audiences is Andromache's duplicitous suicide plan. (The other highly contested place is the play's epilogue, which we shall consider in a moment.) What *is* somewhat surprising, however, is Pamela's specific objection to Andromache's decision to kill herself upon marrying Pyrrhus. Though Pamela does object briefly to the fact that Andromache

---

[38] For an insightful treatment of the functions of female duplicity in *Pamela*, cf. Gwillam, *Fictions of Gender*, ch. 1. For a different interpretation of the function of *The Distrest Mother* in *Pamela*, Part 2, cf. Perry, "Colonizing the breast," 227, n. 69.

reduces the wedding service to a "mere Formality" (4: 98),[39] she criticizes Andromache not so much because of the irreverence and fraudulence of the act she contemplates, but because it seems impractical. "Was it very likely," she asks, "that a Man so wildly in Love with her ... who had shewn, that he would have destroy'd her Son, but for the sake of *her* Person ... would, when disappointed by so great a Rashness, have hazarded his Realms in defence of her Son?" (4: 89–90). As she observes, suicide is a "not very certain" means of coercion (4: 84). Skeptical contemporaries seem to have agreed: "by this egregious Non-performance of the Conditions on *Her* [Andromache's] side," one wrote, "she cancels all *Pyrrhus*'s Obligations on *His*."[40]

Pamela's concern over the viability of the distressed mother's strategies, however, is mild in comparison with her passionate objections to the other most-discussed part of the play, the flippant epilogue spoken by Anne Oldfield, who had acted the part of Andromache.[41] Pamela takes the degradation of Andromache's character much to heart. "I was extremely mortify'd," she says, "to see my favourite (and the only perfect) Character, debas'd and despoil'd ... talking Nastiness to an Audience, and setting it out with all the wicked Graces of Action, and affected Archness of Look, Attitude, and Emphasis" (4: 99). She is horrified to see the men in the audience turn during the epilogue to watch the ladies in the boxes and galleries, "to see how they ... stood" the "Ridicule, not only upon the Play in general, but upon the Part of *Andromache* in particular" (4: 98–99). At one point she even stands up in outrage, only to sit again quickly and carry on her tirade in angry whispers to Mr. B.

Why have I wept ... Why have I been mov'd ... Is it for this? See you not ... that noble *Andromache* ... satirizing her own Sex, but indeed most of all

---

39   The sacrilegious aspects of Andromache's marriage to Pyrrhus were expounded with great heat by the anonymous author of *A Modest Survey* (1712), who objects to Andromache's breaking her "solemn Oaths" (12, 20) and calls her suicide plan a "robbery," since "the Right and Title" to her body belong to Pyrrhus once they are married (13).

40   Anon., *A Modest Survey*, 18.

41   For the text of the epilogue as it appeared in the first edition of *The Distrest Mother*, see the Appendix. Flippancy was, of course, the default mode for Augustan epilogues. This one, attributed to Budgell but probably written or revised by Addison (*Spectator*, 3: 251, n.2), was exceptionally popular with theatre-goers. Budgell claims that Mrs. Oldfield was called on to recite it nine times during the first three performances of the play (*Spectator*, 3: 265, n.4).

      It is a particularly nice irony that the part of Andromache and the epilogue should have been performed by Mrs. Oldfield, who was herself a disturbingly promiscuous maternal figure. See Nussbaum, "Savage mothers" (136) and my "Critical complicities."

ridiculing and shaming, in *my* Mind, that Part of the Audience, who can call for this vile Epilogue? (4: 99)

Pamela insists that the epilogue casts shame on those who enjoy it, but is frustrated to find that only she seems to feel ashamed.

What troubles Pamela most about the epilogue is the easy success with which it ridicules what had seemed sacred and serious before: the epilogue, she complains, seems intent on "inverting the Design of the whole Play" (4: 99). By reducing Andromache to a scheming whore, it makes the disquieting suggestion that even such idealized maternal virtue as hers might be construed as interested and corrupt. If *The Distrest Mother* echoes and validates Pamela's story – a story of violent courtship and coerced maternal behavior – the play's epilogue functions like the "anti-Pamelas" Richardson deplored: it shows that Andromache's experience lends itself equally to both the sentimental, sympathetic interpretation of another distressed mother and the mockery of men intent on detecting in maternal devotion the devious machinations of female sexual and political desire. Pamela wants to believe in the Andromache of the play: a chaste, tender, sacrificial mother. But the epilogue insists on presenting another Andromache, brazen and ambitious, who is never identified as a mother at all. The distressed mother, the epilogue implies, is really just another lustful woman.

One hardly need share Pamela's heightened sensibilities to note the jarring dissonance between play and epilogue. Richardson even allows Mr. B. to have felt it long before he married Pamela: "I never saw this Play, Rake as I was, but the Impropriety of the Epilogue sent me away dissatisfy'd with it, and with human Nature too" (4: 99). But from another perspective, play and epilogue are quite consistent. For both rely on the assumption that maternal virtue cannot exist alongside female sexual desire or political ambition. The play omitted Andromache's sexuality and minimized her public identity in order to represent her as a tender and devoted mother; the epilogue erases her maternal virtue to foreground her sexuality and political volition. Pamela, of course, objects to both the suicide scheme – Andromache's greatest act of self-sacrificial maternal tenderness – *and* the impudence of the epilogue. But the fact that her concern over Andromache's deception of Pyrrhus is moderate in comparison with her fury at the epilogue reveals that for Pamela, maternal duplicity is more acceptable than maternal desire. After all,

Pamela's own position as domestic mother depends on duplicitous dealings reminiscent of Andromache's; and like Andromache's "fine distress," Pamela's maternal virtues often seem devices and disguises, means toward the achievement of hidden desire.

What, we might ask, is the object of that desire? What do mothers want? *The Distrest Mother* provides more than one answer. The play proper suggests that what the virtuous mother wants is to be left in private, away from public power relations, to devote herself to her child. "All I wish for," Andromache declares, "is some quiet Exile where . . . I may conceal my Son, and mourn my Husband" (12).

> Let me go hide him, in some Desart Isle . . .
> To keep him far from Perils of Ambition:
> All, he can learn of me, will be to weep!   (29)

The epilogue, on the other hand, makes a different but equally reductive suggestion: that even the best mothers, like all women, really just want pleasure and power. The Andromache of the epilogue is excited about both "the Charms/Of Love and Life in a young Monarch's Arms" and the "Coronation" that will make her "a Princess, and young Sty a King". What do mothers want? According to *The Distrest Mother* taken entire, they want to care for their children faithfully and without disturbance, but they also want sexual pleasure and political power. It is the play's insistence on keeping all of these options afloat that most distresses Richardson's model mother. Yet ironically, as we shall see, *Pamela*, Part 2 presents multiple answers of its own to the question of maternal desire, and echoes the *The Distrest Mother*'s most disquieting suggestion: that in situations where force is disguised as choice, maternal virtue may not reside only in tender self-sacrifice and withdrawal; it can also include the active deployment of female sexuality and ambition.

Seduction, coercion, and maternal erasure:
Sally Godfrey Wrightson's "kind concurrence"

Richardson's discomfort with a definition of maternal virtue that includes active female sexuality is again made apparent in the episode concerning young Sally Goodwin's adoption by Mr. and Mrs. B. The process is a delicate one because Miss Goodwin already has a living mother and father. Though she calls Pamela "Aunt" and B. "Uncle," the girl is actually B.'s own daughter; her birthmother,

Sarah (Sally) Godfrey Wrightson, lives in social banishment in Jamaica as a result of her loss of virtue to B. Until the marriage between Pamela and B., Miss Goodwin has lived at a boarding school, ostensibly the ward of Lord and Lady Davers. But once Pamela and Mr. B. are married, Pamela adopts the girl.

Soon after Miss Goodwin takes up residence with the B.s, Pamela receives an extraordinary letter from Sally Godfrey Wrightson, who tearfully renounces her claims as young Sally's mother and thanks Pamela in fulsome terms for adopting her child. Despite the rhetoric of gratitude and willingness, however, the pain Sally Wrightson feels at relinquishing her child is palpable. But oddly, neither Pamela nor Lady Davers, with whom Pamela shares the letter, seems to notice. Instead they agree (rather too readily) that the unfortunate story has at last come to an entirely happy end, thanks to Pamela. Nevertheless, the violence of the whole undertaking continues to intrude, both in Sally's letter and in the larger narrative of her daughter's adoption, and undermines yet another of the text's efforts to demonstrate Pamela's exemplary maternal virtue.

Sally Godfrey Wrightson's letter is remarkable for the causal relation it assumes between her sexual fall with B. many years ago and her present position as absent, abdicating mother. Indeed, Sally's remorse over her seduction is so great as to seem almost parodic, and makes Sally herself less a novelistic "character" than a dramatized representative of conduct-book platitudes. "My Heart bleeds," she tells Pamela, "and has constantly bled ever since, at the grievous Remembrance" of "my own odious Weakness" (4: 287–88). She feels continual "Shame and Sorrow," is *"always* guilty," and *"ever penitent"* for having "so deplorably, so inexcusably fallen"; "that Crime turns my very Pleasures to Misery, and fixes all the Joy I *can* know, in Repentance for my past Misdeeds!" (4: 287–89).

Sally describes herself to Pamela as the "unhappy, tho' fond and tender Mother of the poor Infant, to whom your generous Goodness ... has extended itself" (4: 288). Yet when she resigns her child to Pamela's care, she uses language that erases, even denies, her own motherhood.

YOU are her Mamma *now* ... What a Joy is it to me, in the midst of my heavy Reflections on my past Misconduct, that my beloved *Sally* can boast a *virtuous* and *innocent Mamma* ... on my Knees I write it! GOD for ever bless you ... for your generous Goodness to my poor, and, till now, *motherless* Infant. (4: 288–89)

To her daughter, Sally writes, "I transfer my *whole* Right in you" to "your new Mamma" (4: 289).[42] If little Sally should ever be undutiful to Pamela, her distant mother writes, "remember that you have no more a Mamma in me" (4: 289). It is hard to tell whether Sally Wrightson is issuing her lost daughter a threat of contingent future abandonment, or merely announcing her abandonment as an accomplished fact. Indeed, the tone of the letter suggests that the mother herself may not quite know how to define her relation to her daughter at this point. So we can perhaps understand the confusion that surfaces in nearly everything little Miss Goodwin says. "*Dearest dear Mamma*," she writes to Sally Wrightson,

You please me mightily in giving me so dear a new Mamma here. Now I know, indeed, I have a Mamma, and I will love and obey her, as if she was you your own Self ... I am, my honoured Mamma, on the other Side of the Water, and ever will be, as if you was here, *Your dutiful Daughter.* (4: 293)

Miss Goodwin's words seem all but calculated to break the heart of a mother who was forced to abandon her baby. Yet Pamela never observes the suffering and violence inherent in the transaction, its costs to the mother or its necessary commodification of her daughter. Instead, her language in response to Sally Godfrey Wrightson is remarkably callous. She lets Sally know that her consent to the arrangement was not even required:

I was, by Mr. *B.*'s Leave, in actual Possession of my pretty Ward, about a Week before your kind Letter came to my Hands ... judge how welcome your kind Concurrence was to me; and the rather, as, had I known, that a Letter from you was on the Way to me, I should have apprehended, that you had yielded to the Intreaties of your worthy Spouse, and would have insisted upon depriving [us] ... of ... Pleasure ... in the dear Miss. Indeed, Madam, I believe we should one and all have join'd to disobey you, had *that* been the Case; and it is a very great Satisfaction to us, that we are not under so hard a Necessity, as the disputing with a tender Mamma the Enjoyment of her own Child. (4: 292)[43]

The rhetoric of force is disguised, but discernible nevertheless: Pamela would have taken little Sally whether the child's mother

---

[42] Despite this rhetoric, of course, Sally Godfrey's "right" in her daughter could not be so easily alienated. English law made no provision by statute for adoption until 1926; before that date, official adoption could only be effected by a special act of Parliament. Cf. McClure, *Coram's Children*, 129–30.

[43] In later editions, Richardson was to remove Pamela's expression of concern that Sally might have "yielded to the Intreaties" of her husband; its inconsistencies with Pamela's own marital relationship are obvious. "Enjoyment" would also later be changed, ominously enough, to "Possession."

agreed or not – in fact, already *had* taken the girl without that "kind Concurrence," because she had "Mr. *B.*'s Leave." So Sally Godfrey Wrightson's exclamations of gratitude at Pamela's adoption of her child have all the empty "concurrence" of Pamela's earlier claim to be cheerfully obeying Mr. B.'s breastfeeding prohibition, or of Andromache's smiling acceptance of Pyrrhus's hand. Once again, the mother (this time, Sally Godfrey Wrightson) is presented with an ultimatum masquerading as a choice, and is expected to rejoice in the privilege of acquiescence. Like the hiring of Billy's wetnurse and Andromache's acceptance of Pyrrhus's hand, Miss Goodwin's adoption is an act of brutal force; and again brutality is obscured by a not entirely convincing veneer of civility, inevitability, and universal satisfaction. This time, however, the conduit of patriarchal force is Pamela herself, in her role as virtuous (surrogate) mother.

In the remainder of the novel, the oddness of Miss Goodwin's position in the B. home is occasionally emphasized for pathetic effect, but most often the difficulties involved in her confused recognition of both a mother "across the water" and a "new mamma" at home are carefully ignored. Occasionally the situation resonates subversively nevertheless, as in the use of the phrase "on the other side of the water" to describe little Sally's abdicating mother – an echo of "the King across the water," a phrase used by Augustan loyalists to describe the exiled James. But the child's addresses to Mr. B., which Richardson wrings for sentiment, demonstrate the text's strategies for keeping at bay its own most compelling suggestions, even as they make clear the limitations of those strategies. In one early scene, little Sally (with coaching from Pamela) begs Mr. B. to let her come live with him and his new wife: "You should, in Pity, let me live with you, Sir," the little girl says, "for I have no Papa, nor Mamma neither" (4: 19). According to Pamela's narrative, Mr B. is "a little mov'd" at this.

But for fear the young Gentlewoman should take notice of it, How! my Dear, said he, No Papa and Mamma! – Did they not send you a pretty Black Boy to wait upon you, a while ago? Have you forgot that? – That's true, reply'd Miss: But what's a Black Boy to living with my new Aunt? – That's better a great deal than a Black Boy! (4: 19–20)

Miss Goodwin correctly sees that her own mother and (presumed) father in Jamaica have to be erased in order for her to consider the B.s as surrogate parents; but she discovers that Mr. B. resists her efforts to join in their erasure. "How!" B. cries, "Did they not send you a pretty Black Boy?" By conjuring up the figure of the black boy, B. attempts to assure Miss Goodwin that she is not an orphan after all; but the real effect is to keep her orphaned indeed, since her father, B. himself, refuses to own her. B. brings in the black boy as a kind of decoy, protecting himself at the cost of his integrity and denying Miss Goodwin even the most basic self-definition.

But the instrument of this apparent solution – the "pretty Black Boy" – exposes the hypocrisies that maintain B.'s prerogative. For Miss Goodwin herself is in certain respects not unlike the nameless black boy, a commodity shifted from one member of the B. circle to another for the gratification of their vanities and the quieting of their consciences. Like the black boy, Miss Goodwin is emptied of significance as a subject in her own right; she becomes a convenient cipher against whom Pamela's maternal excellence may be defined. Though absent and silent, the black boy nevertheless calls our attention to little Miss Goodwin's confusion and forced compliance, to Pamela's collusion in Mr. B.'s defrauding practices, and to the resonance of those practices beyond the domestic sphere.

The apparently harmonious resolution of Sally Godfrey's maternal plot, then, is built on a series of erasures – of troublesome "fallen" women, children, and racial others.[44] And like the resolution of the breastfeeding crisis, Miss Goodwin's adoption entails a reassertion of the primacy of Mr. B.'s patriarchal position. It is because of B., after all, that Sally Godfrey had to leave the country in the first place and that her new husband cannot adopt Miss Goodwin. Because Mr. B., unlike Sally Godfrey, was free to stay at home and choose at leisure the wife he most desired, Miss Goodwin is at last taken into the care of her own (disguised) father in an act of apparent magnanimity. Despite his self-interest and deceit, Mr. B.'s is the parental story with a happy ending, an ending achieved at the expense of any relationship between a loving mother and her child.

Sally Godfrey Wrightson no longer figures directly in the text after this exchange of letters. But she is difficult to forget nevertheless, especially later when (as we shall see) Pamela tells Miss Goodwin stories that call to mind the violence with which the girl's birthmother was written out of the story in order to make room for Pamela's supposedly more virtuous maternity. The adoption episode

44 Cf. C. Sussman's fine argument about the ideological ramifications of recent critics' erasure of the Sally Godfrey plot (esp. 97–100).

makes painfully clear, furthermore, how little distinguishes the disgraced Sally Godfrey and the virtuous Pamela – only their different responses to B.'s seduction.[45] Pamela's arrogance in claiming Miss Goodwin as daughter is supposedly justified by her resistance to B. in Part 1; and Sally's maternal disenfranchisement, we are to assume, goes with the territory for a "fallen" woman. So the final lesson to be drawn from Richardson's representation of the different maternal experiences of Pamela and Sally Godfrey is that seduction threatens not only virginity and marriage, but motherhood as well. Sally's failure of "virtue" – defined in the reductive, physiological sense at work in *Pamela*, Part 1 – made her an unfit mother from the moment of her daughter's conception and continues forever to exclude her from maternal joys that Pamela is free to usurp. Virtuous maternity – even maternal identity – depends in *Pamela*, Part 2 not on a mother's relationship to her children, but on her relationship to their father.

Maternal virtue and sexual virtue in Pamela's nursery stories

Pamela, Part 2 ends, appropriately enough, with Pamela in the nursery, where she tells morally instructive tales to her children (figure 12).[46] Pamela herself describes the scene in detail in a letter to Lady G. (the former Miss Darnford), placing great emphasis on her own mesmerizing maternal presence.

Miss *Goodwin* imagine you see, on my Right Hand … *Billy* on my Left … My *Davers*, and my sparkling-ey'd *Pamela*, with my *Charley* between them, on little silken Cushions at my Feet, hand in hand, their pleased Eyes looking up to my more delighted ones, and my sweet-natur'd promising *Jemmy* in my Lap; the Nurses and the Cradle just behind us … All as hush and as still, as Silence itself, as the pretty Creatures generally are, when their little watchful Eyes see my Lips beginning to open. (4: 453)

To this rapt audience, Pamela tells a series of tales – a pair for the younger children and a longer "*Woman*'s story" especially for Miss

---

45 Cf. C. Sussman, "Miss Sally Godfrey," 97.
46 The engraving reproduced here is one of a set of twelve produced by Benoist and Truchy and based on Highmore. Today Highmore's paintings are unfortunately scattered among London's National Gallery, the Tate, the Fitzwilliam and the National Gallery of Victoria in Melbourne. Cf. Dick, "Joseph Highmore's vision," (34–35, 41) for further information on Highmore's illustrations and for an intriguing interpretation of the relationship between the engravings and their verbal subtitles.

12 Joseph Highmore. "Pamela and her Children and Miss Goodwin, to whom she is telling her
nursery tales. This last Piece leaves her in full possession of the peaceable fruits of her Virtue." 1743.

Goodwin. Each of the tales features children whose experiences, good or bad, inculcate moral lessons "for Imitation or Warning" to Pamela's young auditors (4: 452). Each also makes much of the experiences of the children's mothers, who by the end of every tale have usurped the children's place at the center of the narrative.

The tale Pamela tells her younger children is concerned with the children of a wealthy married couple and those of an impoverished widow. The children from the two-parent family are genteel at all times: they speak kindly to their servants, study hard, say grace before their meals, "were always clean and neat," and "would not tell a Fib for the World" (4: 454). Even their genders are neatly balanced, two boys and two girls. These children do cheerfully whatever their mother commands: "it was, As my Mamma pleases; My Mamma knows best; and a Bow and a Smile" (4: 454). And needless to say, they grow up to be "good Papas and Mammas" in their turn (4: 455). The children of the poor widow, however, are "three naughty Sons, and One naughty Daughter" who "would do nothing that their Mamma bid them do" (4: 455). All are irreligious, stupid, and unpopular with other children because of "their Unduti-fulness to their poor Mother, who worked hard to maintain them" (4: 456). Eventually these wicked children "impoverish'd their poor Mother, and at last broke her Heart, poor, poor Widow Woman!" (4: 456). After their mother's death, they all come to quick and grisly ends, lamenting too late their dreadful treatment of "so good a Mother" (4: 456). "There," Pamela concludes, "was a sad End of all the Four ungracious Children, who never would mind what their poor Mother said to them; and GOD punished their Naughtiness, as you see!" (4: 456).

Pamela's tale has little to say about fathers (except to make heterosexual union the basis of the first family's wealth, stability, and harmony); instead, Pamela presents the mother as each family's central figure, and makes disobedience to maternal authority a frightening idea. Accordingly, the story of the naughty children elicits tears from every young listener – not for the children, but for their mother. "Poor, poor Widow Woman!" little Billy wails; his distress, Pamela reports, "gave me much Pleasure" (4: 457). While learning the ostensible lesson – "who would not but be good!" (4: 455) – Pamela's children also learn to consider their mother's word to be law, her experience primary, and her authority over them next only to God's.

After dismissing the younger children, Pamela tells a long "*Woman*'s story" especially for Miss Goodwin, who listens with painfully unconvincing rapture: "Now, dear Madam, for your next Character. There are Two more yet to come, that's my Pleasure! I wish there were Ten!" (4: 462). Such attention deserves credit, for the story is convoluted and the ostensible moral obvious from the start: "There is nothing . . . that young Ladies should be so watchful over, as their Reputation" (4: 457). Indeed, what is crucial about the story Pamela tells is not its predictable moralizing or the actual details of its complicated plot; what matters is the relation it implicitly establishes between the sexual chastity of young, unmarried women and the possibility of virtuous maternal authority.

Pamela's "*Woman*'s story" is really a series of four anecdotes featuring young women called Coquetilla, Prudiana, Profusiana and Prudentia. As their names suggest, the first three set negative examples of flirtatiousness, prudery and extravagance, while the last is virtuous and wise. Significantly, the failures or successes of three of the four are directly attributed to their mothers. Ostensibly telling stories about young ladies like Miss Goodwin, Pamela ends up telling stories about their mothers. For instance, it is because Prudiana grows up entirely without maternal influence that she eventually "throws herself" on a servant, becoming "the Outcast of her Family, and the Scorn of all that knew her" (4: 459–60). Ignoring disquieting echoes of Pamela's and B.'s story, Miss Goodwin tractably attributes these misfortunes to the absence of Prudiana's mother. "What a sad, sad Fall was hers!," she cries. "And all owing to the want of a proper Education too! – And to the Loss of such a Mamma, as I have an Aunt . . . I am sure, my dear good Aunt, it will be owing to you, that I shall never be a . . . *Prudiana*" (4: 460).

The most fortunate of Pamela's protagonists, Prudentia, also "lost her Papa and Mamma almost in her Infancy," but "had the Happiness of an Aunt, who loved her, as I do you, and of an Uncle, who doted on her, as yours does" (4: 466). This fortunate young woman concentrates on her education and acts with such care for her reputation that she marries wisely and "shines, to her last comfortable Hour, in all the Duties of domestic Life, as an excellent Wife, Mother, Mistress, Friend and Christian" (4: 467). Obviously, Prudentia is a model designed for Miss Goodwin's emulation not only in her virtue but also in her ability to consider an aunt interchangeable with a mother. But this obvious lesson is complicated by realignments that Miss Goodwin notices with much excitement: the "excellent Wife, Mother, Mistress, Friend and Christian" is a perfect picture of Pamela herself. "PRUDENTIA is YOU!" Miss Goodwin cries; "It *can* be nobody else! – O teach me, good GOD! to follow *your* Example, and I shall be a SECOND PRUDENTIA – Indeed I shall!" (4: 468). "God send you may, my beloved Miss," is Pamela's complacent answer. The model storyteller and surrogate mother has by virtue of her maternal excellence become the center of her own tale, usurping Miss Goodwin's position as implied protagonist and even, in Miss Goodwin's excited syntax, the place of God. As the story shifts imperceptibly from a fable of virtuous maidenhood to a fable of exemplary motherhood, Miss Goodwin becomes a model for female readers who are supposed to wish for nothing so much as to be a second Pamela.

Indeed, maidenhood and motherhood are so closely related in Pamela's "*Woman*'s story" as to be indistinguishable. Maidenly virtue depends on the maintenance of a spotless reputation, and that can only be taught by a mother who is herself perfectly discreet. Coquetilla's mother, a negative example, is "very gay, but ... indiscreet"; she "took not due care of her Daughter's Education" (4: 457–58). Not surprisingly, Coquetilla eventually finds her reputation compromised and her life ruined. The conclusion is so apparent that Miss Goodwin can state it without further prompting from Pamela: "Poor Lady *Coquetilla*! ... what a sad thing it is, to have a wrong Education! and how happy am I, who have so good a Lady to supply the Place of a dear distant Mamma!" (4: 458–59). By presenting tales about the preservation of sexual "reputation" as stories about maternal virtue, and by epitomizing both ideals personally, Pamela links the two parts of her own story, the twin predicaments of seduced maiden and abdicating mother. As in Sally Godfrey's case, maternal disqualification again results from a failure of sexual purity, and maternal virtue is determined by a woman's ability to negotiate delicate, even invisible, boundaries between courtship and compromise, reputation and infamy, seduction and rape. In Pamela's nursery stories, the maintenance of female reputation metamorphoses into praise of Pamela's maternal excellence, excellence as unreproducible, and as compromised, as her famous virtue and its problematic rewards.

From this point, what limited "novelistic" features *Pamela*, Part 2 offers diminish noticeably, until for most of the last fifty pages

Pamela merely sits in state holding forth on correct female conduct. When she drinks tea with Miss Cope and the other young ladies of the neighborhood (who actually take notes on what she says), or when she gathers her children around her to tell them nursery tales, Pamela becomes in effect a barely-embodied conduct book, fulfilling rather too literally Allestree's command: "Let it ... be the care of all Mothers to live a perpetual Lecture to their Children" (222).

To the end, however, Pamela's lessons take narrative forms, "a kind of allegorical or metaphorical Style," as Pamela says, "I know not which to call it" (4: 430). Pamela justifies this procedure as having the most influence with her audience of young girls:

My only Fear ... was, that they would deem me too grave; and so what should fall in the Course of Conversation, would make the less Impression upon them. For even the best Instructions in the world, you know, will be ineffectual, if the Method of conveying them is not adapted to the Taste and Temper of the Person you would engage. (4: 425)

Pamela thus reveals the plan of *Pamela*, Part 2, in which a spoonful of narrative helps the medicine of moral instruction go down. As Richardson once told Lady Echlin, "Instruction ... is the Pill; Amusement is the Gilding."[47]

Narrative "gilding" had been employed in conduct writing before Richardson, perhaps most successfully in Defoe's *Family Instructor*. And the tradition would continue after Richardson. Marriott (1759), for example, describes his poem as "of the didactic, or instructive Kind," intended to give "moral, and religious Precepts, and ... practical Rules of Conduct, and Behaviour, to Female Readers" (ix), and to this end, Marriott permits himself "every Art of Persuasion, and Argument, either by Repetition, Amplification, Tale, Fable, Example, or Allegory, and every pleasing Manner of conveying its Precepts, and enforcing its Doctrine" (ix–x). Haywood's narrative method in the *Female Spectator* provides another example of didacticism made palatable by novelistic "gilding."

Moreover, "gilding" is defined throughout Augustan writing as a strategy of virtuous and effective mothers; the notion links the virtuous mother and the morally upright novelist. In a concluding

---

47   September 1755 (Mullan, *Sentiment and Sociability*, 57). Cf. Richardson's "Preface" to the first edition of *Clarissa*: "in all works of this ... kind, *story or amusement* should be considered as little more than the vehicle to the more necessary *instruction*" (36). Or as he put it in the third edition's "Preface," "It will probably be thought tedious to all such as ... look upon Story in it (interesting as that is generally allowed to be) as its *sole end*, rather than as a vehicle to the Instruction" (1: ix).

defense of the *Female Spectator* against the charge that "since the Second or Third Book ... I moralize too much" and offer "too few Tales," Haywood compares herself to wise (duplicitous) mothers who "anoint with Sweets" the "foremost Parts" of nasty-tasting medicines for children; the children "drink deceiv'd, and so deceiv'd they live" (4: 24: 362–63). Again as in Richardson's comment to Lady Echlin, mother and writer have salutary purposes that must be disguised for the good of their children/readers. "It was necessary," Haywood says, "to engage the Attention of those I endeavoured to reform, by giving them ... Tales, and little Stories" at first; "I was willing to treat them with the Tenderness of a Mother, but not, like some Mothers, to continue my Indulgence to their Ruin" (4: 24: 362–63).

Pamela, Part 2 is nothing if not a lesson in how mothers might best disguise their efforts to wield power. Yet Pamela's story also demonstrates the perils of duplicity, and renders morally problematic the limited, indirect authority it assigns to virtuous mothers. The paradigmatic domestic mother – tender, chaste, nurturant – is all-important and fully accountable; but she is denied the authority to follow her own conscience or choose her own maternal behaviors, even though power in the nursery supposedly compensates her for exclusion from the public sphere. In *Pamela,* Part 2, maternal virtue becomes synonymous with female restriction, submission, and dis-simulation. Such a lesson may have proved nasty medicine indeed for female readers, a "pill" that required every bit of narrative "gilding" Richardson could provide.

Despite Richardson's best efforts to prevent it, the possibility of resistance remains. Andromache's suicide scheme and the aggressive self-promotion that saturates Pamela's "nursery tales" are among its forms; so is Pamela's ringing insistence, during the breastfeeding crisis, on her own freedom of conscience – insistence that continues to resonate long after it is officially silenced, undercutting Pamela's deference to Mr. B., her castigation of Andromache, and her treatment of Sally Godfrey. Pamela's comparison of "the Prerogative of a Husband" to tyrannical political "Doctrine [that] once cost a Prince his Crown" participates in the best tradition of Augustan feminist polemic (it resonates, for instance, with Astell's famous, defiant question, "if all Men are born free, how is it that all Women are born slaves?" (*Reflections upon Marriage,* 76)).

Still, part of the reason *Pamela* Part 2 has not achieved more authority is that it works against these, its own best moments.

Intolerant of dissonance, Richardson silences or tempers recalcitrant maternal voices; *Pamela*, Part 2 never faces squarely the essentially political nature of the domestic relations it depicts and the maternal behaviors it advocates. That would have to wait for Richardson's next novel. *Clarissa* (1747–48) re-opens the debates over maternal agency and accountability initiated in *Pamela*, Part 2, and recasts as tragic uncertainties *Pamela*'s most insistent conclusions about maternal authority and responsibility.

MATERNAL VIRTUE AND MATERNAL FAILURE IN *CLARISSA*

When Richardson makes Clarissa tell Lovelace that he had robbed her of her honour, he must have had strange notions of honour and virtue. For, miserable beyond all names of misery is the condition of a being, who could be degraded without its own consent! (Mary Wollstonecraft)[48]

Believe that even in my deliberateness I was not deliberate. (Gwendolyn Brooks)[49]

Like Pamela, Charlotte Harlowe is an excellent bourgeois mother according to standards set forth in conduct writing during the first half of the eighteenth century. She does not, it is true, breastfeed her own children; it is as if the breastfeeding debate in *Pamela*, Part 2 may be assumed and the mother has already virtuously capitulated to the will of her husband. But except in this, Mrs. Harlowe is a model middle-class mother. Her relations with her children are characterized by affection and tenderness, she instructs them by "example" (7: 43 [1162]) as conduct books never tired of reminding mothers to do, and she practices the kind of indirect authority conduct writing recommended for mothers: "a sweet art ... of conquering by seeming to yield" (7: 43 [1162]).[50] Hers is, in Clarissa's words, "a gentle and sensible mind, which has from the beginning,

---

48   Wollstonecraft, *A Vindication of the Rights of Woman*, 141.
49   Brooks, "The mother."
50   The phrase echoes conduct-book wisdom, derived most directly from Halifax, *The Lady's New-Year's-Gift*. Cf. Lyttleton, "Advice to a Lady," (1733): women's power resides in knowing how to "twist the secret Chains that bind / With gentle Force the captivated Mind" (8); Marriott, *Female Conduct* (1759): women should employ "Insinuating Streams," "lenient Art," and "soothing Blandishment" to get their way (25); and Haywood (*Female Spectator*): "it is not by force our sex can hope to maintain their influence over the men ... whenever we would truly conquer, we must seem to yield." The axiom was not without detractors. Chudleigh's *Ladies Defence* subjects it to withering scorn: "If you wou'd live as it becomes a Wife," her foolish parson earnestly advises women, "You must the useful Art of wheedling try" (10). Nevertheless, the notion that female/maternal authority must be disguised and indirect persisted throughout the century.

on all occasions, sacrificed its own inward satisfaction to outward peace" (7: 30 [54]).

All these virtues, however, also turn out to be vices in Mrs. Harlowe's case, as apparently straightforward standards for maternal excellence are revealed to be problematic – contradictory, contingent on a multitude of shifting factors, and difficult to verify. Even if it were possible to fulfill all the rules for successful domestic motherhood, Mrs. Harlowe's case suggests, such an achievement does not necessarily indicate female virtue or produce domestic accord.[51] Indeed, as in *Pamela*, it is precisely Mrs. Harlowe's maternal righteousness that forces upon her false choices and ambiguous responsibilities. But for Mrs. Harlowe, unlike Pamela, the contradictions inherent in domestic motherhood are never finessed away; her compromised authority is not permitted to masquerade as power, nor her forced compliance as simple choice. The most telling thing about Charlotte Harlowe's maternal failure, in short, is that although she is precisely the sort of woman to whom the standards set down in conduct literature were supposed to apply, and although she follows the dictates of conduct literature admirably, Mrs. Harlowe's motherhood nevertheless proves inadequate, even pernicious.

From the beginning, *Clarissa* places peculiar responsibility for its heroine's tragedy on her mother. It was Mrs. Harlowe who, in Clarissa's words, "connived at" the early secret correspondence with Lovelace, the foundation of his insinuation into Clarissa's life (2: 94 [434]; Cf. Erickson, *Mother Midnight*, 108). Anna Howe blames Mrs. Harlowe for having "spoiled all the three [Harlowe] brothers" by "her indolent meekness" (1: 175 [131]). When Colonel Morden learns that Clarissa is attended on her deathbed by a friend "who is as careful of her, as if she were her mother," he sneers, "and *more* careful too ... or she is not careful at all!" (7: 409–10 [1350]). Latterday critics concur. In Robert Erickson's words, "Charlotte Harlowe misuses the power she has assumed as a mother" and "fails her extraordinary daughter" (114).

Mrs. Harlowe's peculiar guilt rests largely on her failure to exercise the domestic authority she supposedly enjoys as virtuous mother. We are repeatedly told that Clarissa's mother is the best of the Harlowes, but that she is "kept down" by the brutality of the

---

[51]   Cf. Doody, *Natural Passion*, 103.

men, especially her grasping son James.[52] "Your Mother," Anna writes to Clarissa in the novel's opening letter, "admirably well qualified as she is to lead, must submit to be led" (1: 4 [40]).[53] But at the same time, Mrs. Harlowe's powerlessness is also her own fault, a choice she makes for the sake of preserving what she calls domestic "peace" – a code word for maternal comfort. She opposes the early plan to send Clarissa to Scotland because then she would have to take back the "household cares" that Clarissa has shouldered (1: 34 [56]). When she attempts to coerce Clarissa into marrying Mr. Solmes, Mrs. Harlowe constructs the conversation around her own comfort: "I am glad, my love," she says, "you can guess at what I have to say ... I am spared the pains of breaking [it] to you" (1: 95 [89]). And when Clarissa is overwhelmed with distress at being pressured to encourage Solmes, her mother can only cry, "Good girl, distress *me* not thus!" (1: 146 [116], my emphasis). She complains that all this trouble has begun at just the time "when I hoped most comfort from you all" (1: 103 [92]). "Have I not conjured you," she demands of Clarissa, "as you value my peace – What is it that *I* do not give up?" (1: 100 [91]).

When Clarissa's former wetnurse Mrs. Norton pleads with Mrs. Harlowe to intervene on Clarissa's behalf, Charlotte Harlowe objects that "it might cost me the peace of my whole life, at this time, to move for her" (4: 76 [585]). She remains oblivious to her daughter's urgent needs, and never tires of reminding others of "what I have suffered" (1: 283 [189]). "Think for me, my good Norton," she writes.

Think what my unhappiness must be, both as a Wife and a Mother. What restless days, what sleepless nights; yet my own rankling anguish endeavoured to be smoothed over, to soften the anguish of fiercer spirits, and to keep them from blazing out to further mischief ... I myself deserve every one's pity. (4: 74–6 [585]; 7: 36 [1158])

More than anything – more than cultivating justice or maintaining integrity or even, at the end, saving her daughter's life – Mrs. Harlowe wants to avoid unpleasantness, especially for herself. To the last, she cherishes the fiction that she can preserve an increasingly

---

[52] The phrase occurs in the first edition (403); by the third edition, Mrs. Harlowe is no longer "kept down"; instead, she "has no will of her own" (3: 34).

[53] Cf. Augustan defenses of the maternal Queen Anne. According to James Ralph, Anne was "never blameable, but for being govern'd herself, when alike authoriz'd and qualify'd to govern others" (341). And cf. Manley, *New Atalantis*, 110, quoted above, 88.

compromised domestic "peace" by remaining passive in the midst of the storm and by refusing to exert herself on Clarissa's behalf. "I shall endeavour," she says in what is perhaps her most characteristic line, "to be only an observer" (1: 162 [125]).

So no matter how sympathetically we may at times view Mrs. Harlowe, it is impossible completely to excuse her dishonesty, cowardice, and selfishness. But then again, the futility of any efforts she might have made are clear; as Sarah Fielding's Miss Gibson puts it in *Remarks on Clarissa* (1749), "Mrs. *Harlowe* might indeed have suffered with *Clarissa*, but could not have preserved her" (9). Mrs. Harlowe herself expresses the paradoxes of her situation at Clarissa's funeral, when she feels guilt for *not* doing what she was *prevented from* doing: "Oh ... my child!" she cries, "... Why was I not permitted to speak pardon and peace to thee! – Oh forgive thy cruel mother!" (8: 71–2 [1398]). As her language suggests – "I was not permitted ... oh forgive me" – Mrs. Harlowe's maternal agency is a complex tangle of coercions and complicities, not a matter of single, autonomous responsibility, although she construes herself as peculiarly accountable. "What a torment is it to have a will without a power!" she cries (4: 76 [586]). At once subject and object of a domestic tyranny that she perpetuates by her passivity and silence, Mrs. Harlowe demonstrates the impotence of affective sensibility divorced from practical action and the fictitious status of her apolitical maternal self-definition.

Abdication, usurpation, and maternal tyranny

"I had rather all the world should be angry with me than my Mamma!" (Clarissa to Anna Howe)[54]

"What honour is lost, where the *will* is not violated, and the person cannot help it?" (Lovelace to Belford)[55]

Despite Mrs. Harlowe's "indolent passivity," however, Clarissa, Anna Howe, Belford, Aunt Hervey, Lovelace, Mrs. Norton and others all join in pitying Clarissa's mother. "I am equally shocked, and enraged against them all," Anna Howe writes to Clarissa; "Yet would I fain methinks make an exception for your mother" (4: 78 [587]). Anna speaks for all the characters' obsessive (though always frustrated and qualified) need to distinguish Mrs. Harlowe (from)

---

[54] *Clarissa*, 1: 141 (113).   [55] Ibid., 8: 145 (1438).

among the guilty, to believe that the mother remains outside the politicized complexities that make the other members of the family responsible for Clarissa's suffering and death. Clarissa's Aunt Hervey insists that Mrs. Harlowe "is obliged to act a part entirely contrary to her inclinations" (7: 223 [1259]). And shortly after Clarissa's death, Belford admits that he would like to see how the news affects the guilty Harlowes; "Yet," he adds, "who but must pity the unhappy mother?" (8: 38 [1380]). Mrs. Norton too finds Mrs. Harlowe's complaints convincing: "her poor mother is to be pitied," she confides to Anna Howe (4: 70 [582]).

But Miss Howe complicates such feelings in her response to Mrs. Norton:

You pity her mother! – so don't *I*! – I pity no mother that puts it out of her power to show maternal love, and humanity, in order to patch up for herself a precarious and sorry quiet, which every blast of wind shall disturb! I hate tyrants in every form and shape. But paternal and maternal tyrants are the worst of all: For they can have no bowels. (4: 71 [583])

Anna Howe defines parental tyranny paradoxically, not as the arrogation of authority, but as its relinquishment. Clarissa's parents do not merely indulge in "the undue exercise of their natural authority," as Richardson's "Preface" suggests (1: viii [36]). They also fail, paradoxically, to exert their authority *strongly enough*. Clarissa's mother is unpitiable, in Anna's estimation, because she "puts it out of her own power to show maternal love" – she exercises power in the service of her own impotence. Throughout *Clarissa*, Mrs. Harlowe's peculiar form of tyranny is defined as "passiveness" (1: 82 [82]; 2: 12 [211]), a failure to grasp authority that puts authority out of her reach. "Had she been of a temper that would have borne less," Clarissa perceives, "she would have had ten times less to bear" (1: 30 [54]). Yet at the same time, Mrs. Harlowe *is* "obliged" to behave as she does, having little autonomous choice over her own behavior. By abdicating an authority which is also denied her, Mrs. Harlowe acts a complex part, the part of maternal tyrant.

Indeed, *Clarissa* may be read as a book about tyranny as Anna Howe defines it – the abdication of authority, the abandonment of rightful prerogative to usurpers, and the very difficult position into which this puts those with subject status and the duty of obedience.[56] Clarissa understands her own position to be that of a domestic

---

[56]   Cf. Beasley, "Politics," 219; Kay, *Political Constructions*, 166.

subject who owes obedience to her parents based on a natural, unquestionable code of authority and deference. But her parents are only too willing to relinquish their legitimate authority. Their abdication throws into chaos the hitherto reliable system of family governance on which Clarissa depends, and leaves a vacancy that is eagerly filled by a succession of claimants – brother James, sister Arabella, Solmes, and finally Lovelace.

Clarissa struggles against the new state of affairs. She begs to receive commands originating from her parents and not from usurpers.[57] "Let me beseech you, my dear and ever-honoured papa ... that I may have only your's [sic] and my mamma's will, and not my brother's, to obey ... Transfer not, I beseech you, to a brother and sister your own authority over your child" (1: 50 [65]; 2: 33 [221–222]). She defies James's presumption: "If you govern every-body else, you shall not govern me" (2: 194 [306]).[58] And she laments her mother's failures to exert maternal authority. "Would she but exert that authority," Clarissa cries early on, "... all these family-feuds might perhaps be extinguished in their but yet beginnings" (1: 30 [54]). Parental abdication makes Clarissa a kind of moral refugee, searching for the restoration of that human authority ordained for her obedience. The search intensifies as the novel progresses: Clarissa turns to aunts and uncles, to her "mamma" Norton, and even, at the end, to kind strangers, looking for the lost parental relation. She asks Mrs. Lovick to hold her in her illness "saying, She had been a Mother to her, and she would delight herself in thinking she was in her Mamma's arms" (*Clarissa*, 7: 412 [1351]). As Belford observes after the rape,

Never having been, till very lately, from under her parents wings, and now abandoned by all her friends, she is for finding out something *paternal* and *maternal* in everyone ... to supply to herself the father and mother her dutiful heart pants after! (6: 306 [1082])[59]

The heroine's poignant search for legitimate authority figures is not simply a personal quest in *Clarissa*; it is also a representation, from a particular Tory point of view, of the predicament of Augustan Britain, a nation orphaned by the abdication (or, for some, the

---

[57] *Clarissa*, 1: 31 [54]; 1: 265 [179].

[58] James's domestic usurpation has become a critical commonplace. Cf. for example Todd, *Women's Friendship*, 15. Todd follows critical tradition in seeing James, Jr.'s usurpation as merely economic.

[59] Cf. Erickson, *Mother Midnight*, 171.

usurpation) of its rightful king in 1688 and struggling ever since to locate legitimate authority. Lest we fail to observe the relation between the domestic abdications and usurpations of the Harlowe family and those of public politics, Clarissa herself makes the connection clear: "Shall we wonder," she says,

> that Kings and Princes meet with so little controul in their passions, be they ever so violent, when in a private family, an Aunt, nay, even a Mother in that family, shall chuse to give up a once favoured child against their own inclinations, rather than oppose an aspiring young man, who had armed himself with the authority of a father? (7: 226 [1260])

Lovelace too, with his usual acuity, instantly recognizes the political stakes implicit in the situation.

> Whose property, I pray thee, shall I invade, if I pursue my schemes of love and vengeance? Have not those who have a right in her, renounced that right? ... Shocking as these principles must be to a reflecting mind, yet such thou knowest are the principles of thousands ... and as often carried into practice, as their opportunities or courage will permit – Such therefore have no right to blame *me*. (4: 355 [717])

Lovelace's arrogant pronouncement combines with the political language that consistently informs discussions of domestic relations in *Clarissa* ("tyranny," "abdication," "prerogative," "usurper," "cabal," "phalanx," "peace and union") and the more prominent works of literature used to motivate or comment on the novel's action (Dryden's poetry, *Venice Preserved, A Tale of a Tub*) to suggest that what is at stake in Clarissa's struggle against domestic usurpers is not only the purity and protection of the heroine's individual female body, but also the purity of conscience and moral justification of the Augustan body politic.[60]

The problematic situation of the governed when rulers abdicate would have been peculiarly resonant for Richardson's readers, who struggled to construct and maintain political allegiances at a time when the very idea of legitimate authority was undergoing radical revision. And as Margaret Doody has shown, Richardson was among those who felt nostalgia for lost monarchical ideals and discomfort with Whiggish principles.[61] So when *Clarissa* defines tyranny as the withdrawal of rightful authority, and oppression as the torment experienced by the dutiful subject who cannot recognize the person to whom her allegiance belongs, it rephrases the most troubling

---

[60]   Cf. Keymer, *Richardson's Clarissa*, 116–120.
[61]   Doody, "Richardson's Politics," 119–26.

political questions of its day.[62] In the figure of Mrs. Harlowe, Richardson reformulates the dilemmas of a generation of loyalists struggling to make sense of their unprecedented position as subjects of an absent king.

The connections *Clarissa* draws between domestic tyranny in the Harlowe home and the tyrannical abdications of Augustan monarchs are not merely metaphorical. On the contrary, the novel's language and thematic preoccupations – especially its portrayal of Charlotte Harlowe's passive political agency – offered eighteenth-century readers a particular, partisan interpretation of recent political events. *Clarissa* actively enters Augustan controversy over the location of legitimate authority (controversy that had boiled over as recently as 1745 in the battle of Culloden); the novel is an *agent in* public debate, not a *deflection from* it. By using a fictional, domestic power struggle to influence readers' attitudes toward public politics, *Clarissa* deftly undermines the notion that there are two unconnected sites of interaction, public and private. And by representing a mother who by her very abjection helps to perpetuate tyranny, *Clarissa* exposes the fiction that affective maternal sentiment has significance apart from practical, discursive empowerment.

The contradictions and vulnerabilities that define Mrs. Harlowe's avowedly apolitical position as domestic mother are manifested particularly in the duplicity that enables her maternal authority. Mrs. Harlowe's speech, indeed her whole persona, are characterized by indirect manipulative strategies that Clarissa, in an idealistic reminiscence late in the story, defines for Anna Howe as the essence of virtuous maternal power.

Here was my MOTHER, one of the most prudent persons of her Sex, married into a family, not perhaps so happily tempered as herself; but every one of which she had the address, for a great while, absolutely to govern as she pleased by her directing wisdom, at the same time that they knew not but her prescriptions were the dictates of their own hearts; such a sweet art had she of conquering by seeming to yield. Think, my dear, what must be the pride and the pleasure of such a mother ... With what a noble confidence could she look upon her dear Mr. Harlowe, as a person made happy by her; and be delighted to think, that nothing but purity streamed from a fountain so pure! (7: 43 [1162])

---

[62] Kay makes a similar observation about *Pamela*: noting that Pamela's "most important trait" is dutifulness, Kay reads Part 1 as an examination of the difficulty of doing one's duty "if rules are unclear" (*Political Constructions*, 141).

But despite Clarissa's positive gloss, the strategic indirection she attributes to her mother has its dark side. Mary Wollstonecraft's astute attack on "the winning softness so warmly, and frequently, recommended, that governs by obeying" might be read as a comment on Clarissa's tribute to her mother: "How insignificant," Wollstonecraft cries, "is the being ... who will condescend to govern by such sinister methods!" (*Vindication*, 89). Indeed, it is often hard to distinguish the covert power plays that characterize Mrs. Harlowe's supposedly irreproachable maternal behavior – even in Clarissa's admiring description – from the "dissembling" advocated by Halifax and less ingenuously denounced in later conduct writing. *The Ladies Library*'s description of "crafty" persons who "can never avoid those very Inconveniences which they labour to shun" (2: 173) suggests only too strongly Clarissa's acute estimate of her mother's failed strategies: "she has too often forfeited that peace of mind which she so much prefers, by her over-concern to preserve it" (7: 113 [1200]).

Despite her fulsome praise of maternal duplicity as "purity," Clarissa had long before recognized that the indirect tactics her mother habitually uses to consolidate her own authority are disguised manifestations of cowardice and even cruelty. Consider for example Clarissa's transcription of a particularly painful early interview with her mother. Mrs. Harlowe has insisted that Clarissa marry "the odious Solmes," and Clarissa is so upset that she cannot speak. Mrs. Harlowe deviously pretends to mistake her daughter's silence for assent:

I see, my dear, said she, that you are convinced. Now, my good child, now, my Clary, do I love you! It shall not be known, that you have argued with me at all ... All your scruples, you see, have met with an indulgence truly maternal from me ... I advise as a friend, you see, rather than command as a mother – So adieu, my love. And again she kissed me, and was going. (1: 110 [96])

"Oh my dear mamma," Clarissa cries, "forgive me! – But surely you cannot believe, I can ever think of having that man!" (1: 110–11 [97]). In exposing her mother's duplicitous practices, Clarissa forces her to reveal the complicity between her apparent tenderness and the men's brutal force: "She was very angry ... She threatened to turn me over to my Father and my uncles" (1: 111 [97]). Clarissa remarks on the incident in a letter to Anna:

Did not this seem to border upon *cruelty*, my dear, in so indulgent a Mother? – It would be wicked (would it not!) to suppose my Mother capable of *art* – But she is put upon it; and obliged to take methods to which her heart is naturally above stooping; and all intended for my good. (1: 110 [97])

It is crucial to recognize that the excuses Clarissa provides for her mother are, in fact, legitimate: Mrs. Harlowe *is* "put upon it," and she *does* want the best for Clarissa. Yet at the same time, she *could* act more effectively. In Mrs. Harlowe's maternity, good intentions and true tenderness exist alongside – indeed, as part of – self-interest and deceit. Where she is not actively complicit in Clarissa's oppression, she is culpably passive. Mrs. Harlowe is both innocent and guilty, both victim and perpetrator of her own failed authority.

Thus *Clarissa* goes far beyond the simplistic maternal politics of *Pamela*, Part 2, complicating and interrogating the duplicitous and manipulative tactics which *Pamela* so blithely held up as models of virtuous and potent maternal authority. In *Clarissa*, Richardson undermines distinctions between the "sweet art . . . of conquering by seeming to yield" and "Craft," between the apolitical sphere of the home and the political "world outside." *Clarissa* refuses to reduce or mystify the political nature of private affairs and their participation in the very issues that obsessed Augustan public politics: overdetermined choice, contested authority, and ambiguous agency.

Perhaps the largest question raised by Mrs. Harlowe's experience is whether, apart from a wholesale revision of domestic relations and the social relations in which they participate, there can be a maternal authority *not* dependent on the coercions and frauds Mrs. Harlowe exemplifies, a maternal resistance not neutralized in its very formation. This question, finally, is not just about maternal authority, but about all authority – about whether legitimacy and integrity can survive in any relation of power and subordination. In his representation of Mrs. Harlowe, Richardson represents not only the compromised authority of the virtuous domestic mother, but also the complicities and contingencies of authority itself and the complex problems inherent in any attempt definitively to assign responsibility for its failure.[63]

The problem of assigning accountability for maternal failure in *Clarissa* was a troubling one for contemporary readers. In *Remarks on Clarissa* (1749), for instance, Sarah Fielding's fictional group of amateur critics discusses Mrs. Harlowe's responsibility for Clarissa's

---

[63] Cf. Kay, *Political Constructions*, 167–69.

tragedy. "Totally to justify Mrs. *Harlowe* was not attempted; on the contrary, it was unanimously agreed, that she was to blame" (9). But at the same time, all agree that Mrs. Harlowe is "the least guilty" of the Harlowe family (44). The most astute of Fielding's readers, Miss Gibson, sums up the paradox:

To preserve any Charity in censuring her, I think it should be considered, how much a Woman must be embarrassed, who has for many Years accustomed herself to obey the very Looks of another, where a Point is preemptorily insisted on, which, to comply with, must gall her to the Heart ... And perhaps she flatter'd herself, that she might gain more Influence by seeming to comply, than if she had attempted absolutely to resist the Storm gathering in her Family. And this I think, the many Hints she gives, that if she was left to herself, it would be otherwise, is a full Proof of. (9)

Mrs. Harlowe's motives are pure, in other words, despite her reprehensible (in)actions, and her good intentions matter more than what she actually does. The problem is not how she acted, but that she was not "left to herself."

In this evaluation of Mrs. Harlowe's maternal virtue, Fielding's characters rehearse a central fantasy that occupies Clarissa in regard to her mother: that if the mother were a free agent, things would be essentially different. "Oh, Mr. Lovelace," Clarissa declares, "you know not, sir, half the excellencies of my dear mamma! and what a kind heart she has, when it is left to follow its own impulses" (4: 311 [695]). Clarissa's poignant words, like Miss Gibson's extenuation of Mrs. Harlowe's guilt, depend on the cherished ideal of a domestic mother whose purely affective relationship with her children could conceivably inhabit a space free from the coercions and complicities of material circumstances and hierarchical social relationships. But as *Clarissa* so painfully demonstrates, Mrs. Harlowe has no maternal existence outside the relations of dominance and subordination that define family life at Harlowe Place, and no hope of exoneration from their results. Lovelace puts it with magnanimous deflation: "her mother had been faultless, had she not been her father's wife" (1: 210 [145]).

Fielding's critics attempt to address the question of maternal agency with finality, but find themselves unable to do so. Significantly, at this difficult juncture Miss Gibson broadens the question of accountability for maternal failure to include not only Mrs. Harlowe, but also Richardson himself. "Miss *Gibson* desired Mrs. *Harlow's* Faults might not be thrown on the Author, unless it could be proved that he himself intended her Conduct should deserve no Censure" (9). The author's *intention*, like the fictional mother's, becomes the most important criterion for determining whether he is responsible for the dissonance we hear in *Clarissa* as a supposedly powerful and loving mother takes a passive part in the destruction of her child.

But the strategy runs the same risk for the author that it did for the mother. Adapting Miss Gibson's evaluation of Mrs. Harlowe, one might suggest that an author who uses his innocent intentions for self-exoneration merely "flatters himself" that the devious, indirect methods of fiction can have positive moral influence while protecting authorial innocence. It is impossible finally to determine what action Mrs. Harlowe might have taken if "left to herself," or to imagine virtuous maternal authority outside the codes, compromises, evasions, and duplicities of a particular political and material situation. Likewise, the novelist's intention, however pure, is necessarily complicated and subverted by its imbeddedness in destabilizing particularities that compromise firm moral positions – in this case, the instability of the epistolary method and the impossibility of controlling readers' interpretations.

In this light, *Clarissa*'s insistence that the virtuous mother inhabits an exceptional position outside (domestic) politics becomes not simply mistaken but actively pernicious: by denying maternal complicity, and by insistently defining maternal difference as moral exemption, the text discourages readers from identifying authentic resistance in Mrs. Harlowe's behaviors. As long as her words and actions are construed as outside political struggle, her unknowable "intention" more important than her visible behaviors, Mrs. Harlowe can be falsely relieved of political agency. And in her image, motherhood can be denied status as a corporate social function participating effectively in public structures and processes, and reduced to the merely personal behaviors of isolated individual women.

Innocent guilts: seduction, rape, and maternal responsibility

Say not all the blame and all the punishment is yours. I am as much blamed and as much punished as you are; yet am more innocent. (Charlotte Harlowe to Clarissa)[64]

---

[64]   *Clarissa*, 1: 160 (124).

The third book of Henry Fielding's *Joseph Andrews* (1742) includes an often-overlooked interpolated tale in which a vain young woman, Leonora, casts off a faithful lover of many years in favor of a fop who in turn deserts her when he learns that she has no dowry. The trite story is narrated by an anonymous woman who insists on complicating its obvious interpretation (i.e., the woman is to blame for her own unhappiness). Fielding's narrator reminds her listeners that Leonora was very young and had been taught virtually nothing; furthermore, she deserted her fiancée at the urging of a trusted aunt (the maternal figure in the story) and with the approval of her careless, absent father. Under these circumstances, the assignment of responsibility for her misery becomes more difficult. Leonora is "unfortunate" the narrator says, only "if one can justly call a Woman unfortunate, whom we must own at the same time guilty and the Author of her own Calamity" (102).

Fielding's tale – predictable, yet disturbing – has surprising pertinence for Richardson's representation of maternal failure in *Clarissa*. For the complicating question posed by Fielding's narrator – the question of agency – is the same question *Clarissa* raises about Charlotte Harlowe's maternal failure, a failure that, as we have seen, constitutes at once both an active transgression and a passive victimization. Furthermore, Leonora's story also illuminates Clarissa's: in both, the victims of seduction are also agents of their own ruin, but even as agents they are always victims. Both are seduced, but both are also, in a sense, raped. Leonora's and Clarissa's stories overlap with Mrs. Harlowe's on the critical site of agency.

Narratives of seduction, rape, and maternal failure are obsessive and closely connected in Augustan discourse. And in all three, the operative questions are the same. Who is responsible? Who is innocent, and who is guilty? What might constitute innocence or guilt when victims help to create the circumstances of their own victimization? May we "justly call a woman unfortunate whom we must own at the same time guilty and the author of her own calamity?" Fielding's question is *Clarissa*'s question, both the question Clarissa cannot answer about her own experience and the question elaborated in Charlotte Harlowe's maternal failure. Furthermore, the question epitomizes one of the most troubling political problems that confronted Richardson's (and Fielding's) contemporaries. In the experiences of Clarissa and her mother, an apparently private loss of explicitly female authority and autonomy makes necessary – and reveals as impossible – a central effort of the generations that followed the Glorious Revolution: the effort to assign responsibility for the failure of political authority, to label such failure as either abdication or usurpation, and thus to demarcate a position of unsullied innocence.

The difficulty of evaluating Mrs. Harlowe's responsibility for Clarissa's fate is structurally very like the problem we encounter when attempting to locate an agent responsible for Clarissa's errors. In the novel's very first letter, the heroine's status as dominated-but-still-responsible agent is emphasized. "Every eye,... is upon you with the expectation of an example," Anna Howe writes; and she adds, with unconscious irony, "I wish to heaven you were at liberty to pursue your own methods" (1: 4 [40]). Later, Clarissa's parents allow her to visit Anna, but insist that she not see Lovelace there; as Clarissa observes, she cannot forbid visitors to someone else's house, yet if Lovelace visits she will be blamed (1: 37 [58]). Clarissa's impossible position is made apparent again when Anna struggles to excuse her friend for maintaining a secret correspondence with Lovelace. "Who, as things are situated, can blame you?" Anna asks. "You are drawn in by a perverse fate against inclination: But custom ... will reconcile the inconveniency and *make* an inclination" (1: 62 [71]). Only too typically, Mrs. Harlowe, who initially encouraged Clarissa to correspond with Lovelace, later leaves Clarissa to deal alone with what had become a dangerous situation: "I will not be in your secret," she says disingenuously. "I will not know that you did correspond" (1: 161 [124]).

Undoubtedly, the most powerful representations of Clarissa's compromised agency occur in the context of her escape with Lovelace from Harlowe Place. Was Clarissa seduced into compliance at the garden gate, or forcibly and fraudulently abducted? The question obsesses Richardson's correspondents. Writing to Anna Howe shortly after leaving home, Clarissa wishes that she had remained for what she is now convinced would have been the final trial with Solmes:

Would to heaven, that I had stood it ...! Then, if I had afterwards done, what now I have been prevailed upon, or perhaps foolishly frightened to do, I should not have been stung so much by inward reproach as now I am ... God forgive those of my friends who have acted cruelly by me! but their faults *are* their own, and not excuses for mine ... Had I stayed, ... my friends would then have been answerable ..., but now, I have this *one* consolation left me ... that I have cleared *them* of blame, and taken it all upon *myself*! (2: 335–38 [381–82])

Clarissa's belief in her own responsibility increases as hopes for reconciliation and autonomy fade. She regrets "the power my indiscretion has given him over me" (3: 25 [398]). "Oh this artful, this designing Lovelace! – Yet I must repeat, that most ought I to blame myself for meeting him" (3: 256 [508]). She feels she may "be easy" as to her own innocence, "excepting the fatal, tho' involuntary step of *April* 10" (7: 107 [1197]). To the end, Clarissa cannot help returning obsessively to her error, and blaming herself for its results. "My fault," she tells Colonel Morden shortly before her death, "is the foundation of all" (7: 417 [1353]).

Characteristically, Anna Howe interprets the elopement/abduction otherwise, repeatedly attempting to exonerate Clarissa, but never quite succeeding.

I think, your *provocations* and *inducements* considered, you are free from blame: at least, the freest, that ever young creature was who took such a step.
But *you took it* not – You were *driven on one side*, and, possibly *tricked on the other*. – If any on earth shall be circumstanced as you were, and shall hold out so long as you did, against her persecutors on one hand, and her seducer on the other, I will forgive her for all the rest. (3: 38 [405])
...
The penitence you talk of – It is for *them* to be penitent, who hurried you into evils you could not well avoid ... Upon my honour, I think you faultless in almost every step you have taken. (6: 234–35 [1043])

Anna's difficulty absolving Clarissa is as palpable as her desire to do so, and thus to exempt her friend from responsibility for the abduction (or elopement) – to construe the event as a rape rather than as a seduction, and to construe rape and seduction as entirely discrete matters.

Many other characters make some judgment on Clarissa's elopement/abduction, making it perhaps the most internally commented-upon episode in the novel. Lovelace, for instance, joins Anna in the attempt to acquit Clarissa.

The step she so freely blames herself for taking, was truly what she calls *compulsatory*; for tho' she was provoked to *think* of going off with me, she intended it not ... neither would she ever have had the *thought* of it, had her relations left her free ... with me, she has done more honour to the sex in her fall, if it be to be called a fall (in truth it ought not) than ever any other could do in her standing. (6: 56 [1036–37])

And Dr. Lewen voices a similar sentiment: "I will not look back upon the measures which you have either been *led* or *driven* into: but will only say ... that I think you are the least to blame" (7: 208 [1251]). But Clarissa's mother is much more harsh: "Her fault," she says, "was a fault of *premeditation*, of cunning, of contrivance. She has deceived everybody's expectations. Her whole sex, as well as the family she sprung from, is disgraced by it" (4: 74 [585]).

Critics too have concentrated on the problem of agency in the crucial scene at the garden gate. Sarah Fielding's Miss Gibson makes a case for Clarissa's innocence, describing Lovelace's machinations in language that suggests the scene of rape later in the novel:

That *Clarissa* positively did not intend to go off with *Lovelace* when she met him, to me is very plain; nor could he have prevailed on her, had not the Terrors raised in her Mind ... almost robbed her of her Senses, and hurried her away, not knowing what she did ... She was vexed to her soul afterwards to find she was tricked, as she calls it, out of herself ... she did not know all his Design, for if she had, she would certainly have left him. (16–17)

But recently some have argued for a more complex reading. Castle contends that Clarissa is "attracted" by Lovelace's willingness to listen to her speak without interrupting, "the most seductive ... of tactics" (*Clarissa's Ciphers*, 81–83). Eagleton says that Clarissa is tricked, yet calls the event an "elopement"; he criticizes others for reducing the complexities of agency in the scene.[65] In short, when it comes to the all-important matter of agency, the episode at the garden gate has proven much more problematic than the rape, which is carefully constructed to eliminate ambiguity about Clarissa's own volition. When Clarissa opens the garden gate, she compromises her integrity and muddies the waters of accountability. Lovelace realizes this at once: "The moment I heard the door unbolt," he brags to Belford, "I was sure of her" (3: 27 [399]). Despite extenuating circumstances that almost – but don't quite – exonerate her, Clarissa's complicity at this moment will haunt her to the end. Her ruminations on this fatal episode, more than any other, bring her slowly to recognize what Eagleton calls "the most demoralizing double bind of all: the truth that it is not so easy to distinguish resistance to power from collusion with it" (82). Or as Richardson

---

65 Eagleton, *Rape of Clarissa*, 64–67. Eagleton attacks Van Ghent, *The English Novel*, Watt, *The Rise of the Novel*, and Warner, *Reading Clarissa*. Cf. Scheuermann, *Her Bread to Earn*, 60. Eaves and Kimpel say that *meeting* Lovelace was Clarissa's "only voluntary fault"; Richardson "obviously did not want anyone to think that she was at fault in the elopement" (*Samuel Richardson*, 211).

himself put it in a pamphlet designed to clarify his intentions, Clarissa is "not drawn absolutely perfect"; she has "something to blame herself for, tho' not in Intention."[66]

At one point Clarissa asks Anna to share some of her resistant "spirit," but Anna demurs: "It will not sit naturally upon you. You are your Mother's girl, think what you will" (1: 54 [67]). Anna is right – Clarissa and her mother have only too much in common when it comes to the possibility of effective resistance. Like Clarissa, Mrs. Harlowe has "something to blame herself for, tho' not in Intention"; in her case as in her daughter's, agency and responsibility are finally indeterminable. Anna could be addressing Mrs. Harlowe when she tells Clarissa, "you will have more of it, and more still, as you bear it" (1: 170 [129]). Furthermore, Mrs. Harlowe also shares with Clarissa the experience of violation at the hands of men. Mrs. Harlowe's situation at home is one of forced and unwilling compliance, of "struggling ... against the attempts" of her "ungovernable" and "violent" son and brothers (1: 284 [189], 1200), and against the abdicating despotism of her husband (who, though notably absent and passive, nevertheless is habitually described by Richardson and his contemporaries as a "tyrant"[67]). Mr. Harlowe threatens her directly, "as she valued her own peace," to join in pressuring Clarissa to marry Solmes (1: 135 [110]); he forces her to permit, even to seem to countenance, behaviors to which she does not consent (7: 223 [1259]). Mrs. Harlowe's language, like Clarissa's, eventually degenerates into what Sarah Fielding's critic Bellario calls "broken half-utter'd Sentences ... Pictures of the broken timorous Spirit of Meekness tyrannised over" (38).

Yet, as we have seen, it is hard to feel unequivocally sorry for Mrs. Harlowe, whose meekness is not only "tyrannized over," but also tyrannizing. Like an Augustan subject falling back on the doctrine of passive obedience, or like the "nonprotective" mother of a sexually abused child, who by doing nothing effectively collaborates in her child's abuse, Mrs. Harlowe is culpably unresistant.[68] Her tragedy,

[66] Eaves and Kimpel, "An unpublished pamphlet," 402.
[67] Commentators frequently remark on the cipher-like status of Mr. Harlowe (e.g., Eaves and Kimpel, *Samuel Richardson*, 251), yet the term most often used to describe him, in the eighteenth century and even now, is "tyrant" (5: 230 [852]; S. Fielding, *Remarks*, 38. Cf. Braudy, "Penetration," 268; Dussinger, *Discourse of Mind*, 83–4; Scheuermann, *Her Bread to Earn*, 81). The apparent paradox is important, as we shall see shortly.
[68] Cf. McCormick, *Mothers*, 7. I borrow the language of Jacobs's perceptive and pertinent study of the mothers of incest victims. Though Clarissa never suffers incest (except perhaps symbolically), she is certainly abused; and all the characters in *Clarissa*, including the

like Clarissa's, involves both the compromised agency of the seduced maiden and the unwilling violation of the victim of rape. Her failure to exert maternal authority – like Clarissa's exit at the garden gate – is simultaneously active and passive, a violent, even brutal, divestment in which the victim is at crucial steps complicit. And the duplicitous failures of both mother and daughter repeat the pattern of what to Richardson was perhaps his nations's greatest tragedy – the strangely active-and-passive flight of King James II in 1688, a flight that had been famously represented by Delarivier Manley as that of an "excessively grieved" mother, "irresolute" and "ruined," who recognizes too late that she is at once the victim of "treachery" and the perpetrator of "injustice."[69] Both unlucky and unwise, at once the agent of his own ruin and a helpless victim besieged by enemies, James haunts *Clarissa* much as his memory continued throughout the 1740s to haunt English consciences. Behind *Clarissa*'s most powerful representations of lost authority and ambiguous agency stands the unforgettable figure of the fallen king, the paradigmatic guilty victim.

May we "justly call a woman unfortunate whom we must own at the same time guilty and the author of her own calamity?" In Mrs. Harlowe's experience, as in Clarissa's, apparently distinct categories – seduction and rape, abdication and usurpation, agency and passivity – resist differentiation; they shift and merge unpredictably, disquietingly. The complex, multiple, and oblique agencies responsible for Mrs. Harlowe's failure (not least her own) reposition and represent the questions about female autonomy and responsibility raised by her daughter's experience and expose the myth of monolithic agency, whether for mothers, maidens, or kings.

Other mothers in Clarissa

As critics have often observed, Mrs. Harlowe is not the only mother in *Clarissa*.[70] In fact, nearly all the adults in the novel are, in some sense, Clarissa's parents, and one of the heroine's main problems is that she has altogether too many parental figures to answer to. "Our Uncles consider us as their own children," Clarissa brags early on to

heroine, share with the daughters in Jacobs's study a contradictory need to separate the mother from male abuse while holding her responsible for it.
69 *New Atalantis*, 202–03.
70 E.g., Erickson, *Mother Midnight*, 171; Scheuermann, *Her Bread to Earn*, 80.

Anna "... they are advised with upon every article relating to us, or that may affect us" (1: 35 [56]; cf. 6: 306 [1082]). In particular, Mrs. Howe, Mrs. Sinclair, and Mrs. Norton serve as surrogate mothers for the heroine and as alternate versions of maternal possibility in the novel. Remarkably, each of these "other mothers" exists outside the conjugal bond. If, as we saw in *Pamela*, heterosexual marriage enforces female submission and so permits the reduction of complex questions of maternal agency to simple matters of wifely obedience, then the singleness of these mothers seems to promise greater maternal autonomy than Mrs. Harlowe could possibly enjoy. (As Clarissa puts it, "Would any-body, my dear Miss Howe, wish to marry, who sees a wife of such a temper, and blessed with such an understanding as my Mother is noted for ... deprived of all power?" [1: 101 (92)].) But the suggestion that the maternal authority denied to Augustan wives might be available to unmarried mothers is one that Richardson's text works hard to contain.

The widowed Mrs. Howe, for instance, an expert on economic questions and matters of inheritance, is sole parent to her daughter Anna and, as she tells Clarissa's Uncle Antony, enjoys having "nobody to control me" (4: 172 [631]).[71] Nevertheless, her maternal potency is increasingly defined as only another kind of weakness, and her parenting becomes largely ineffectual and unsatisfying. "I have not your consent to marry?" she asks Anna, directly (if ironically) reversing the tyrannical exercise of parental authority over children in *Clarissa*'s main plot (4: 168 [630]). Exasperated at Anna's continued correspondence with Clarissa despite frequent prohibitions, Mrs. Howe at last, with supreme unconscious irony, appeals for help to Clarissa herself:

Pray, miss, don't make my Nancy guilty of your fault; which is that of disobedience. I have charged her over and over not to correspond with one who has made such a giddy step. It is not to her reputation, I am sure. (6: 108 [975])

Mrs. Howe is dissatisfied with the small authority she enjoys over her daughter ("Not that I stand in fear of my daughter neither: it is not fit I should" [4: 171 (631)]) but, not unlike Mrs. Harlowe, she finds it

---

[71] Widows were traditionally powerful figures in English society. Mendelson finds in the records of widows with children a "matriarchal model" ("Stuart women's diaries," 199). The power and freedom conferred by widowhood tended to be class-specific, however. As Mendelson shows, aristocratic dowagers enjoyed the most authority, and widows from the minor gentry could expect financial independence, but most widows were economically dependent.

impossible to exert herself more effectively. Her very resoluteness as a mother, ironically, undercuts her ability to deal with Anna, who complains that Mrs. Howe "is grown so much into *mother*, that she has forgotten she ever was a *daughter*" (2: 76 [245]).

So despite the appearance of autonomy afforded by her status as independent widow, Mrs. Howe's authority to order her own life (even, toward the end, to dispose of her own assets) is offset and finally neutralized by her inability to control Anna and by the degree to which her motherhood is increasingly manipulated by others. Eventually she is reduced to a tool of the Harlowe men, one of whom actually makes her rejection of Anna the condition of matrimonial alliance. Fortunately, the ultimatum presents few difficulties for Mrs. Howe: "one would not chuse, you know, Sir," she tells Clarissa's Uncle Antony, "to enter into any affair, that, one knows, one must renounce a Daughter for, or she a Mother – Except indeed one's heart were *much* in it; which, I bless God, mine is not" (4: 172 [631]). But as cheering as it is to hear Mrs. Howe thus dispose of Antony's pretensions, this moment of resistance does little to mitigate the truth of Anna's observation that the Harlowe men "only have borrowed my Mother's lips ... for a sort of speaking-trumpet for them" (3: 90 [432]).

Mrs. Howe's experience dramatizes the special questions raised by Augustan conduct literature about the authority of widows over their children. A widow had to "supply the Place of both *Parents* ... she should put on the Affections of both, and to the Tenderness of a Mother, add the Care and Conduct of a *Father*" ([Steele,] *Ladies Library*, 2: 349[72]). But any version of matriarchal authority that might have seriously rivaled or revised male dominance was consistently resisted. *The Ladies Library* reluctantly acknowledges the necessary authority of the widow-mother, but moves immediately to mitigate that authority by arguing that the obedience owed by children to their widowed mothers is uniquely contingent:

When the *Mother* is the only *Parent*, then her Authority increases, and she is then solely to be regarded. Indeed the Civil *Laws* do generally free the *Sons* at such an Age, supposing them the Masters of the Family, and by the Advantage of their *Sex* and *Education*, fit to govern and dispose of themselves and their Affairs. The Daughters, 'tis true, are kept longer in Subjection ... There cannot be any exact Rules in such Cases; For the Wisdom of either *Parent* or *Children* must necessarily make some alteration in the measure of *Obedience*. (*Ladies Library*, 2: 34–35)

[72] Cf. John Hill, *Management*, 10–17.

Mrs. Howe's potentially empowering difference as a widowed mother – independence from the "control" of a husband – brings with it, as if necessarily, a mitigation rather than an expansion of her parental authority. As a woman alone, *Clarissa* makes clear, Mrs. Howe is unable to raise her child adequately. She is represented as unequal to the task of motherhood precisely because she is *not* limited by the greater authority of the father.

"Mother" Sinclair's maternal difference is unequivocally for the bad, her independence a transparent sham. The brothel she presides over is the site of constant degradation of women by men, and she herself is not immune. True, Lovelace is Sinclair's instrument, as he gradually comes to recognize; but she is also his tool. Sinclair does not want Clarissa around – she and her girls repeatedly complain that Clarissa's presence is bad for business – but they are powerless against Lovelace. The business exists at all only because Sinclair, though as well-born as Mrs. Harlowe, was once seduced and "ruined" herself. An unmarried "mother," a manlike whore, Sinclair is a kind of monster or beast, a much more violent and threatening version of *Pamela*'s Mrs. Jewkes, but equally the tyrannized instrument of a cruel and powerful man.[73]

Of the three unattached mothers, Clarissa's "Mamma Norton" is the freest and her moral authority least undermined. Indeed, Richardson's portrayal of the wetnurse as surrogate mother is so positive as to make it virtually unique in Augustan writing. Norton's maternal tenderness for Clarissa stands throughout the novel as potentially the most healing relationship available to the beleaguered heroine, second only to Clarissa's relationship with Anna Howe. Clarissa calls her "my dear mamma Norton" (7: 115 [1200]), and Norton refers repeatedly to her "maternal" affection for Clarissa. At Clarissa's funeral, Mrs. Harlowe "told Mrs. Norton, that the two mothers of the sweetest child in the world ought not, on this occasion, to be separated" (8: 86 [1407]). "Yours, . . . was this child," Mrs. Harlowe says to Mrs. Norton another time, "and your glory as well as mine" (4: 72 [584]).

Richardson even turns on its head the popular notion that a child imbibes its nurse's character (and sometimes her physical characteristics) with her milk.[74] Augustan conduct books frequently used this idea as a threat to pressure mothers to breastfeed. But Richardson

---

[73]   Cf. Erickson and Castle (*Ciphers*) for detailed discussions of Sinclair as an evil anti-mother.

[74]   This myth had a long history: it appears regularly in the sixteenth and seventeenth

employs it quite otherwise, to validate Mrs. Norton's role. As Mrs. Harlowe tells Mrs. Norton, "Many of [Clarissa's] excellencies were owing to yourself; and with the milk you gave her, you gave her what no other nurse in the world could give her" (1: 74 [584]). Clarissa is so extraordinary, Richardson makes clear, because she has benefited from the influence of *two* mothers – her biological mother and her nurse.

Nevertheless, Mrs. Norton too is prevented, despite her fervent desire, from practicing effective maternal care. Her own motherhood gets in the way when she is unable to go to London and care for the dying Clarissa because of a son's serious illness. So do the limitations associated with her social position: as economic inferior and outsider to the family, she fears the Harlowes and is obligated to obey them. For their part, the Harlowes exploit both their power over Norton and Norton's influence with Clarissa, knowing that Clarissa feels "filial regard" for her old nurse (1: 260 [177]). They command Norton to visit Clarissa, then they command her to stay away; always, she submits. In "Mother Norton," the parallel limitations inherent in lower-class existence and in motherhood – limitations of choice, mobility, autonomy, and authority – come together, rendering her at once a figure of moral power and practical impotence. Although she is able to provide some comfort to Clarissa, she cannot save her.

There are still other mothers in *Clarissa*. Lovelace's mother makes shadowy but recurrent appearances, always as the originary guilty party behind her son's brutality. "How would my sister Lovelace have reproached herself for all her indulgent folly to this favourite boy of hers, had she lived til now," Lord M. reflects (6: 220–1 [1036]). And Lovelace himself agrees:

Why, why did my mother bring me up to bear no controul? Why was I so educated, *as that to my very tutors it was a request, that I should not know what contradiction of disappointment was?* – Ought she not to have known what cruelty there was in her kindness? (8: 132 [1431])

The villain echoes conduct books' wisdom on too-doting mothers, whose children "are usually spoiled by it, made insolent and untractable" (Allestree, *The Ladies Calling*, 208; Steele, *Ladies Library*, 2: 191), as well as another staple of Augustan conduct discourse, mother-blame. Allestree calls on mothers of wayward offspring to

centuries (e.g., Phaer's *Boke of Children*; Guillemeau's *Nursing of Children*), and can still be found in late eighteenth-century explanations for Samuel Johnson's scrofula.

"look on their Childrens faults as the product of their own" (221).
And a 1754 treatise declares that

the Happiness of a Parent depends upon the Conduct of her Children; and
it is fit it should be so ... as it will be owing to her Care that it is good, or to
her Neglect that it will be otherwise. (J. Hill, *Management of Children*, 11–12)

In *Pamela*, Part 2, Sally Godfrey's failure is attributed to the
machinations of her "designing Mother," who according to Lady
Davers "sought artfully to intrap" Mr. B. (3: 40). Following this
powerful tradition, Richardson makes clear his assignment of blame
to Lovelace's mother in a letter to Lady Bradshaigh:

Mr. Lovelace's Mother is often hinted at in the Progress of the Story, as
having by her faulty indulgence to him in his early Youth, been the
Occasion of that uncontroulableness of Will, which proved so fatal to many
Innocents and in the End to himself. (*Selected Letters*, 116)

Lovelace's mother, then, emerges as the initiator of all the novel's
heartache, the one ultimately responsible for her son's criminality.
Yet she is already dead before the novel even begins; in this
supremely cacaphonous text, her voice is never heard. She stands as
the paradigm for a version of motherhood still influential today: the
mother who is by definition entirely responsible, yet who is also
almost entirely invisible.[75]

Lovelace's mother is not, however, the most nearly-invisible
mother in *Clarissa*. That distinction belongs to Clarissa herself, whose
ambiguous maternal status, though all but ignored in critical discourse, constitutes an important crux in the narrative and makes
available a new kind of response to the problems of maternal agency
and accountability that vex the representations of all the other
mothers in the novel.

Was Clarissa pregnant? Motherhood, indeterminacy and subversion at Clarissa's death

Throughout *Clarissa*, there are allusions to the heroine's maternal
attributes. As the book opens, she has largely changed roles with her
mother; she acts with maternal indulgence and benevolence toward
"her poor"; Anna Howe argues that Clarissa is a better maternal

---

[75] Cf. Rich, *Of Woman Born*, esp. 66–71; Chodorow, *Reproduction*. Sprengnether's *Spectral
Mother* provides a perceptive critique of the persistence of mother-blame in both object-
relations and Lacanian theory (6–10; 182–220).

influence than Anna's own mother (3: 89 [432]). Clarissa even extends maternal comfort to herself: at a moment of desperation at what Lovelace cold-heartedly describes as his own "perfectly eloquent ... vows and protestations," Clarissa "dropt into the next chair; her charming face, as if seeking for a hiding-place (which a mother's bosom would have best supplied) sinking upon her own shoulder" (5: 216 [844]). In each of these cases, Clarissa is acting in ways we might call maternal, but is not in fact anyone's mother. Only at the end, when she is already starting her long progress toward death, does the possibility of bodily motherhood arise for Clarissa.

The question of Clarissa's motherhood erupts when it becomes apparent to the Harlowes that she has actually lost her virginity to Lovelace: immediately, they are intent on discovering whether she is pregnant. For his part, Lovelace hopes so, and attributes Clarissa's failing health to this cause. He had long cherished the hope that Clarissa would bear his children, believing that such a circumstance would ensure her complete subjugation:

Let me perish, Belford, if I would not forgo the brightest diadem in the world, for the pleasure of seeing a twin Lovelace at each charming breast ... the pious task, for physical reasons, continued for one month and no more!

I now, methinks, behold this most charming of women in this sweet office: her conscious eye now dropped on one, now on the other, with a sigh of maternal tenderness; and then raised up to my delighted eye, full of wishes, for the sake of the pretty varlets, and for her own sake, that I would deign to legitimate; that I would condescend to put on the nuptial fetters. (4: 334 [706])

But for Clarissa's family, motherhood is the only circumstance that could make her situation worse than it already is, and her Uncle John demands to know the truth. "You *must* answer this," he storms, "before any-thing can be resolved upon about you" (7: 99 [1192]). But Clarissa is no longer interested in their resolutions about her.

As to the question required of me to answer ... "A *little* time, and much *less* time than is imagined, will afford a more satisfactory answer to my whole family, and even to my *Brother* and *Sister*, than I can give in words." (7: 108 [1197])

The "little time" Clarissa refers to might be the period of gestation which she knows has already begun. On the other hand, when she promises a "satisfactory answer" Clarissa almost certainly refers to her own impending death, as she does also in the "meditation" based on the seventh chapter of Job which she "stitched to the bottom" of Uncle John's demanding letter "with black silk."

> *O That thou wouldst hide me in the grave! That thou wouldst keep me secret, till Thy wrath be past! . . .*
> *I have sinned! What shall I do unto thee, O thou Preserver of men! Why hast Thou set me as a mark against Thee; so that I am a burden to myself! . . .*
> *My soul chuseth strangling, and death rather than life . . .*
> *Yet all the days of my appointed time will I wait, till my change come.* (7: 100–1 [1192–93])

The language of this anguished prayer is especially interesting when set against the anxious letter from Uncle John to which it responds – in fact, Clarissa's poem literally "embroiders on" Uncle John's letter. Clarissa shifts her uncle's suggestion that she might have what Augustan slang denoted "a burden in the belly" to cry "I am a burden to myself." She refers obliquely to a usual method of infanticide in eighteenth-century England – strangling – applying its violence and desperation to herself. Her insistence on an "appointed time" and a coming "change," likewise, suggests pregnancy as well as death. Although on the face of it Clarissa's meditation is about death and not about maternity, those two categories – always closely linked in discourse as in experience in the eighteenth century – from this moment become inseparable in *Clarissa*.

So it seems strangely appropriate that to her uncle's question about whether she is pregnant Clarissa should answer "I'm dying." Just as we never know the truth about Clarissa's supposed pregnancy, we never really know whether she abdicates life willfully or whether her life is forcibly usurped by unbearable trials. At her final moments, Clarissa's ambiguous motherhood literally conflates with her ambiguous death; similar uncertainties about agency and responsibility resonate around both.

If Clarissa were pregnant, then her death, already morally dubious, would be more problematic by far. For Clarissa's death is not physically inevitable (a partial justification, perhaps, for the Harlowes' and Lovelace's reluctance to believe it imminent) and her responsibility for it remains an issue to the very end. According to Belford, "her apothecary . . . gave it as the doctor's opinion, as well as his own, that she would recover, if she herself desired to recover, and would use the means" (6: 397 [1127]). Though she asks the doctor to assure her that she is innocent of "any imputations of curtailing, thro' wilfulness or impatiency ... a life that might other-wise be prolonged," that assurance never comes. Richardson never provides a convincing empirical cause for Clarissa's death (though he was clearly convinced of its moral and aesthetic inevitability: "Clarissa," he told Lady Bradshaigh, "... could not be rewarded in this World" [December 15, 1748; *Selected Letters*, 108]).

So it is impossible to settle even so apparently fundamental a question as whether Clarissa is killed or kills herself – whether by allowing herself to die she does or does not commit suicide. Like the lost fetuses in the "dead baby poems" of Barbara Johnson's brilliant discussion, Clarissa's "deadness ... cannot be named" (Johnson, "Apostrophe," 36).[76] The problem of passive agency – the defining problem of Mrs. Harlowe's maternity and the most troubling political question inherited by Richardson's generation – is epitomized in Clarissa's peculiar death, a death made intensely problematic by the possibility that Clarissa might be pregnant.

Indeed, what is most important is not whether Clarissa is or is not pregnant, but the fact that the book never decides. Critics tend to overlook this fact. Eaves and Kimpel, for instance, declare that "the question is not whether Clarissa *is* pregnant, (she is not) but whether Lovelace could possibly have thought so."[77] The critics' inference appears in parenthesis, as if it were too obvious to state; yet it is by no means certain. After all, why shouldn't Clarissa be pregnant?[78] The reluctance of critics even to recognize this obvious possibility suggests the persistence of assumptions about motherhood not far removed from those at work in *Clarissa*. Again the fundamental issue is one of agency. Lovelace assumes that if Clarissa is pregnant, she will be constrained to live. By impregnating her, he believes, he exercises ultimate power over her, forcing her to continue existing – raping her, as it were, to life. But by refusing to answer the question, Clarissa denies life to the idea of an heir conceived in rape, and exercises over Lovelace the uniquely female power that resides in maternity.

---

[76] By extension, Mrs. Harlowe stands in the place of the aborting mother, an "agent" who "is not entirely autonomous" who "has not chosen the conditions" under which she "must choose" (Johnson, "Apostrophe," 33). For a different interpretation of Clarissa's death, cf. Doody, *A Natural Passion*, 172.

[77] Eaves and Kimpel, "An unpublished pamphlet," 407.

[78] The only critic who attempts to eliminate the possibility of conception is Judith Wilt, who argues in a well-known essay that at the moment for which he has waited so long, Lovelace is impotent.

Thus Richardson leaves open all possibilities – the possibility of autonomous choice (in regard to motherhood and to life), the opposite possibility of abject victimization, and numberless possibilities between the two. Clarissa might not have been pregnant; she might not have known whether she was pregnant; she might have decided to die in either case; or she might have wished to live but found herself overtaken by death and too weakened to resist it. Each of these interpretations has textual support, but no single one is adequate. In both Clarissa's death and her (possible) motherhood, agency is the problem that will not resolve. Clarissa ends the cycle of compromised and usurped agency by refusing either to accept or to deny responsibility, making it impossible for others to close off their interpretations of her and parcel out blame. When she chooses to focus on her impending death rather than on her possible pregnancy, Clarissa refuses to bow to a fundamental assumption at work in her culture's discourse on motherhood and still operative in debates over reproductive choice in our own day – the assumption that a pregnant woman's responsibility to her unborn child outweighs her responsibility to her own autonomy. The novel's final subversion lies in allowing Clarissa to die while leaving the question of her pregnancy undecided.

Richardson avoids directly considering whether Clarissa is pregnant at her death; but he does argue, both within the text and outside it, that it is impossible to imagine Clarissa as a mother. Indeed, whether characters recognize the impossibility of Clarissa's physical motherhood becomes a touchstone for their sensibilities. Lovelace and Uncle John Harlowe do not scruple to imagine such a possibility. Lovelace simply assumes, in his vanity, that Clarissa must be pregnant, having been penetrated by such a potent fellow as himself: her motherhood, he says, "will be very surprising to me if it do not happen" (7: 14 [1147]). But the more perspicacious Belford sees Clarissa's maternity as a contradiction in terms. She is too much "mind" to undertake the physical work of motherhood, Belford writes, too much "an angel" to "be plunged so low as into the vulgar offices of domestic life ... For why ... should not the work of bodies be left to *mere* bodies?" (4: 11 [555])

Richardson made the same argument in a letter to Lady Bradshaigh, who hoped that Clarissa and Lovelace would marry after all:

Let us suppose the Story to end, as you, Madam, would have it ... See her an excellent Wife, an excellent Mistress, and even an excellent Mother, struggling thro' very delicate and very painful Circumstances ... What is there unusual in all this? ... We will imagine her to have repeatedly escaped the Perils of Child birth. How many Children shall we give her? Five? Six? Seven? How many, Madam? Not less I hope.[79]

As William Warner notes, Richardson's portrait of Clarissa as mother is intentionally "grotesque and implausible"; there is implied a certain "incongruity" in making Clarissa, like Pamela, "an efficient producer of babies" (*Reading Clarissa*, 172). Clarissa is simply too delicate, too spiritual, too intellectual – all qualities assumed to be antithetical to mothering. "Is this ... the Condition of Life, to which we are so solicitous to prefer a Creature perfected by Sufferings and already ripened for Glory?" Richardson asks.[80] Although he coyly suggests to Lady Bradshaigh that "Mr. Belford perhaps has too high Notions of her Excellencies,"[81] Belford clearly speaks for Richardson's own belief – a belief enormously degrading to virtually every woman of his time, including his own wife – that motherhood is the lowest form of physical labor, rightly undertaken by "mere bodies." With this gesture Richardson makes motherhood, the measure of female virtue in conduct literature and in *Pamela*, Part 2, not only uninteresting but actually bestial, and certainly incompatible with his "angelic" notions of female virtue. Thus Clarissa's rarity debases other women, as did the excellence of the Virgin Mary, of Queen Elizabeth, and of Pamela; and in all these cases, that debasement occurs specifically in the context of motherhood.

Perhaps the disturbing suggestion that motherhood and female excellence are somehow essentially incompatible is not really, as it seems, an aberration cropping up suddenly at the end of *Clarissa*. For the fact is that in both *Pamela*, Part 2 and *Clarissa*, Richardson consistently implies the same idea by failing to show a single example of maternal authority that does not to some degree undercut the purported virtue of the woman in question, and by closely tying narratives of maternal failure to stories of lost female virtue. From first to last, mothers in Richardson are deceptive and deceived: they are victimizing victims whose honor and authority, when they have any, are limited and compromised, if not actually fraudulent. Both *Pamela*, Part 2 and *Clarissa* demonstrate the inadequacy of Augustan Britain's maternal ideals by constructing complicity   indeed,

---

[79] 15 December 1748. *Selected Letters*, 106–07.
[80] Richardson, *Selected Letters*, 108.
[81] Ibid., 107.

identity – between failed motherhood, lost female virtue, and contested political legitimacy.

In *Pamela*, Part 2, Richardson managed, though with difficulty, to sustain the myth of the powerful-because-submissive domestic mother by deploying devices characteristic of conduct literature: reduction of characters to flat exponents of theses, reliance on exhortation over dramatic enactment, refusal to admit doubt or analyze assumptions. *Clarissa*, on the other hand – though also didactic and also raising an impossible standard for female excellence – begins with the theses *Pamela* had argued already in place, then proceeds to blow them up one by one, exposing the contradictions implicit in its own portrait of a virtuous mother. That domestic harmony may be achieved by the submission of wives to the commands of their husbands even over the dictates of a wife's own conscience and reason; that mothers, though naturally possessing greater tenderness for their children, are rightly subordinated to fathers and find satisfaction and power in that subordination; that domestic spaces and political spaces are distinct, parallel spheres capable of metaphorical comparison but not of conflation – all these notions are exposed as untenable in *Clarissa*, where a submissive wife is guilty *because of* her submission, where the fraudulence of her maternal virtue and authority is made painfully apparent, and where the compromised agency of the mother, like that of her daughter, is represented in the language of public politics. In the connections it draws between maternal failure and the seduction of female innocence, *Clarissa* rephrases Augustan society's most urgent public questions – questions about the responsibilities of subjects and the possibilities for integrity in a world where victimization necessarily involves complicity and where legitimate authority has been ambiguously displaced.

Going public: the case of Lady Sarah Pennington

Out of confusion new voices will arise, voices recognized not so
much by the content of the truths they enunciate as by the
honesty and courage of enunciation. They will be at once
familiar and original, these voices arising out of maternal
practice, affirming its own criteria of acceptability, insisting that
the dominant values are unacceptable and need not be accepted.

Sara Ruddick[1]

In 1761, an aristocrat named Sarah Pennington produced a surprise
bestseller, a conduct book entitled *An Unfortunate Mother's Advice to Her
Absent Daughters*. The work appeared under particularly dramatic
conditions. Pennington had been publicly discarded by her husband
Sir Joseph – and so, by eighteenth-century law, was permanently
separated from their children. Even letters were forbidden. Yet
Pennington felt keenly that maternal instruction was, as conduct
literature taught, her "indispensable duty" (Pennington, 1). Caught
like Pamela between the requirements of maternal virtue and the
edict of an implacable husband, she hit upon a novel solution: she
published, as *An Unfortunate Mother's Advice*, a private letter to her
eldest daughter Jenny (and through her, to the younger daughters),
hoping that the text would gain notoriety sufficient to bring it to the
girls' attention. Of course, this expedient eliminated the possibility of
genteel anonymity for the aristocratic Lady Sarah. Resourcefully
fulfilling conduct literature's mandate to instruct her daughter, she
simultaneously transgressed an arguably more fundamental requirement by doing so *in print*, under her own name, and against the
wishes of her husband.

By going public with a personal letter between members of a
family, Pennington participates in the transgressions of the epistolary
novelist – indeed, she exceeds them. For Pennington's *Advice* at once

[1] Ruddick, "Maternal thinking," 357. Cf. Ruddick, *Maternal thinking*, 40.

exploits the public forum of print in order to engage in an intimate communication with her daughter, and exploits her intimate relationship with her daughter in order to make public her grievances against Sir Joseph. The duties of motherhood, that most private of relations, take place in print, that most public of spaces. Pennington's letter is not simply a private communication masquerading as a public one; nor is it a public statement disguised as a personal letter. Simultaneously public and private, it calls the distinction into question more radically than any text we have examined.

Under such circumstances, Pennington is obliged to defend her claim to virtuous maternal authority, without which her advice would be of little value. She meets this challenge by emphasizing her discomfort with the "impropriety" of her situation as publishing mother and her reluctance to move out of her "proper sphere" (1, 25). "Was there any probability that a letter from me would be permitted to reach your hand alone," she assures Jenny in the letter's opening sentence, "I should not have chosen this least eligible method of writing to you" (1). Though she breaks all the rules for domestic motherhood and openly defies her husband by going public, the fact that she does not *choose* this course, but is forced into it, makes taking the "least eligible method" an act consistent with maternal virtue for Lady Sarah.

Pennington explicitly advises her daughters to disobey their father (and future husbands) if necessary. "Obedience," she counsels, becomes "impracticable" when commands are "contrary to the higher obligations of morality" (56).

Where this happens ... keep steady to your principles, and neither by persuasion or threats be prevailed with to act contrary to them. All commands repugnant to the laws of Christianity it is your indispensable duty to disobey; all requests that are inconsistent with prudence ... it is your interest to refuse ...; for a man capable of requiring from his wife what he knows to be in itself wrong, is equally capable of throwing the whole blame of such misconduct on her. (57)

Pennington goes so far as to attribute her present separation from the children to submissions she previously made to their father against her own better judgement. What transgressions she may be guilty of, she says, were committed "by his absolute command (which, contrary to reason, and my own interest, I was, for more than twelve years, weak enough implicitly to obey)" (5). "I ... cannot, upon reflection," she says, accuse myself of any thing, but too absolute, too unreserved an obedience to every injunction, even where they were plainly contrary to the dictates of my own reason. – How wrong such a compliance, was clearly evinced by many instances of it having been since most ungenerously and most ungratefully urged as circumstantial arguments against myself. (84–85)

In Pennington's transgressive letter, in other words, the lesson of *Pamela*, Part 2 is directly refuted. Pennington insists on the priority of a wife's own reason and conscience in determining her maternal behavior, and rejects the code of passive obedience in the domestic sphere.

Pennington does not place the blame for her present difficulties entirely on Sir Joseph. She also accepts responsibility for a youthful carelessness about maintaining coherence between her public and private existences, carelessness that later made her vulnerable to slander. "My private conduct," she recalls, "was what the severest prude could not condemn; my public, such as the most finished coquet alone would have ventured upon" (4). As a result, when the malicious Sir Joseph seeks to destroy his wife's reputation by "a public accusation" of wrongdoing (6), he is readily believed. Like other mothers in eighteenth-century writing, Pennington finds that pre-marital transgressions threaten to undermine her potential for maternal authority, even to disqualify her as a mother.

But in Pennington's case, unlike any other we have witnessed, there is escape from this predicament. And ironically enough, it is the *Advice* – itself a dramatic instance of maternal transgression – that exonerates her. The degree to which the *Advice* and her subsequent writings[2] brought Pennington public respect as a mother is demonstrated in the obituary the *Gentleman's Magazine* published in the year of her death, 1783. To modern readers aware of Pennington's notorious personal history, it might come as something of a surprise that the *Gentleman's Magazine* includes no whisper of scandal in its eulogy. Instead, we find fulsome praise of Pennington's

extraordinary abilities, long since displayed to the world, in her excellent and much-admired writings, which could only be equalled by her piety, charity, and benevolence, united to that patient and unreserved resignation, with which she sustained (through the course of many years) a series of very severe and uncommon afflictions. (918)

In its commendatory tone and in its careful but pointed allusions to

---

[2] Pennington's subsequent works include *The Child's Conductor* (London: 1777) and *Letters on Different Subjects* (4 v., Dublin: 1766).

Sir Joseph's cruelty, the *Gentleman's Magazine* seems to reflect the late eighteenth century's consensus on Lady Sarah Pennington. As Kathryn Shevelow has observed, Pennington's contemporaries not only "exonerated" her, but "even made her a martyr" ("Lady Sarah Pennington," 246).

When Pennington published her letter to her daughter, she broke unwritten laws against speaking publicly *as a mother*. More fundamentally, she dispensed advice to hundreds of readers and manipulated her husband's public persona, and so challenged her culture's invisible but potent boundaries between what is acceptably public and what is necessarily private. Rejecting the notion that maternal virtue and a publicly defiant maternal voice are separate and mutually exclusive, Lady Sarah Pennington addressed the world and her child in one voice simultaneously intimate and oracular, pious and rebellious. And she got away with it: her contemporaries made the unlikely effort to imagine her transgression as a new kind of virtuous maternal act. By violating her society's most precious myth about maternity – that it is a wholly private affair, separated naturally from public life and discourse – Lady Sarah undid the error of her youth at last, and gained a public reputation consonant with her private merit.

Pennington insists that the *Advice* is not a narrative of her personal history (tantalizingly described as "full of incidents of a nature so uncommon as to be scarcely credible" [7–8]), and that she does not intend it to "prove" the injustice of her situation (8). On the contrary, the letter's purported design is more modest and entirely consistent with standard prescriptions for virtuous motherhood: "to remind you, that you have still an affectionate mother, anxious for your welfare, [and] to give you some advice with regard to your conduct in life" (8). But a more explosive letter to the children – one that by telling the "whole truth" will expose Sir Joseph – is still to come. In fact, Pennington says, she has already completed this second letter, and merely waits for the children to grow up before she delivers it ("you are all yet too young to enter into things of this kind" [8]). Sir Joseph, meanwhile, can contemplate not *whether* but *how* he would like the next letter to reach them. "That future letter," Pennington says,

must contain the relation of many events, which, for the sake of the person, concerned in them, I could wish (my heart being really void of all angry resentment) there was no necessity of making public. If therefore I can find a certain means of conveying the narrative to your brothers, sisters, and yourself only, when you are all arrived at a proper age to receive and understand it, that method will be preferred; if not, I must again have recourse to this channel. (87–88)

Pennington's threats seem to have achieved their objective: among her subsequent publications, none is devoted to telling the children "the whole truth" about her life with their father. Perhaps Sir Joseph saw the wisdom of a private correspondence between mother and children after all.

But despite the resourcefulness with which Pennington opposes the combined restrictions of patriarchal privilege, maternal disenfranchisement, and the code of domestic motherhood, she remains haunted by anxiety.

So many have been the instances of falsehood and deceit I have met with ... that it may justify a precaution against my name being hereafter made use of, without my knowledge. (87)

Such fears were well founded, for there was little to prevent anyone, including Sir Joseph, from writing a letter to the children and calling it Lady Sarah's. The problem was the medium of print itself, with its simultaneously promising and dangerous materiality. Pennington's letter substitutes for her bodily presence (it "suppl[ies] the deprivation of a constant, tender, maternal care" [9; cf. 86]) and allows the absent, silenced mother to make herself heard. But in the process it also reduces her to a disembodied voice – and voices can be ventriloquized, their authenticity faked, and their authority usurped. Under such circumstances, Pennington rightly wonders how to protect her children from misrepresentation. How will they know the mother's own voice?

In response to this new predicament, Pennington once again develops an impressive strategy. If the mother can be present to her children only in printed language, which is subject to co-optation, then the answer is to make public maternal language physically particular and thus irreproducible. "Whilst I live," she says,

I shall write my name to whatever is by me addressed to any of you.
Depend upon it, therefore, my dear, most certainly, that I am not the author of any epistle which bears not the manual sign of
Your affectonate mother,
S. Pennington. (88)

Lady Sarah remained as good as her word: although *An Unfortunate*

Mother's Advice went into three editions in the first year of publication
and many more before the author's death, Pennington did her best
to ensure throughout her life that every copy carried a manuscript
signature (figure 13). Of course, there were the usual piratings, and
the *Advice* almost immediately began appearing in conduct-book
collections like the 1773 *Instructions for a Young Lady* from which our
citations are taken. Pennington could not possibly have supervised all
such reprints; she probably did not even know about many of them.
But so far as legitimate, separate editions are concerned, Pennington
herself seems to have signed every copy of the first three (1761) and
fourth (1767) editions.[3] The medium of print may be vulnerable and
insufficient, but the mother's presence can be reliably evoked nevertheless – not in the printed text *per se*, but in the signature *on* the text.
The "manual sign" gives authenticity and authority to the printed
text; and that text in turn becomes context – even pretext – for the
ink of the mother's signature, the sign of continuing maternal
presence, even in absence.

Thus Pennington's *Advice* continues a tradition we have observed
throughout this book, in which an absent or inadequate mother is
represented at key moments by some agent or proxy. When Queen
Anne, on first stepping out as national mother, attempts to subsume
her own maternal particularity by wearing another queen's costume;
when Amy pushes Roxana's children through their aunt's door and
hurries away (and later, when she seems herself to support the grown
children); when Victorinus's nurse cares for him while his mother
works, and feels "Tenderness more than equal to that which Mothers
ordinarily feel for their own Children" (Haywood, *Rash Resolve*, 106);
when Pamela instructs Miss Goodwin; when Clarissa leans on Mrs.
Lovick's breast – at each of these highly charged moments, the active
maternal agent is a substitute. The mother herself is hidden, spoken
for, impersonated, even replaced. In Pennington's *Advice*, the surrogate has become considerably more abstract: the maternal representative (at least initially) is conduct writing itself – ironically, the genre
explicitly devoted to enforcing domestic motherhood. And when that
surrogate proves insufficiently reliable, its role is assumed by the

---

[3] In the fifth and sixth editions (1770, 1773), when the letter had already won extraordinary
attention and was universally familiar, Pennington's "signature" is printed, with the
bookseller's manuscript signature beneath. The seventh edition, unsigned, appeared post-
humously in 1784. Shevelow reviews the work's publication history during the nineteeth
century (246).

(96)

effectually fecure you from the Poffibility of being impofed upon, by any pretended pofthumous Letter of mine ; and, whilft I live, fhall *write* my Name to whatever is by me addreffed to any of you.

DEPEND upon it, therefore, my Dear, moft certainly, that I am not the Author of any Epiftle, which bears not the MANUAL SIGN of,

Your affectionate Mother,

S. Pennington

13 Lady Sarah Pennington, *An Unfortunate Mother's Advice to her Absent Daughters.*
      Third edition, 1761. Final page, with manuscript signature.

mother's signature – a liquid, physical, temporal, intimate, yet entirely public connection between herself and her child.

It is important to recognize at this point that Pennington's text is for the most part a conventional, even predictable, conduct book. In terms of content, Pennington's heterodoxy is limited to the insistence we have already noted that a woman must disobey a husband's commands if they go against her conscience, an anomalous piece of rebellion directly derived from Pennington's own experience. Otherwise, she is given to admonishing her daughters in Halifaxian style –

to religious duty, thrift, avoidance of speculative or intellectual learning (because "a sensible woman will soon be convinced, that all the learning her utmost application can make her mistress of, will be, from the difference of education, in many points inferior to that of a schoolboy" [24]), and strategic dissimulation in dealing with husbands. The text's largest transgressions take place, in other words, on entirely different levels than that of content: in the very fact of its existence as a public document, and in the handwritten signature that guarantees its legitimacy and authority.

We have examined a number of efforts in early eighteenth-century British discourse to define maternal virtue and control maternal authority – to re-present and reposition motherhood for modernity. These efforts, as we have seen, met with considerable success: even today, mothers continue to labor under assumptions formulated in the Augustan age, particularly the assumption that good motherhood is naturally separate from (and uniquely threatened by) participation in the public world. And today as in the eighteenth century, it is sometimes difficult to imagine how virtuous motherhood might coexist with public maternal presence, ambition, and authority, or with active female sexual desire.

Sarah Pennington's *Advice* encourages us to take heart. It reminds us that although Augustan Britain reached a significant degree of consensus on the question of maternal authority, resistance was still possible. In Pennington's extraordinary text we see an unusually vivid working out of ideas about maternal virtue that run counter to those conduct writing presented as universally and exhaustively true. We hear an undeniably tender and solicitous maternal voice; but the fact that we do hear it, the simple fact of that voice's presence in public discourse, destabilizes the notion that maternal tenderness is necessarily hidden and private, a notion precious to many in Pennington's day, as in our own. In *An Unfortunate Mother's Advice*, we witness maternal virtue that is compatible with – even a function of – aggressive participation in public discourse. And we find, once again, that the most intimate relations are intensely political.

Perhaps under more "fortunate" circumstances, Pennington's motherhood would have taken shape in the behaviors taught by Augustan conduct writers – constant physical presence, breast-feeding, personal instruction, withdrawal to domesticity. But when these behaviors demand the compromise of integrity or permit the abdication of responsibility, maternal virtue may be less reliably indicated by a mother's conformity with cultural norms than by her courage to resist them – to make her own choices, speak in her own voice, define her own sexuality, and deploy her own representations. To be sure, those representations will always be incomplete. But as Pennington's text demonstrates, at any particular historical moment the expedients available for imagining and making present new versions of virtuous motherhood may prove sufficient after all, if we can summon the courage to make them our own.

Epilogue to "The Distrest Mother"
(Spoken by Mrs. Oldfield)

I hope you'll own, that with becoming Art,
I've play'd my Game, and topp'd the Widow's Part;
My Spouse, poor Man! could not live out the Play,
But dy'd commodiously on [his] Wedding-Day,
While I, his Relict, made at one bold Fling,
My self a Princess, and young Sty a King.
　　You Ladies who protract a Lover's Pain,
And hear your Servants sigh whole Years in vain;
Which of you all would not on Marriage venture,
Might she so soon upon her Jointure enter?
　　'Twas a strange Scape! Had *Pyrrhus* liv'd till now,
I had been finely hamper'd in my Vow.
To die by one's own Hand, and fly the Charms
Of Love and Life in a young Monarch's Arms!
'Twere an hard Fate – e're I had undergone it,
I might have took one Night – to think upon it.
　　But why you'll say was all this Grief exprest
For a first Husband, laid long since at Rest?
Why so much Coldness to my kind Protector?
– Ah, Ladies! had you known the good Man *Hector*!
Homer will tell you (or I'm misinform'd)
That when enrag'd the *Grecian* Camp he Storm'd,
To break the ten-fold *Barriers* of the Gate,
He threw a Stone of such prodigious Weight
As no two Men could lift: not even of those
Who in that Age of thund'ring Mortals rose:
– It would have sprain'd a Dozen modern Beaux.
　　At length howe'er I laid my Weeds aside,
And sunk the Widow in the well-dress'd Bride.
In you it still remains to grace the Play,
And bless with Joy my Coronation Day:
Take then, ye Circles of the Brave and Fair,
The Fatherless and Widow to your Care.

Works cited

PRIMARY WORKS

Addison, Joseph. "The campaign." London: 1705.

    The Guardian, no.105. Ed. John Calhoun Stephens. Lexington: University Press of Kentucky, 1982. 365–67.

Allestree, Richard. *The Ladies Calling.* 1673. Fifth Impression. Oxford: 1677.

Anonymous. *A Collection of all the Addresses that have been presented to Her Majesty, since March the 25th, 1710.* London: 1710.

    A Collection of the Parliamentary Debates in England; From the Year MDCLXVIII to the Present Time. 21 volumes. London: 1741. Vol 5.

    A Copy of the Royal Charter, Establishing an Hospital for the Maintenance and Education of Exposed and Deserted Young Children. London: Osborn, 1739.

    The Covetous Old Mother; Or, The terrible Overthrow of Two Loyal Lovers. Newcastle-upon-Tyne: 1720.

    The Cruel Mother. Being a strange and unheard-of Account of one Mrs. Elizabeth Cole ... that threw her own Child into the Thames on Sunday Night last. 1708.

    A Dissertation on Mr. Hogarth's Six Prints Lately publish'd, viz. Gin-Lane, Beer-Street, and the Four Stages of Cruelty. London: Dickinson, 1751.

    "England's Triumph, Or An Occasional Poem on the Happy Coronation of Anne Queen of England." London: 1702.

    The Forced Virgin; or, the Unnatural Mother. A True Secret History. London: W. Trott, 1730.

    "The Generous Muse. A Funeral Poem, in Memory of his late Majesty K. James the II." London: 1701.

    The Life of her Late Majesty, Queen Anne. London: 1721.

    The Miscarriages of the Whig-Ministry Discovering the Intriegues [sic] of that Party for the First Eight Years of the Late Reign ... London: 1714.

    A Modest Survey of that Celebrated Tragedy the Distrest Mother, So often and so highly Applauded by the Ingenious Spectator. London: 1712.

    Mother Gin, A Tragi-Comical Eclogue: being a Paraphrastical Imitation of the Daphnis of Virgil. London: 1737.

    "A New Ballad. To the Tune of the Black-Smith." *Whig and Tory: or, Wit on Both Sides.* 1710–11. London: 1712. Part 1: 22–24.

"Nonsense Authenticated and Consemated [sic] by a Vow of our Late English Convention to be the Main Fundamental of our new Government; Or, The Modern State or Meaning of the Word Abdicate, Parrabel'd [sic] by Diverse Instances." *A Collection of All the Secret Poems and Lampoons Wrote During the Reigne of the Late King William.* n.d. Regenstein MS. 559: 23–24.

"On the Death of Her Late Majesty, Queen Anne." *The Loyal Mourner for the Best of Princes: Being a Collection of Poems Sacred to the immortal Majesty Queen Anne. By a Society of Gentlemen.* Ed. Charles Oldisworth. London; Dublin: S. Powell, 1716. 32–34.

A Pittilesse Mother. That most unnaturally at one time, murthered two of her owne Children ... upon holy thursday last 1616. The ninth of May. Beeing a Gentlewoman named Margret Vincent, wife of Mr. Jarvis Vincent ... With her Examination, Confession and true discovery of all the proceedings in the said bloody accident. [London: 1616.]

"The Queen's and the Duke of Ormond's New Toast." London: 1712.

Sorrowes Joy. Or, A Lamentation for our late deceased Soveraigne Elizabeth. Cambridge: 1603.

The Unnatural Grand Mother, or a True Relation of a Most Barbarous Murther. London: Thomas Higgins, 1659.

The Unnatural Mother and Ungrateful Wife, a narrative: founded on true and very interesting facts. London: n.d.

The Unnatural Mother: Being a Full and True Account of One Elizabeth Kennet, a Marry'd Woman ... who, on Tuesday the 6th of April, 1697, privately Delivered herself, and afterwards flung her Infant in the Fire, and Burnt it all to Ashes, but a few of the Bones. London: 1697.

The Unnatural Mother: Or, Innocent Love Persecuted. London, 1734.

The Unnatural Mother: The Scene in the Kingdom of Siam. London, 1698.

Astell, Mary. *Reflections Upon Marriage.* 1700. *The First English Feminist: Reflections Upon Marriage and Other Writings by Mary Astell.* Ed. Bridget Hill. New York: St. Martin's Press, 1986. 69–132.

Barker, Jane. *Love Intrigues ... The Amours of Bosvil and Galesia.* 1713. *The Entertaining Novels of Miss Jane Barker.* 2 volumes. London: E. Curll, 1719. Vol. 2.

Behn, Aphra. "A Congratulatory Poem to Her Most Sacred Majesty, on the Universal Hopes of all Loyal Persons for a Prince of Wales." London: Canning, 1688.

Blackmore, Richard. "Eliza: an epick poem. In ten books." London: 1705.

Blower, John. *A Sermon Preach'd in the Parish Church of St. Martin in York ... Upon the Death of... Dr. John Sharp, Late Archbishop of York.* London: 1714.

Boyer, Abel. *The English Theophrastus: or, The Manners of the Age.* 3rd edition. London: 1722.

The History of the Life and Reign of Queen Anne, with all the Medals, and Other Useful Cuts. London: 1722.

The History of Queen Anne . . . Illustrated with a Regular Series of All the Medals that were Struck . . . [in] this Reign. London: 1735.

Memoirs of Queen Anne. London: 1729.

Br., J. "A Letter to *Mareschal* Tallard. *Made* English *out of* French." 1705. *Poems on Affairs of State, from the year 1620 to the year 1707.* Vol. 4. London: 1716. 42–48.

Brownlow, John. *The History and Objects of the Foundling Hospital, with a Memoir of the Founder.* 1858. 4th edition. London: 1881.

Buchan, William. *Domestic Medicine; Or, A Treatise on the Prevention and Cure of Diseases by Regimen and Simple Medicines.* 1769. 2nd ed. London: 1772.

Burnet, Gilbert. *History of His Own Time.* 2 volumes. London: Ward, 1724.

[Cadogan, William.] *An Essay upon Nursing, and the Management of Children, from Their Birth to Three Years of Age, by a Physician. In a Letter to one of the Governors of the Foundling Hospital. Published by Order of the General Committee for transacting the Affairs of the said Hospital.* London: 1748. Rpt. *Three Treatises on Child Rearing.* Ed. Randolph Trumbach. *Marriage, Sex and the Family in England, 1660–1800.* New York: Garland, 1985.

Chester, Joseph Lemuel, ed. *The Marriage, Baptismal and Burial Registers of the Collegiate Church or Abbey of St. Peter, Westminster.* The Publications of the Harleian Society. Vol. 10. London: 1876.

Chudleigh, Mary (Lee), Lady. *The Ladies Defence: Or, The Bride-Woman's Counsellor Answer'd: a Poem. In a Dialogue Between Sir John Brute, Sir William Loveall, Melissa, and a Parson. Written by a Lady.* London: 1701.

"On the Death of his Highness the Duke of *Glocester.*" *Poems on Several Occasions . . . Together with the Song of the Three Children Paraphras'd.* London: 1703. 1–13.

"To the Queen's Most Excellent Majesty." *Poems on Several Occasions.* 1703. 41–45.

"To the Queen's Most Excellent Majesty" [a different poem]. *Poems on Several Occasions.* 1703. 121–25.

Cibber, Colley. *Apology For the Life of Mr. Colley Cibber, Comedian, and Late Patentee of the Theatre-Royal.* 2 volumes. Ed. Robert W. Lowe. London: J. C. Nimo, 1889. Vol. 2.

Clarendon, Henry Hyde, Earl of. *The Correspondence of Henry Hyde, Earl of Clarendon and of his Brother Laurence Hyde, Earl of Rochester; with the Diary of Lord Clarendon from 1687 to 1690 . . . and the Diary of Lord Rochester.* Ed. Samuel Weller Singer. 2 volumes. London: Henry Colburn, 1828. Vol. 2.

Clerk, John. *Memoirs of the Life of Sir John Clerk . . . Extracted by Himself from His Own Journals 1676–1755.* Ed. John M. Gray. Pubs. of the Scottish History Society. Vol. 13. Edinburgh: Edinburgh University Press, 1892.

Clinton, Elizabeth Knevitt, Countess of Lincoln. *The Countesse of Lincolnes Nurserie.* Oxford, 1628. Rpt. Walter J. Johnson, Inc. Theatrum Orbis Terrarum, Ltd. Amsterdam and Norwood, N.J. 1975. *The English*

Experience: Its Record in Early Printed Books Published in Facsimile, Number 720.

Cobb, Samuel. "Honour Retriev'd. A POEM Occasioned By the Later Victories." London: 1705.

Collier, N. *A Sermon on Queen Anne's Death.* London: R. Knaplock, 1714.

Congreve, William. "A Pindarique Ode, Humbly Offer'd to the Queen." London: Tonson, 1706.

Cooper, Maria Susannah. *The Exemplary Mother: Or, Letters Between Mrs. Villars and her Family. Published by a Lady.* 2 volumes. London: 1769.

Davys, Mary. *The Ladies Tales: Exemplified in the Vertues and Vices of the Quality, with Reflections.* London: 1714.

Defoe, Daniel. *A Hymn to Victory.* London: J. Nutt, 1704.

    The Family Instructor. In Three Parts. 1715. Fifteenth edition. 2 volumes. London: C. Hitch, 1761. Vol. 1.

    The Fortunes and Misfortunes of the Famous Moll Flanders. 1722. Ed. G. A. Starr. New York: Oxford University Press, 1981.

    The Life and Strange Surprizing Adventures of Robinson Crusoe. 1719. Ed. J. Donald Crowley. New York: Oxford University Press, 1972.

    [attrib.] *No Queen; Or, No General. An Argument, Proving The Necessity Her Majesty was in . . . to Displace the D— of M—borough.* London: 1712.

    Roxana, The Fortunate Mistress. 1724. Ed. Jane Jack. New York: Oxford University Press, 1981.

    A Review of the State of the British Nation. 9 volumes. 1704–13. Vol. 5: London: 1709. Ed. Arthur Wellesley Secord. 22 volumes. New York: Columbia University Press, 1938. Vols. 13, 14.

Diderot, Denis. "Éloge de Richardson." 1762. *Oeuvres Complètes.* 22 volumes. Ed. Jean Varloot et al. Paris: Hermann, 1975. Vol. 13, *Arts et Lettres 1739–1766.* 192–208.

Dunton, John [attrib.]. N—, H—. *The Ladies Dictionary; Being a General Entertainment for the Fair-Sex: A Work Never Attempted Before in English.* London: 1694.

Dussinger, John. *The Discourse of Mind in Eighteenth-Century Fiction.* Paris: Mouton, 1974.

Drake, Judith [attrib]. *An Essay in Defence of the Female Sex . . . In a Letter to a Lady. Written by a Lady.* 1696. 3rd ed., 1697.

Eliot, George [Mary Ann Evans.] *Daniel Deronda.* 1876. Ed. Barbara Hardy. New York: Penguin, 1967.

Fénelon, François de Salignac de La Mothe. *Éducation des filles.* Paris: P. Aubouin, 1687. Trans. and revised by George Hickes. *Instructions for the Education of a Daughter, By the Author of Telemachus. To which is added, A Small Tract of INSTRUCTIONS for the Conduct of Young Ladies of the Highest Rank. With Suitable Devotions ANNEXED.* London: Bowyer, 1707.

Fenton, Elijah. "An Ode to the Sun for the New Year." London: Tonson, 1707.

"To the Queen, On Her Majesty's Birth-Day." London: Benjamin Tooke, n.d. [1706].

Fielding, Henry. *Joseph Andrews*. London: 1742. Ed. Martin C. Battestin. Middletown, Connecticut: Wesleyan University Press, 1967.

The Covent Garden Tragedy. London: J. Watts, J. Roberts, 1732.

Fielding, Sarah. *Remarks on Clarissa*. 1749. Intro. Peter Sabor. The Augustan Reprint Society Pub. nos. 231–32. Los Angeles: William Andrews Clark Memorial Library, 1985.

Filmer, Robert. *Patriarcha*. London: 1690. *Two Treatises of Government, By John Locke, With a Supplement Patriarcha by Robert Filmer*. Ed. Thomas I. Cook. New York: Hafner, 1947. 249–310.

Fleetwood, William. *A Discourse Concerning the Education of Children*. London: Thomas Newborough, 1702.

Franklin, Benjamin. *Autobiography: a Genetic Text*. Ed. J. A. Leo Lemay and P. M. Zall. Knoxville: University of Tennessee Press, 1981.

Gaius, Seius [pseud.]. *The Mother's Looking Glass*. London: 1702.

The Gentleman's Magazine. London: 1783. Vol. 53, part 2, no. 5. (November, 1783).

Gibbs, James. *The Holy Bible, Illustrated by J. Gibbs ("The Kitto Bible")*. 60 volumes. London: 1836. Vol. 11: *Exodus*, Part 1.

Granger, James. *A Biographical History of England, from Egbert the Great to the Revolution*. Extra-illustrated by Richard Bull. 36 volumes. London: 1769. Vol. 23.

Grant, John. *Deborah and Barak the glorious instruments of Israel's deliverance. A sermon preach'd at the cathedral church of Rochester on the seventh of September, 1704*. London: W. Rogers, 1704.

Guillemeau, Jacques. *The Nursing of Children*. London: A. Hatfield, 1612.

Halifax, George Savile, Marquess of. *The Lady's New-Year's-Gift: Or, Advice to a Daughter. The Complete Works of George Savile, First Marquess of Halifax*. Ed. Walter Raleigh. New York: Augustus M. Kelley Reprints, 1970. 1–46.

Harrison, Conyers. *An Impartial History of the Life and Reign of her Late Majesty Queen Anne of Immortal Memory*. London: 1744.

Haywood, Eliza. *The Female Spectator*. 4 volumes. London: Gardner, 1745. Vols. 1, 4.

The Force of Nature. Secret Histories, Novels, and Poems. 4 volumes. 2nd ed., London: 1725. Vol. 4.

The Rash Resolve; or, The Untimely Discovery. A Novel. In Two Parts. *The Works of Mrs. Eliza Haywood*. 4 volumes. London: 1724. Vol. 4.

Highmore, Joseph, L. Truchy, and A. Benoist. *Twelve Plates Illustrating Pamela*. London: 1745.

Hill, John [attrib.]. *The Conduct of a Married Life ... in a series of letters written by ... Juliana-Susannah Seymour ... to a young lady*. London: R. Baldwin, 1753.

On the Management and Education of Children, A Series of Letters Written to a Niece. By Juliana-Susannah Seymour. London: R. Baldwin, 1754.

Hume, David. *The History of England, from the Invasion of Julius Caesar to the Revolution in 1688*. 1763. 6 volumes. London: T. Caddell, 1778. Indianapolis: Liberty Classics, 1983. Vol. 6.

"Of Chastity and Modesty." *A Treatise of Human Nature*. Ed. L. A. Selby-Bigge. 2nd ed., Rev. P.H. Nidditch. Oxford: Clarendon Press, 1978. 570–73.

Joceline, Elizabeth. *The Mothers Legacie, to her unborne Childe*. London: 1635.

Johnson, Samuel. *The Life of Savage*. 1744. Ed. Clarence Tracy. Oxford: Clarendon Press, 1971.

The Journals of the House of Commons. 152 volumes. London: House of Commons, 1803. Vols. 10, 16.

[Kendrick, William.] *The Whole Duty of A Woman, Written by a Lady: or a Guide to the Female Sex, From the Age of 16 to 60*. London: 1707.

Leigh, Dorothy. *The Mothers Blessing*. Fifth edition. London: 1618.

Locke, John. *Some Thoughts Concerning Education*. London: 1690.

Two Treatises of Government. Ed. Thomas I. Cook. New York: Hafner, 1947.

[Lyttleton, George.] "Advice to a Lady." London: Gilliver, 1733.

Macpherson, James, Ed. *Original Papers; Containing the Secret History of Great Britain, From the Restoration, to the Accession of the House of Hanover. To Which are Prefixed Extracts from the Life of James II as Written by Himself*. 2 volumes. London: Strahan and Cadell, 1775.

Manley, Delarivier. "A Modest Enquiry into the Reasons of the Joy Expressed by a Certain Sett of People Upon the Spreading of a Report of Her Majesty's Death." London: 1714.

The Secret History of Queen Zarah. Parts 1 and 2. 1705. *The Novels of Mary Delariviere Manley*. Ed. Patricia Koster. 2 volumes. Gainesville, Fl: Scholars' Facsimiles and Reprints, 1971. Vol. 1.

New Atalantis. 1709. Ed. Rosalind Ballaster. NY: Penguin, 1991.

Marchmont, Patrick, Earl of, et al. A Selection from the Papers of the Earls of Marchmont ... Illustrative of Events from 1685 to 1750. Ed. G. H. Rose. 3 volumes. London: 1831.

Marlborough, Sarah Jennings Churchill, Duchess of. *An Account of the Conduct of the Dowager Duchess of Marlborough. From Her First Coming to Court to the Year 1710*. London: 1742.

Private Correspondence of Sarah, Duchess of Marlborough, Illustrative of the Court and Times of Queen Anne; with Her Sketches and Opinions of Her Contemporaries, and the Select Correspondence of her Husband, John, Duke of Marlborough. 2 volumes. London: Henry Colburn, 1938.

Marlborough, John Churchill, Duke of; Godolphin, Sidney; et alia. *The Marlborough-Godolphin Correspondence*. Ed. Henry L. Snyder. 3 volumes. Oxford: Clarendon Press, 1975.

Marriott, Thomas. *Female Conduct: Being an Essay on the Art of Pleasing. To be practiced by the Fair Sex, Before, and After Marriage. A Poem, in Two Books*. London: 1759.

Marshall, Mr. *Mr. Marshall's Character of Her late Majesty. The Loyal Mourner for the Best of Princes: Being a Collection of Poems Sacred to the Immortal Memory of Her late Majesty Queen Anne. By a Society of Gentlemen.* Charles Oldisworth, ed. London; Dublin: 1716. 5–8.

Master, T. "The Virgin Mary: A Sermon Preached at St. Mary's College ... Oxon., March 15, 1641." *Conjugal Duty: Set Forth in a Collection of Ingenious and Delightful Wedding-Sermons.* London: J. Watson, 1732.

[Meredith, Royston.] *Mr. Steele Detected: Or, The Poor and Oppressed Orphan's Letters to the Great and Arbitrary Mr. Steele; Complaining of the Great Injustice done, to the Publick in General, and to Himself in Particular, by the LADIES LIBRARY; Publish'd by Mr. Steele. Together with Mr. Steele's Answers; and some Just Reflections on them.* London: 1714.

Mist, Nathaniel. *Mist's Weekly Journal: A Collection of Miscellany Letters, Selected out of Mist's Weekly Journal.* 4 volumes. 1722. London: 1727.

Nelson, James. *An Essay on the Government of Children, Under Three General Heads: viz. Health, Manners and Education.* London: 1753.

Newcome, Henry. *The Compleat Mother.* London: J. Wyat, 1695.

Oldmixon, John. *The History of England, During the Reigns of the Royal House of Stuart.* London: 1730.

Otway, Thomas. *Venice Preserved.* London: 1682.

Parker, Martin [attrib.]. *No naturall Mother, but a Monster. Or, the exact relation of one, who for making away her owne new borne childe, about Brainford neere London, was hang'd at Teyborne* [sic], *on Wednesday the 11. of December, 1633.* 1634.

The Parliamentary History of England, from the Earliest Period to the Year 1803. Cobbett's Parliamentary History. 10 volumes. London: 1806–20. Vol. 6. London: 1810.

[Peck, Francis.] "Sighs Upon the Never Enough Lamented Death of Queen Anne." London: 1719.

Pennington, Sarah. *An Unfortunate Mother's Advice to her Absent Daughters.* 1761. *Instructions for a Young Lady, in every Sphere and Period of Life.* Edinburgh: A. Donaldson, 1773. 1–88.

Phaer, Thomas. *Boke of Children.* 1545.

Phillips, Ambrose. *The Distrest Mother. A Tragedy.* London: S. Buckley, 1712.

Pix, Mary. "A Poem. Humbly Inscribed ... [On the] Union." London: 1707.

Pope, Alexander. *The Dunciad.* 1728. *The Poems of Alexander Pope.* Ed. John Butt. London: Methuen, 1963.

Povey, Charles. *An Enquiry into the Miscarriages of the Four Last Years Reign.* London: 1714.

[Prior, Matthew.] "A Prologue, Spoken at Court Before the Queen." London: 1704.

The Proceedings on the King's Commission of the Peace ... at Justice Hall in the Old Bailey. London: 1680–1820. Harvester Microfilm, 1984.

[Ralph, James.] *The Other Side of the Question: or, An Attempt to Rescue the*

Characters of the Two Royal Sisters Q. Mary and Q. Anne Out of the Hands of the D—— D—— of ——. By A Woman of Quality. London: 1742.

Rapin-Thoyras, Paul de. *Histoire d'Angleterre.* 10 volumes. 1724–27. Trans. Nicholas Tindal. *The History of England.* 4 volumes. London: 1732–47. Vols. 3, 4.

Reeve, Clara ["C.R."]. *The Progress of Romance Through Times, Countries, and Manners* ... 2 volumes in 1. Dublin: Price, Exshaw, 1785. Vol. 1.

Richardson, Samuel. *Clarissa, or The History of a Young Lady.* 1747–48. Ed. with Intro. Angus Ross. New York: Penguin, 1985.

Clarissa, or The History of a Young Lady. 3rd ed., 1751. 8 volumes. Rpt. with Intro. by Florian Stuber. *The Clarissa Project.* New York: AMS Press, 1990. 8 volumes. Vols. 1–8.

Pamela, or Virtue Rewarded. 4 volumes. London: S. Richardson, 1742.

Pamela; or, Virtue Rewarded [Part One]. 1740. 14th ed., 1801. Ed. Peter Sabor. New York: Penguin Books, 1980.

Selected Letters of Samuel Richardson. Ed. John Carroll. Oxford: Clarendon Press, 1964.

Rogers, Timothy. *The Character of a Good Woman, Both in a Single and Marry'd State. In a Funeral Discourse* ... *Occasioned by the Decease of Mrs. Elizabeth Dunton.* London: John Harris, 1697.

Rousseau, Jean-Jacques. *Emile, or On Education.* 1762. Intro., Trans., and Notes by Allan Bloom. New York: Basic Books, 1979.

Salmon, Thomas. *The Life of Her Late Majesty* ... *Wherein her Conduct During the Last Four Years* ... *is* ... *Vindicated.* London: Rivington, 1721.

Savage, Richard. "The Bastard." *The Works of Richard Savage, Esq., Son of the Earl Rivers, With an Account of the Life and Writings of the Author, by Samuel Johnson, LL.D.* 2 volumes. London: T. Evans, 1777. Vol. 2. 89–95.

Settle, Elkanah. *Distres'd Innocence: Or, The Princess of Persia, A Tragedy.* London: 1691.

"Threnodia Britannica: A Funeral Oblation to the Memory of ... John Duke of Marlborough." London: 1722.

"Threnodia Britannica: A Funeral Poem to the Memory of Our Late Sovereign Lady Anne." London: 1714.

Sharp, Jane. *The Midwives Book.* London: S. Miller, 1671. New York: Garland Press, 1985.

Sharp, John. *A Sermon Preach'd at the Coronation of Queen Anne.* London: 1702.

Sherlock, William. *A Sermon Preach'd Before the Queen* ... *on the 7th of September, 1704.* London: 1704.

Shute, James. "A Pindarick Ode, Upon Her Majesties Sending His Grace the Duke of Marlborough to Command the English Forces in Holland." London: 1703.

Smith, Joseph. *The Duty of the Living to the Memory of the Dead. A Sermon upon the Death of her Most Sacred Majesty Queen Anne.* London: Richard Smith, 1714.

Smollett, Tobias. *The History of England, from the Revolution to the Death of George the Second. Designed as a Continuation of Mr. Hume's History.* 1748. 4 volumes. London: Longman, 1848. Vols. 1, 2.

The Adventures of Roderick Random. 1748. Ed. Paul-Gabriel Bouce. New York: Oxford University Press, 1979.

The Spectator. London: 1711–12, 1714. Ed. with an Intro. and Notes by Donald F. Bond. 5 volumes. Oxford: Clarendon Press, 1965.

Steele, Richard [supposed author]. *The Ladies Library.* 3 volumes. London: Jacob Tonson, 1714.

Strickland, Agnes. *The Lives of the Queens of England from the Norman Conquest; with Anecdotes of their Courts.* 12 volumes. Philadelphia: Lea and Blanchard, 1848. Vols. 11, 12.

Swift, Jonathan. *Jonathan Swift: The Complete Poems.* Ed. Pat Rogers. New Haven: Yale University Press, 1983.

[attrib.] *A Fable of the Widow and Her Cat.* London: J. Morphew, 1712.

The History of the Four Last Years of the Queen. 1758. Ed. Harold Williams. Oxford: Blackwell, 1973.

Memoirs of the Last Four Years of the Reign of Queen Anne, From 1710, to her Death. London: T. Cooper, 1742.

A Tale of a Tub. London: 1704.

Tate, Nahum. "The Muses Memorial of Her Late Majesty." Ed. Charles Oldisworth. *The Loyal Mourner for the Best of Princes . . . a Collection of Poems Sacred to the Immortal Memory of . . . Queen Anne. By a Society of Gentlemen.* Charles Oldisworth, Ed. London: 1716. 1–16.

The Tatler. London: 1709–1711. Ed. with an Introduction and Notes by Donald F. Bond. 3 volumes. Oxford: Clarendon Press, 1987.

Theobald, Lewis. *The Mausoleum. A Poem Sacred to the Memory of her Late Majesty Queen Anne.* London: Jonas Brown, 1714.

Trusler, John. *The Works of Mr. Hogarth Moralized.* London: 1768.

Trusty, John. *The Speech of John Trusty, aged eleven years, a poor boy belonging to the workhouse . . . to Her Sacred Majesty Queen Anne.* London: 1702.

Wesley, Samuel. *Marlborough: Or, the Fate of Europe. A Poem.* London: Charles Harper, 1705.

Wilkes, Wetenhall. *A Letter of Genteel and Moral Advice to a Young Lady.* 1740. Fifth Edition. London: C. Hitch, 1748.

Willis, Richard. *A Sermon Preach'd before the Queen . . . Published by Her Majesty's Special Command.* London: H. Hills, 1705.

Wollstonecraft, Mary. *A Vindication of the Rights of Woman.* 1790. *The Works of Mary Wollstonecraft.* Ed. Janet Todd and Marilyn Butter. 7 vols. New York: New York University Press, 1989. Vol. 5.

Woolf, Virginia. *The Voyage Out.* London: The Hogarth Press, 1975.

Young, Edward. "On the Late Queen's Death, and His Majesty's Accession to the Throne." London: 1714.

SECONDARY SOURCES

Althusser, Louis. "Ideology and ideological state apparatuses." *Lenin and Philosophy and Other Essays*. New York: Monthly Review Press, 1971. 127–86.

Armstrong, Nancy. *Desire and Domestic Fiction: A Political History of the Novel.* New York: Oxford University Press, 1987.

"The gender bind: women and the disciplines." *Genders* 1:3 (Nov., 1988): 1–23.

"The rise of the domestic woman." *The Ideology of Conduct: Essays on Literature and the History of Sexuality.* Ed. Nancy Armstrong and Leonard Tennenhouse. New York: Methuen, 1987. 96–141.

Aston, Margaret. *England's Iconoclasts.* Volume 1: *Laws Against Images.* Oxford: Clarendon Press, 1988.

Badinter, Elisabeth. *The Myth of Motherhood: An Historical View of the Maternal Instinct.* Trans. R. DeGaris. London: Souvenir Press, 1980.

Balbus, Isaac. "Disciplining women: Michel Foucault and the power of feminist discourse." *After Foucault: Humanistic Knowledge, Postmodern Challenges.* Ed. Jonathan Arac. New Brunswick: Rutgers University Press, 1988. 138–60.

Ball, Donald L. "*Pamela II*: a primary link in Richardson's development as a novelist." *Modern Philology* 65 (1968): 334–42.

Ballaster, Ros. *Seductive Forms: Women's Amatory Fiction from 1684 to 1740.* Oxford: Clarendon Press, 1992.

Barash, Carol L. *Augustan Women's Mythmaking: English Women Writers and the Body of Monarchy, 1660–1720.* Dissertation, Princeton University, 1989.

Barber, C. L. "The family in Shakespeare's development: tragedy and sacredness." *Representing Shakespeare.* Ed. Murray M. Schwartz and Coppelia Kahn. Baltimore: Johns Hopkins University Press, 1980. 188–202.

Barker-Benfield, G. J. *The Culture of Sensibility: Sex and Society in Eighteenth-Century Britain.* Chicago: University of Chicago Press, 1992.

Bartky, Sandra Lee. "Foucault, femininity, and the modernization of patriarchal power." *Feminism and Foucault: Reflections on Resistance.* Ed. Irene Diamond and Lee Quinby. Boston: Northeastern University Press, 1988. 61–86. Rpt. *Femininity and Domination: Studies in the Phenomenology of Oppression.* New York: Routledge, 1990. 63–82.

Bassoff, Evelyn Silten. *Between Mothers and Sons: The Making of Vital and Loving Men.* New York: Penguin, 1994.

Bate, W. J. *Samuel Johnson.* New York: Harcourt, 1977.

Beasley, Jerry C. "Eliza Haywood." *British Novelists, 1660–1800, Part I.* Ed. Martin C. Battestin. *Dictionary of Literary Biography.* 137 volumes. Detroit: Gale, 1985. 39: 251–59.

"Politics and moral idealism: the achievement of some early women novelists." *Fetter'd or Free? British Women Novelists, 1670–1815.* Ed. Mary

Anne Schofield and Cecilia Macheski. Athens, OH: Ohio University Press, 1986. 216–36.

Bell, Ian. "Crime and comfort." *Daniel Defoe's Moll Flanders.* Ed. Harold Bloom. New York: Chelsea, 1987. 95–111.

Bender, John B. *Imagining the Penitentiary: Fiction and the Architecture of Mind in Eighteenth-Century England.* Chicago: University of Chicago Press, 1987.

Birdsall, Virginia Ogden. "Out of the jaws of destruction." *Daniel Defoe's Moll Flanders.* Ed. Harold Bloom. New York: Chelsea, 1987. 113–32.

Bowers, Toni. "Critical complicities: *Savage* mothers, Johnson's mother, and the containment of maternal difference." *The Age of Johnson* 5 (1992). New York: AMS Press. 115–46.

"Sex, lies and invisibility: amatory fiction from Behn to Haywood." *The New Columbia History of the Novel.* Ed. John J. Richetti. New York: Columbia University Press, 1994. 50–72.

Braudy, Leo. "Daniel Defoe and the anxieties of autobiography." *Genre* 6 (1973): 76–97.

"Penetration and impenetrability in *Clarissa.*" *Modern Essays on Eighteenth-Century Literature.* Ed. Leopold Damrosch, Jr. New York: Oxford University Press. 261–81.

Brooks, Gwendolyn. "The Mother." *Blacks.* Chicago: The David Company, 1987. 21.

Brown, Beatrice Curtis. *The Letters and Diplomatic Instructions of Queen Anne.* London: Cassell, 1935.

Brown, JoAnne. "Professional language: words that succeed." *Radical History Review* 34 (1986): 33–51.

Bruce, Susan. "The flying island and female anatomy: gynaecology and power in *Gulliver's Travels. Genders* 1:2 (Summer, 1988): 60–76.

Castle, Terry. " 'Amy, who knew my disease': a psychosexual pattern in Defoe's *Roxana.*" *English Literary History* 46 (1979): 81–96.

Clarissa's Ciphers: Meaning and Disruption in Richardson's Clarissa. Ithaca: Cornell University Press, 1982.

Masquerade and Civilization: The Carnivalesque in Eighteenth-Century English Culture and Fiction. Stanford: Stanford University Press, 1986.

"P/B: *Pamela* as sexual fiction." *Studies in English Literature* 22 (1982): 469–89.

Chaber, Lois A. " 'This Affecting Subject': An 'Interested' Reading of Childbearing in Two Novels by Samuel Richardson." *Eighteenth-Century Fiction* 8:2 (Jan., 1996): 193–250.

"From moral man to godly man: 'Mr. Locke' and Mr. B. in Part 2 of *Pamela.*" *Studies in Eighteenth-Century Culture* 18 (1988): 213–61.

"Matriarchal mirror: women and capital in *Moll Flanders.*" *Publication of the Modern Language Association* 97:2 (Mar., 1982): 212–26.

Chamberlain, Frederick. *The Sayings of Queen Elizabeth.* New York: Dodd, Mead, 1923.

Chodorow, Nancy and Susan Contratto. "The fantasy of the perfect mother." *Rethinking the Family: Some Feminist Questions.* Ed. Barrie Thorne with Marilyn Yalom. New York: Longman, 1982. 54–75.

Feminism and Psychoanalytic Theory. New Haven: Yale University Press, 1989.

The Reproduction of Mothering: Psychoanalysis and the Sociology of Gender. Berkeley: University of California Press, 1978.

Clark, J. C. D. *English Society 1688–1832: Ideology, Social Structure and Political Practice During the Ancien Regime.* New York: Cambridge University Press, 1985.

Coward, Rosalind. *Patriarchal Precedents: Sexuality and Social Relations.* Boston: Routledge and Kegan Paul, 1983.

Crawford, Patricia. "The construction and experience of maternity in seventeenth-century England." *Women as Mothers in Pre-Industrial England.* Ed. Valerie Fildes. New York: Routledge, Chapman and Hall, 1990. 3–38.

Curtis, Gila. *The Life and Times of Queen Anne.* London: Weidenfeld and Nicolson, 1972.

Daly, Brenda O. and Maureen T. Reddy. "Introduction." *Narrating Mothers: Theorizing Maternal Subjectivities.* Knoxville: University of Tennessee Press, 1991.

de Lauretis, Teresa. *Technologies of Gender: Essays on Theory, Film, and Fiction.* Bloomington: Indiana University Press, 1987.

Delaney, Carol. "The meaning of paternity and the virgin birth debate." *MAN: The Journal of the Royal Anthropological Institute.* Sept., 1986: 494–513.

Diamond, Irene and Lee Quinby. *Feminism and Foucault: Reflections on Resistance.* Boston: Northeastern University Press, 1988.

Dick, Miriam. "Joseph Highmore's vision of *Pamela.*" *English Language Notes.* 24:4 (June, 1987): 33–42.

Doody, Margaret Anne. *A Natural Passion: A Study of the Novels of Samuel Richardson.* Oxford: Clarendon Press, 1974.

"Richardson's politics." *Eighteenth-Century Fiction* 2:2 (January, 1990): 113–26.

Durant, David. "Roxana's fictions." *Studies in the Novel* 13 (1981): 225–36.

Eagleton, Terry. *The Rape of Clarissa: Writing, Sexuality and Class Struggle in Samuel Richardson.* Minneapolis: University of Minnesota Press, 1982.

Earle, Peter. *The Making of the English Middle Class: Business, Society, and Family Life in London, 1660–1730.* London: Methuen, 1989.

Eaves, T. C. Duncan and Ben D. Kimpel. "An unpublished pamphlet by Samuel Richardson." *Philological Quarterly* 63:3 (Summer, 1984): 401–9.

Samuel Richardson: A Biography. Oxford: Clarendon Press, 1971.

Elton, G. R. *Studies in Tudor and Stuart Politics and Government. Papers and Reviews, 1983–1990.* Vol. 4. Cambridge: Cambridge University Press, 1992.

Erickson, Robert. *Mother Midnight: Birth, Sex and Fate in the Eighteenth-Century Novel.* New York: A.M.S. Press, 1986.

Faller, Lincoln B. *Crime and Defoe: A New Kind of Writing. Cambridge Studies in*

Eighteenth-Century English Literature and Thought 6. Eds. Howard Erskine-Hill and John Richetti. Cambridge: Cambridge University Press, 1993.

Ferguson, Ann. "On conceiving motherhood and sexuality: a feminist materialist approach." *Mothering: Essays in Feminist Theory.* Ed. Joyce Trebilcot. Totowa: Rowman and Allanheld, 1984. 153–82.

Fildes, Valerie. *Breasts, Bottles and Babies.* Edinburgh: Edinburgh University Press, 1986.

"Maternal feelings re-assessed: child abandonment and neglect in London and Westminster, 1550–1800." *Women as Mothers in Pre-Industrial England.* Ed. Valerie Fildes. New York: Routledge, Chapman, and Hall, 1990. 139–78.

Wet-Nursing: A History from Antiquity to the Present. Oxford: Basil Blackwell, 1988.

Flax, Jane. "The conflict between nurturance and autonomy in mother-daughter relationships and within feminism." *Feminist Studies* 4.1 (1978): 171–89.

Fliegelman, Jay. *Prodigals and Pilgrims: The American Revolution Against Patriarchal Authority, 1750–1800.* New York: Cambridge University Press, 1982.

Flint, Christopher. "The anxiety of affluence: family and class (dis)order in *Pamela: or, Virtue Rewarded.*" *Studies in English Literature* 29 (1989): 489–514.

"Orphaning the family: the role of kinship in *Robinson Crusoe.*" *English Literary History* 55 (1988): 381–419.

Flynn, Carol Houlihan. "Defoe's idea of conduct: ideological fictions and fictional reality." *The Ideology of Conduct: Essays on Literature and the History of Sexuality.* Ed. Nancy Armstrong and Leonard Tennenhouse. New York: Methuen, 1987. 73–95.

Foucault, Michel. *The History of Sexuality.* 3 volumes. Trans. Robert Hurley. New York: Vintage Books, 1980. Vol. 1: "An Introduction."

"Questions of method." *After Philosophy: End or Transformation?* Ed. Kenneth Baynes et al. Cambridge, MA: M.I.T. Press, 1987. 100–18.

"What is Enlightenment?" *The Foucault Reader.* Ed. Paul Rabinow. New York: Pantheon Books, 1984.

Frye, Susan. *Elizabeth I: The Competition for Representation.* New York: Oxford University Press, 1993.

Gallagher, Catherine. "Embracing the absolute: the politics of the female subject in seventeenth-century England." *Genders* 1:1 (Spring 1988): 24–39.

Gallop, Jane. "The monster in the mirror: the feminist critic's psychoanalysis." *Feminism and Psychoanalysis.* Ed. Richard Feldstein and Judith Roof. Ithaca: Cornell University Press, 1989. 13–24.

"Reading the mother tongue: psychoanalytic feminist criticism." *Critical Inquiry* 13:2 (Winter, 1987): 314–29.

Garner, Shirley Nelson. "Constructing the mother: contemporary psycho-analytic theorists and women autobiographers." *Narrating Mothers: Theorizing Maternal Subjectivities.* Ed. Brenda O. Daly and Maureen T. Reddy. Knoxville: University of Tennessee Press, 1991. 76–93.

Garner, Shirley Nelson, Claire Kahane, and Madelon Sprengnether, eds. *The (M)other Tongue: Essays in Feminist Psychoanalytic Interpretation.* Ithaca: Cornell University Press, 1985.

Gelpi, Barbara Charlesworth. "The nursery cave: Percy Bysshe Shelley and the maternal." *The New Shelley: Later Twentieth-Century Views.* Ed. G. Kim Blank. New York: Macmillan, 1991. 42–63.

  Shelley's Goddess: Maternity, Language, Subjectivity. New York: Oxford University Press, 1992.

George, M. Dorothy. *London Life in the Eighteenth Century.* 1925. New York: Penguin, 1966.

Giddens, Anthony. *A Contemporary Critique of Historical Materialism.* 2 volumes. Macmillan, 1981. Volume 1: *Power, Property, and the State.*

Goldberg, Jonathan. "Fatherly authority: the politics of Stuart family images." *Rewriting the Renaissance: The Discourses of Sexual Difference in Early Modern Europe.* Ed. Margaret W. Ferguson, Maureen Quilligan, and Nancy J. Vickers. Chicago: University of Chicago Press, 1986. 3–32.

Gordon, D. J. *The Renaissance Imagination.* Ed. Stephen Orgel. Berkeley: University of California Press, 1975.

Green, David. *Sarah, Duchess of Marlborough.* New York: Scribners, 1967.

Greenfield, Susan. "The maternal bosom and the slave trade: bodies in *Belinda*." Paper presented at the Northeast American Society for Eighteenth-Century Studies, 1992.

Gregg, Edward. *Queen Anne.* Boston: Routledge and Kegan Paul, 1980.

  "Was Queen Anne a Jacobite?" *History* 57 (Oct., 1972): 358–75.

Gwillam, Tassie. *Samuel Richardson's Fictions of Gender.* Stanford: Stanford University Press, 1993.

Hagstrum, Jean. *Sex and Sensibility: Ideal and Erotic Love from Milton to Mozart.* Chicago: University of Chicago Press, 1980.

Haigh, Christopher. *The English Reformation Revised.* Cambridge: Cambridge University Press, 1987.

Hamilton, David. *The Diary of Sir David Hamilton, 1709–1714.* Ed. Philip Roberts. Oxford: Clarendon Press, 1975.

Harris, Barbara J. "Property, power and personal relations: elite mothers and sons in Yorkist and early Tudor England." *Signs* 15 (Spring, 1990): 606–32.

Harris, Tim. *Politics Under the Later Stuarts: Party Conflict in a Divided Society 1660–1715.* New York: Longman, 1993.

Heisch, Allison. "Queen Elizabeth and the persistence of patriarchy." *Feminist Review* 4 (1980): 45–56.

  Ed. *Queen Elizabeth I: Political Speeches and Parliamentary Addresses, 1558–1601.* Forthcoming.

Hill, Bridget. *Women, Work, and Sexual Politics in Eighteenth-Century England.* New York: Blackwell, 1989.

Hirsch, Marianne. "Incorporation and repetition in *La Princesse de Clèves.*" *Yale French Studies* 62 (1981): 67–87.

The Mother-Daughter Plot: Narrative, Psychoanalysis, Feminism. Bloomington: Indiana University Press, 1989.

Hobby, Elaine. *Virtue of Necessity: English Women's Writing, 1646–1688.* London: Virago Press, 1988.

Hoffer, Peter C. and N. E. H. Hull. *Murdering Mothers: Infanticide in England and New England, 1558–1803.* New York: New York University Press, 1981.

Hollway, Wendy. "Gender difference and the production of subjectivity." *Changing the Subject: Psychology, Social Regulation and Subjectivity.* Julian Henriques, Wendy Hollway, Cathy Urwin, Couze Venn, and Valerie Walkerdine. London: Methuen, 1984. 227–63.

Holmes, Geoffrey. *British Politics in the Age of Anne.* 1967. Rev. Ed., London: Hambledon Press, 1987.

Homans, Margaret. *Bearing the Word.* Chicago: University of Chicago Press, 1986.

Horn, Robert D. *Marlborough: A Survey: Panegyrics, Satires, and Biographical Writings, 1688–1788.* New York: Garland, 1975.

Hunter, J. Paul. *Before Novels: The Cultural Contexts of Eighteenth-Century English Fiction.* New York: Norton, 1990.

Huston, Nancy. "The matrix of war." *The Female Body in Western Culture.* Ed. Susan Suleiman. Cambridge: Harvard University Press, 1985. 119–36.

Iau, Marcia. *Remembering the Phallic Mother: Psychoanalysis, Modernism, and the Fetish.* Ithaca: Cornell University Press, 1993.

Illick, Joseph. "Child-rearing in seventeenth-century England and America." *The History of Childhood.* Ed. Lloyd de Mause. New York: Psychohistory Press, 1974. 303–50.

Irigaray, Luce. "And the one doesn't stir without the other." Trans. Hélène Vivienne Wenzel. *Signs* 7.1 (1981): 60–67.

This Sex Which Is Not One. Trans. Catherine Porter with Carolyn Burke. Ithaca: Cornell University Press, 1985.

Jacobs, Janet Liebman. "Reassessing mother blame in incest." *Ties That Bind: Essays on Motherhood and Patriarchy.* Ed. Jean F. O'Barr et alia. Chicago: University of Chicago Press, 1990. 273–87.

Jarrett, Derek. *England in the Age of Hogarth.* New York: Viking Press, 1974.

Johnson, Barbara. "Apostrophe, animation, and abortion." *Diacritics* (Spring, 1986): 29–39.

"Mallarmé as mother: a preliminary sketch." *Denver Quarterly* (Spring, 1984). Rpt. *A World of Difference.* Baltimore: Johns Hopkins University Press, 1987. 137–43.

Jones, J. R., Ed. *Liberty Secured? Britain Before and After 1688.* Stanford: Stanford University Press, 1992.

Kahn, Madeleine, *Narrative Transvestism: Rhetoric and Gender in the Eighteenth Century English Novel*. Ithaca: Cornell University Press, 1991.

Kaplan, E. Ann. *Motherhood and Representation: The Mother in Popular Culture and Melodrama*. New York: Routledge, 1992.

Kay, Carol. *Political Constructions: Defoe, Richardson, and Sterne in Relation to Hobbes, Hume, and Burke*. Ithaca: Cornell University Press, 1988.

Kenyon, J. P. "The birth of the old pretender." *History Today* 13 (1963): 418–26.

   Revolution Principles: The Politics of Party 1689–1720. New York: Cambridge University Press, 1977.

Kern, Jean B. "The fallen woman, from the perspective of five early eighteenth-century women novelists." *Studies in 18th-Century Culture*. 10 (1981): 457–68.

Keymer, Tom. *Richardson's Clarissa and the Eighteenth-Century Reader*. Cambridge: Cambridge University Press, 1992.

Kinkead-Weekes, Mark. *Samuel Richardson: Dramatic Novelist*. Ithaca: Cornell University Press, 1973.

Klein, Carol. *Mothers and Sons*. Boston: G. K. Hall, 1985.

Koon, Helene. "Eliza Haywood and the *Female Spectator*." *Huntington Library Quarterly* 42:1 (1978–79): 43–55.

Kristeva, Julia. "Psychoanalysis and the polis." Trans. Margaret Waller. *Critical Inquiry* 9 (Sept., 1982): 77–92.

   "Héréthique de l'amour." *Tel Quel* 74 (Winter 1977): 30–49.

Kunzle, David. "William Hogarth: the ravaged child in the corrupt city." *Changing Images of the Family*. Ed. Virginia Tufte and Barbara Myerhoff. New Haven: Yale University Press, 1979. 99–140.

Laqueur, Thomas. *Making Sex: Body and Gender from the Greeks to Freud*. Cambridge: Harvard University Press, 1990.

Larson, Kerry. " 'Naming the writer': exposure, authority, and desire in *Pamela*." *Criticism* 23:2 (Spring, 1981): 126–40.

Laslett, Peter. *The World We Have Lost, Further Explored*. London: Methuen, 1983.

Lerenbaum, Miriam. "A woman on her own account." *Daniel Defoe's Moll Flanders*. Ed. Harold Bloom. New York: Chelsea, 1987. 37–56.

MacDonald, Michael. *Mystical Bedlam: Madness, Anxiety, and Healing in Seventeenth-Century England*. New York: Cambridge University Press, 1981.

Maddox, James H. "On Defoe's *Roxana*." *English Literary History* 51 (1984): 669–91.

Malcolmson, R. W. "Infanticide in the eighteenth century." *Crime in England, 1550–1800*. Ed. J. S. Cockburn. Princeton: Princeton University Press, 1977.

Martin, Biddy. "Feminism, criticism, and Foucault." *Feminism and Foucault: Reflections on Resistance*. Ed. Irene Diamond and Lee Quinby. Boston: Northeastern University Press, 1988. 3–19.

Marx, Karl. *Grundrisse. The Marx-Engels Reader*. Ed. Robert C. Tucker. 2nd edition. New York: W. W. Norton, 1978. 221–93.

McBurney, William H. "Mrs. Penelope Aubin and the early eighteenth-century English novel." *Huntington Library Quarterly* 20 (May, 1957): 245–67

McClure, Ruth K. *Coram's Children: The London Foundling Hospital in the Eighteenth Century*. New Haven: Yale University Press, 1981.

McCormick, Marjorie. *Mothers in the English Novel: From Stereotype to Archetype*. New York: Garland, 1991.

McKeon, Michael. *The Origins of the English Novel 1600–1740*. Baltimore: Johns Hopkins University Press, 1987.

McLaren, Angus. "The pleasures of procreation: traditional and bio-medical theories of conception." *William Hunter and the Eighteenth-Century Medical World*. Ed. W.F. Bynum and Roy Porter. Cambridge: Cambridge University Press, 1985. 323–41.

McLaren, Dorothy. "Marital fertility and lactation 1570–1720." *Women in English Society, 1500–1800*. Ed. Mary Prior. New York: Methuen, 1985. 22–53.

Mendelson, Sara Heller. "Stuart women's diaries and occasional memoirs." *Women in English Society, 1500–1800*. Ed. Mary Prior. New York: Methuen, 1985. 181–210.

Minh-ha, Trinh T. "Not you/like you: post-colonial women and the interlocking questions of identity and difference." *Inscriptions* 3:4 (1988): 71–77.

Mohanty, Chandra Talpade. "Under western eyes: feminist scholarship and colonial discourse." *Third World Women and the Politics of Feminism*. Bloomington: Indiana University Press, 1991. 51–80.

Molloy, Fitzgerald. *Queen's Comrade: The Life and Times of Sarah Duchess of Marlborough*. 2 volumes. London: Hutchinson, 1901.

Montrose, Louis A. *"A Midsummer Night's Dream* and the shaping fantasies of Elizabethan culture: gender, power, form." *Rewriting the Renaissance: The Discourses of Sexual Difference in Early Modern Europe*. Ed. Margaret Ferguson, Maureen Quilligan, and Nancy J. Vickers. Chicago: University of Chicago Press, 1986. 3–32.

Mullan, John. *Sentiment and Sociability: The Language of Feeling in the Eighteenth Century*. Oxford: Clarendon Press, 1988.

Mulvey, Laura. *Visual and Other Pleasures*. New York: MacMillan, 1989.

Neale, R. S. *Class in English History 1680–1750*. Oxford: Basil Blackwell, 1981.

Nichols, R. H. and F. A. Wray. *The History of the Foundling Hospital*. London: Oxford University Press, 1935.

Nicolson, Benedict. *The Treasures of the Foundling Hospital*. Oxford: Clarendon Press, 1972.

Nussbaum, Felicity. *The Autobiographical Subject: Gender and Ideology in Eighteenth-Century England*. Baltimore: Johns Hopkins University Press, 1989.

"The other woman: polygamy, *Pamela*, and the prerogative of empire." *Women, "Race," and Writing in the Early Modern Period.* Ed. Margo Hendricks and Patricia Parker. New York: Routledge, 1994. 138–59.

"'Savage' mothers: narratives of maternity in the mid-eighteenth century." *Cultural Critique* 20 (Winter, 1991–92): 123–51.

Orgel, Stephen. "Nobody's perfect: or why did the English stage take boys for women?" *South Atlantic Quarterly* 88:1 (Winter, 1989): 7–29.

"Prospero's wife." *Rewriting the Renaissance: The Discourses of Sexual Difference in Early Modern Europe.* Ed. Margaret Ferguson, Maureen Quilligan, and Nancy Vickers. Chicago: University of Chicago Press, 1986. 50–64.

O'Shaughnessy, Toni [Toni Bowers]. "Fiction as truth: personal identity in Johnson's *Life of Savage*." *Studies in English Literature* 30 (1990): 487–501.

Pateman, Carole. *The Sexual Contract.* Stanford: Stanford University Press, 1988.

Paulson, Ronald. *Hogarth: His Life, Art, and Times.* 2 volumes. New Haven: Yale University Press, 1971. Vol. 2.

Ed. *Hogarth's Graphic Works.* 3rd Ed. London: The Print Room, 1989.

Perkin, Harold James. *The Origins of Modern English Society 1780–1880.* Second Edition. Boston: Ark, 1985.

Perkins, Jean. "Changing concepts of motherhood: a case study." Paper presented at the American Society for Eighteenth-Century Studies Annual Conference. Pittsburgh, 1991.

Perry, Ruth. "Colonizing the breast: sexuality and maternity in eighteenth-century England." *Journal of the History of Sexuality* 2:2 (Oct, 1991): 204–34.

Peters, Dolores. "The pregnant Pamela: characterization and popular medical attitudes in the eighteenth century." *Eighteenth-Century Studies* 14:4 (Summer, 1981): 432–51.

Phillips, John. *The Reformation of Images: Destruction of Art in England, 1535–1660.* Berkeley: University of California Press, 1973.

Pocock, J. G. A. *The Ancient Constitution and the Feudal Law.* Cambridge: Cambridge University Press, 1957, 1987.

Politics, Language, and Time: Essays on Political Thought and History. New York: Atheneum, 1971.

Pollak, Ellen. "*Moll Flanders*, incest, and the structure of exchange." *The Eighteenth Century: Theory and Interpretation* 30:1 (Spring, 1989): 3–21.

Pollock, Linda A. "Embarking on a rough passage: the experience of pregnancy in early-modern society." *Women as Mothers in Pre-Industrial England.* Ed. Valerie Fildes. New York: Routledge, Chapman, and Hall, 1990. 39–67.

Forgotten Children: Parent-Child Relations from 1500 to 1900. New York: Cambridge University Press, 1983.

Pope, Deborah, Naomi Quinn, and Mary Wyer, Eds. "The ideology of mothering: disruption and reproduction of patriarchy." *Signs* 15 (1989): 441–46.

Porter, Carolyn. "History and literature: 'after the new historicism.'" *New Literary History* 21:2 (Winter, 1990): 253–72.

Rackin, Phyllis. "Foreign country: the place of women and sexuality in Shakespeare's historical world." *Enclosure Acts: Sexuality, Property, and Culture in Early Modern England.* Ed. Richard Burt and John Michael Archer. Ithaca: Cornell University Press, 1994. 68–95.

Rich, Adrienne. "Compulsory heterosexuality and lesbian existence." *Powers of Desire: The Politics of Sexuality.* Ed. Ann Snitow, Christine Stansell, and Sharon Thompson. New York: Monthly Review Press, 1983. 177–205.

Of Woman Born: Motherhood as Experience and Institution. 1976. Second Edition. New York: W. W. Norton, 1986.

"Women and honor: some notes on lying." *Heresies* 1:1 (1975). *On Lies, Secrets and Silence: Selected Prose, 1966–1978.* New York: W. W. Norton, 1979. 185–94.

Richetti, John J. "The dialectic of power." *Daniel Defoe's Moll Flanders.* Ed. Harold Bloom. New York: Chelsea, 1987. 19–36.

Roof, Judith. "'This is not for you': the sexuality of mothering." *Narrating Mothers: Theorizing Maternal Subjectivity.* Ed. Brenda O. Daly and Maureen T. Reddy. Knoxville: University of Tennessee Press, 1991. 157–73.

Rothman, Barbara Katz. *Recreating Motherhood: Ideology and Technology in a Patriarchal Society.* New York: W.W. Norton, 1989.

Ruddick, Sara. "Maternal thinking." *Feminist Studies* 6:2 (1980): 342–67.

Maternal Thinking: Toward a Politics of Peace. Boston: Beacon Press, 1989.

Safouan, Maustafa. "Feminine sexuality in psychoanalytic doctrine." *Feminine Sexuality: Jacques Lacan and the École Freudienne.* Ed. Juliet Mitchell and Jacqueline Rose. Trans. Jacqueline Rose. New York: MacMillan, 1982. 123–36.

Sawicki, Jana. "Feminism and the power of Foucaldian discourse." *After Foucault: Humanistic Knowledge, Postmodern Challenges.* Ed. Jonathan Arac. New Brunswick: Rutgers University Press, 1988. 161–78.

Scharfman, Ronnie. "Mirroring and mothering." *Yale French Studies* 62 (1981): 88–106.

Schellenberg, Betty A. "Enclosing the immovable: structuring social authority in *Pamela*, Part II." *Eighteenth-Century Fiction* 4:1 (Oct., 1991): 27–42.

Scheuermann, Mona. *Her Bread to Earn: Women, Money, and Society from Defoe to Austen.* University Press of Kentucky, 1993.

Schochet, Gordon. *Patriarchalism in Political Thought.* New York: Basic Books, 1975.

Schofield, Mary Anne. "'Descending angels': salubrious sluts and pretty prostitutes in Haywood's fiction." *Fetter'd or Free? British Women Novelists, 1670–1815.* Ed. Mary Anne Schofield and Cecilia Macheski. Athens, OH: Ohio University Press, 1986. 186–200.

Eliza Haywood. Boston: Twayne, 1985.

"Exposé of the popular heroine: the female protagonists of Eliza Haywood." *Studies in Eighteenth-Century Culture* 12 (1983): 93–103.

Quiet Rebellion: The Fictional Heroines of Eliza Fowler Haywood. Washington, DC: University Press of America, 1982.

Schofield, Roger. "Did the mothers really die? three centuries of maternal mortality in 'the world we have lost.'" *The World We Have Gained: Histories of Population and Social Structure.* Ed. L. Bonfield, R. M. Smith and K. Wrightson. Oxford: Blackwell, 1986. 231–60.

Scott, Joan Wallach. *Gender and the Politics of History.* New York: Columbia University Press, 1988.

Scott, James C. *Domination and the Arts of Resistance.* New Haven: Yale University Press, 1990.

Sharpe, Kevin. *Politics and Ideas in Early Stuart England: Essays and Studies.* New York: Pinter, 1989.

Sharpe, Kevin and Steven N. Zwicker, eds. *Politics of Discourse: The Literature and History of Seventeenth-Century England.* Berkeley: University of California Press, 1987.

Shevelow, Kathryn. "Lady Sarah Pennington." *A Dictionary of British and American Women Writers, 1660–1800.* Ed. Janet Todd. Totowa: Rowman and Allanheld, 1985. 245–46.

Shinagel, Michael. *Defoe and Middle-Class Gentility.* Cambridge: Harvard University Press, 1968.

"The maternal paradox in *Moll Flanders*: craft and character." *Moll Flanders: An Authoritative Text, Backgrounds and Sources, Criticism.* Ed. Edward Kelly. New York: W.W. Norton, 1973. 404–14.

Shorter, Edward. *The Making of the Modern Family.* New York: Basic Books, 1975.

Siemon, James R. *Shakespearean Iconoclasm.* Berkeley: University of California Press, 1985.

Speck, W. A. "The Orangist conspiracy against James II." *Historical Journal* 30 (1987): 453–62.

Stability and Strife: England, 1714–1760. Cambridge, MA: Harvard University Press, 1977.

Sprengnether, Madelon. *The Spectral Mother: Freud, Feminism, and Psychoanalysis.* Ithaca: Cornell University Press, 1990.

Stanton, Domna C. "Difference on trial: a critique of the maternal metaphor in Cixous, Irigaray, and Kristeva." *The Poetics of Gender.* Ed. Nancy K. Miller. New York: Columbia University Press, 1986. 157–82.

Starr, George. *Defoe and Casuistry.* Princeton: Princeton University Press, 1971.

Stephanson, Raymond. "Defoe's 'malade imaginaire': the historical foundation of mental illness in *Roxana.*" *Huntington Library Quarterly* 45 (1982): 99–118.

Stone, Lawrence. *The Family, Sex, and Marriage in England, 1500–1800.* Abridged Edition. New York: Harper and Row, 1979.

Works cited   255

Strong, Roy. *The Cult of Elizabeth: Elizabethan Portraiture and Pageantry.* London: Thames and Hudson, 1977.

Sturrock, June. "The completion of *Pamela.*" *Durham University Journal* 74:2, n.s. 43:2 (June 1982): 227–32.

Suleiman, Susan Rubin. "Writing and motherhood." *The (M)other Tongue: Essays in Feminist Psychoanalytic Interpretation.* Ed. Shirley Nelson Garner et al. Ithaca: Cornell University Press, 1985. 352–77.

Sussman, Charlotte. " 'I wonder whether poor Miss Sally Godfrey be living or dead': The married woman and the rise of the novel." *Diacritics* 20.1 (1990): 88–102.

Sussman, George. *Selling Mothers' Milk: The Wet-Nursing Business in France, 1715–1914.* Chicago: University of Illinois Press, 1982.

Tennenhouse, Leonard. *Power on Display: The Politics of Shakespeare's Genres.* New York: Methuen, 1986.

Thompson, E.P. "Eighteenth-century English society: class struggle without class?" *Social History* 3 (1978): 133–65.

Todd, Janet. *Women's Friendship in Literature.* New York: Columbia University Press, 1980.

Travitsky, Betty S. " 'A pittilesse mother'? reports of a seventeenth-century English filicide." *Mosaic* 27:4 (December, 1994): 55–79.

Trumbach, Randolph. *The Rise of the Egalitarian Family: Aristocratic Kinship and Domestic Relations in Eighteenth-Century England.* New York: Academic Press, 1978.

Tyacke, Sarah. *English Map-Making, 1500–1650.* London: The British Library Board, 1983.

Van Dyke, Carolynn. *The Fiction of Truth: Structures of Meaning in Narrative and Dramatic Allegory.* Ithaca: Cornell University Press, 1985.

Van Ghent, Dorothy. *The English Novel: Form and Function.* New York: Rinehart, 1959.

Walker, Nigel. *Crime and Insanity in England.* 2 vols. Edinburgh: Edinburgh University Press, 1967–73. Vol. 1.

Warner, Marina. *Alone of All Her Sex: The Myth and Cult of the Virgin Mary.* New York: Knopf, 1976.

Warner, William Beatty. *Reading Clarissa: The Struggles of Interpretation.* New Haven: Yale University Press, 1979.

"Reading Rape: Marxist-Feminist figurations of the literal." *Diacritics* 13:4 (Winter, 1983): 12–32.

Watt, Ian. *The Rise of the Novel.* Berkeley: University of California Press, 1957, 1964.

Weber, Max. *The Protestant Ethic and the Spirit of Capitalism.* New York: Scribner, 1958.

Weil, Rachel. "The politics of legitimacy: women and the warming-pan scandal." *The Revolution of 1688–89: Changing Perspectives.* Ed. Lois G. Schwoerer. New York: Cambridge University Press, 1992. 65–82.

Williams, Raymond. *Marxism and Literature*. New York: Oxford University Press, 1977.

Wilt, Judith. "He could go no farther: a modest proposal about Lovelace and Clarissa." *PMLA* 92(1977): 19–32.

Wittig, Monique. "The straight mind." *Feminist Issues* 1:1 (Summer, 1980): 103–11.

Yates, Frances A. *Astrea: The Imperial Theme in the Sixteenth Century*. London: Routledge and Kegan Paul, 1975.

Yeazell, Ruth Bernard. *Fictions of Modesty: Women and Courtship in the English Novel*. Chicago: University of Chicago Press, 1991.

Young, Iris Marion. "Breasted experience: the look and the feeling." *Throwing Like a Girl and Other Essays in Feminist Philosophy and Social Theory*. Bloomington: Indiana University Press, 1990. 189–209.

Zimbardo, Rose. *At Zero Point: Politics, Discourse and Satire in Restoration England*. Manuscript in progress.

Index

Index